DAWN OF A KINGDOM

The message of 1 Samuel

by

Gordon J. Keddie

EVANGELICAL PRESS
16/18 High Street, Welwyn, Hertfordshire, AL6 9EQ, England

© Evangelical Press 1988
First published 1988

Unless otherwise stated, all Scripture references are taken from
the New International Version, Hodder & Stoughton Ltd., 1984
edition.

British Library Cataloguing in Publication Data

Keddie, Gordon
    Dawn of a kingdom.
    1. Bible. O.T. Samuel. 1st – Commentaries
    I. Title
    222'.4307

ISBN 0–85234–248 9

Typeset by Alan Sutton Publishing Ltd., Gloucester
Printed by The Bath Press, Avon

Contents

Preface

It is often said that the Christian faith is a historic faith. 'Sure,' says someone, 'everyone knows it's been around for a long time.' The point, however, is not that Christianity is old but that it is rooted in the mighty acts of God in history. Our faith is neither myth nor legend, but the revelation of God to real men in a real past and in real manifestations of his power and glory.

This is why the study of the Old Testament is of crucial importance to the church of Jesus Christ. I believe that the church has retreated from the Old Testament and, apart from the famous 'Sunday School stories' like David and Goliath, is largely ignorant of the flow of biblical history. I have often been asked why I preach 'so much' from Old Testament books – I usually have an Old Testament exposition somewhere in my weekly ministry. The short answer can be summed up in the well-known couplet about the relationship between the Old and New Testaments:

> The New is in the Old concealed;
> The Old is in the New revealed.

'*All* Scripture is God-breathed' and none of it is dispensable if we are to grasp the fulness of God's plan of redemption for the world. Indeed, there are compelling reasons for the need of a resurgence of preaching of the Old Testament.[1]

Three factors suggest themselves as relevant to the current situation.

The first is the prevailing tendency to see one's Christian faith in purely *individualistic terms*. It is not an accident that the Old Testament is treated like an 'optional extra' at a time when faith in Christ has been reduced to an inward-looking individual experience. Ours is the 'what Jesus means to *me*' generation. The Christian faith – the 'born-again' experience – has been psychologized into a kind of mind-cure, divorced from the all-embracing claims of God upon every aspect of our life and destiny. It is simply assumed that the Old Testament, with its strongly corporate and covenant emphasis centring in the life of a single nation, together with a core of legal and ceremonial teaching and practice, has little to say to our spiritual health and progress in today's world. Indeed, in the generally anti-historical and anti-intellectual climate of society as a whole, an interest in Scripture history seems quaintly antiquarian to many Christians. Furthermore, the world's outlook is affecting Christians very significantly and that outlook includes the feeling that if the future looks bad, just look at the past! So the past is shunned – we're looking for better things! And that means we are looking inwards – into ourselves – and seeking personal satisfaction and peace of mind for the life we are trying to live right now. The truth is, however, that the Old Testament provides the historical depth for New Testament faith and demonstrates the lordship of God over history itself. The scope is all-embracing. From creation to new creation, God is the Lord of all. World history is God dealing with the human race! And the destiny of the world, the nations and each and every individual is in the Lord's hands. To ignore this is to put ourselves in danger of misunderstanding the very plan and purpose of redemption itself and, by reducing the gospel to little more than a personal psychological prop, to court the mistake of those who came to Christ with the claim that they had done great things for him, when in fact they had not (Matthew 7:22).

A second factor is the influence of *positive self-image psychology* on the way Christians apply the teaching of God's Word to their lives and their thinking. We live in the days of what I call 'home on the range' theology. You know the words of the famous cowboy song:

> Home, home on the range,
> Where the deer and the antelope play,
> And never is heard a discouraging word,
> And the skies are not cloudy all day.

There is just too much blood and judgement in the Old Testament for a lot of modern Christians. It is too 'negative' and tends to be depressing. In any case, they would say, the New Testament is the 'positive' message that was given to supplant it! The old heresy of Marcion (second century A.D.) finds a modern echo in the sentimental, 'power of positive thinking' religion of the present day. Marcion thought the God of the Old Testament was different from, and inferior to, the God of the New Testament. The Jews' God, he said, was full of wrath, whereas Jesus' God was full of grace. This interpretation overlooked the teaching of both Testaments, of course, and was and is decisively rejected by the church. Nevertheless, many Christians shy clear of the Old Testament. There is too much of sin, of death and of judgement there, as they see it, and we would not be 'balanced' as Christians if we dwelt too much upon it. The contrary is the truth, however, for the whole of Scripture presents us as we really are and realistically faces us with the alternatives, to the end that we might hear the voice of the Lord and come to him in repentance and faith so that we might be saved.

A third factor is an *antinomian* (i.e., anti-law) *spirit* which has infiltrated the practice of many Christians today. There is a negative attitude to God's law. Little attention is given to the detailed prescriptions of God's Word for the holiness of each believer's life. The Old Testament law has fared particularly poorly in this regard. Partly this has been due to the stress placed, correctly, on the fulfilment of the ceremonial and sacrificial aspects of the law of Moses in the person and work of Jesus Christ. The rest of the law has come to be viewed as shadowy and superseded and so the case law of the Old Testament has tended to go the way of the ceremonies and the dietary regulations, almost by default. But, it must be said, this neglect of the principles and practice of the Old Testament case law is a culpable retreat from a body of revealed truth that has a wealth of searching application to the New Testament era. Could it be that the very precision with which the law details the practice of holy living is a stumbling-block to people who are happier with a faith that lets them 'love God and do as they like'? It is also no accident that we live in a time when immorality is rearing its head as never before in the ranks of the leadership of evangelical churches and is being dealt with more as an illness than as an abomination in the sight of God. The Old Testament starkly confronts the issues of life and undergirds the New Testament focus upon Christ as the Saviour and the Judge of the world.

The books of Samuel are, of course, historical narratives of God's dealings with his people. They touch upon the law and the ceremonies as these are relevant to this particular moment in the life of God's people. We are thereby provided with a window into the exercise of a godly life – both the individual and corporate dimensions of holiness to the Lord. And precisely because they are histories we see the rough and tumble of real lives and, with that, the blessings of godliness and the curses of wickedness. That it took place 3,000 years ago in some ways enhances the vividness of the lessons. We have to think our way into the shoes of people who lived in times so distant from our own. And as we do this, the intervening millennia will dissolve and the immediacy of the Word will forcibly engrave itself upon our lives with the utmost urgency and relevance. And then the fact that the Old Testament exposes us, in Derek Kidner's expression, to 'the bones and sinews that underlie the fair surface of the New,'[2] brings us face to face with Jesus Christ as the only Redeemer of God's elect.

This volume on 1 Samuel has grown out of week-to-week preaching ministry in a local congregation. The emphasis is therefore upon the meaning of the text for our real day-to-day lives. Those who delight in technical exegesis will have to look elsewhere and will find some indications where to do so in the references given for each chapter. I am, as always, indebted to my patient and discerning 'better half', Jane, who read the manuscript and made many practical suggestions.

Gordon J. Keddie
State College,
Pennsylvania,
USA

References

[1] For an illuminating and persuasive exposition of this theme, see Derek Kidner, *Preaching from the Old Testament*, (Edinburgh; Rutherford House, 1983) 15pp.
[2] Kidner, p.5.

Introduction

The goal of all Old Testament study ought to be a more perfect discipleship to the Lord. All of God's Word is directed towards the moulding of heart and mind and the transformation of behaviour, to the end that we might be holy as God is holy. Sad to say, modern biblical scholarship has all but abandoned this calling in favour of a kind of technical exegesis which, while meticulous in its dissection of the text and abounding in ingenious and intricate theories of its origins, is strangely arid and virtually devoid of any contemporary application. The secularization of modern life, having banished the Bible from every sphere of human existence except the realm of private faith, has now succeeded in expelling faith from the Bible itself! It seems hardly possible, I know, but a half-hour study of many of the modern commentaries – even those that are ostensibly conservative and evangelical – will reveal a disturbing unwillingness to make concrete application of the teaching of the Word of God to our lives. Biblical scholarship has ceased to be devotional both in its very nature and in its thrust. Secular methodology has hijacked biblical study. It is academically unacceptable today to expound Scripture in terms of its redemptive, devotional and prophetic purposes. A chasm has been opened between 'serious' study ('scholarly' commentaries) and 'devotional' or 'layman's' exposition. And here's the rub: the life-changing power of the Word of God has been relegated to the realm of the non-scholarly, the private and the relatively uninformed!

Current studies in the historical books of the Old Testament are particularly blighted with this plague of secular intellectualization. If you are looking for commentaries that

will warm your soul and stir you to refreshed discipleship to
Christ, you will look in vain. I cannot whole-heartedly
recommend even one, although Keil and Delitzsch, now
over a century old, does include some directions and
exhortations. The older evangelical commentators, like
Charles Simeon, Thomas Scott and Matthew Henry were, of
course, committed to pressing home the message of the
Word – they knew that scholarship was nothing if it did not
point people to Christ! Of the modern writers, R. P.
Gordon's *1 & 2 Samuel* is the most recent and the best. But
you will need to go to Matthew Henry and A. W. Pink's *Life
of David* for something to touch your soul.

1 Samuel is a book about three men in the same boat. It
traces the development of Israel from the anarchy of the
period of the judges to the establishment of the theocratic
monarchy, that is, a monarchy in which the kings were
appointed by God and acted as agents of Israel's true King,
the Lord. The three men are Samuel, the prophet and
king-maker; Saul, the people's choice as king; and David,
the Lord's heir-presumptive, who would succeed Saul (in 2
Samuel).

The narrative spans the hundred-year period from the
birth of Samuel to the death of Saul on Mount Gilboa (c.
1010 B.C.). Samuel was a contemporary of Samson. Saul
probably began to reign only a few years after Samson's
death. We begin, therefore, in the twilight of the period of
the judges – the theocratic Hebrew republic – and end with
the establishment of the theocratic monarchy, which was to
flower, ever so briefly, under David and Solomon.

Three principal themes are intertwined throughout this
account.

1. *The development of the theocratic monarchy*
The significance of this is not merely political or socio-
logical, but theological, spiritual and eschatological. It is
theological, because it concerns the rule of God among his
people; it is spiritual because it concerns the faith of those
who love the Lord and are committed to him as his
disciples; and it is eschatological because it points, in its
very form, to the coming of God's Son, the Lord Jesus
Christ, in the fulness of time to be the messianic and

mediatorial King who must reign until all things are put under his feet (1 Corinthians 15:25). Christ is central to any understanding of the thrust of 1 Samuel. To see it only in terms of narrow contextual considerations is to miss the point, which is cosmic in scope and redemptive in focus – in the person and work of the coming Messiah. In this respect, the history of 1 Samuel must not be divorced from the content of the psalms, many of which are distinctly prophetic of Jesus Christ and most of which came from the pen of David, a leading actor in the whole story.

2. *The absolute sovereignty of God*
Behind all the visible wars in which the Lord's people were involved an invisible war was being waged. God was doing his will among the armies of heaven and with the inhabitants of the earth. All the machinations of evil cannot thwart his purpose. Indeed, the very wickedness of men is turned in on itself and accomplishes in the end the purposes of God. The miserable end of Saul's reign underscores the legitimacy of that of David. There is a divine purpose in history. He commands the affairs of men and overthrows their plans as it suits his purposes. And his purpose is good in itself and brings divine blessing into the lives of his faithful people. God is with his people and reveals himself to them. We are not left to ourselves, alone in the universe, at the mercy of dark impersonal forces. The Lord is King!

3. *The triumph of God's righteousness*
The holy and righteous God does all things well. Hope, ultimately centring in Christ, shines through the darkest times for the Lord's people. We are shown the true consequences of rebellion against the Lord. There is no glamour in the Bible's representation of sin. 'The wages of sin is death' is stamped across the pages of 1 Samuel. Sin does not work. Its pleasures and advantages are temporary and illusory. Only the righteousness of God remains and bears fruit. Saul clings to his sins and perishes. Samuel and David cleave to the Lord and are clothed with the robes of redemption. We are pointed to the victory of Christ, who is saving his people from their sins to this very day.

Israel's history is our history. Israel's future is our reality.

The Saviour, who was believed 'from a distance' by faithful Abraham and that great catalogue of saints recorded in the eleventh chapter of Hebrews, is preached to us in the Lord's dealings with his Old Covenant people, Israel. Let us hear with willing ears God's Word for our day and rejoice in a living faith in the only Saviour of sinners, the Lord Jesus Christ!

PART I: Samuel - prophet and king-maker

1.

A childless woman

Please read 1 Samuel 1:1–20

'He settles the barren woman in her home as a happy mother of children' (Psalm 113:9).

Everyone's story begins with a mother. And the stories of remarkable children frequently have their genesis in extraordinary mothers. There are surely few more remarkable children in the annals of world history than the prophet Samuel. Indeed, so notable was his childhood, and especially his encounter with God in the tabernacle (3:4–14), that our first remembrance of him is not as the elder statesman of Israel, but as the child prophet of Shiloh. It is altogether appropriate and not at all surprising, therefore, that our first glimpse of this great servant of Yahweh and maker of kings should be through the window of his mother, Hannah, the wife of Elkanah.

They did not know it at the time, but the period when Israel was ruled by the 'judges' had begun to draw to a close. About the year 1100 B.C., the hill country of Ephraim enjoyed a time of relative peace under the judgeship of Tola of Issachar (Judges 10:1). Not far to the south of Tola's home in Shamir lay the town of Ramathaim Zuphim – better known to us, perhaps, as the Arimathea of the New Testament (Matthew 27:57).[1] A Levite named Elkanah lived there with his two wives: Hannah, who was childless, and Peninnah, who had many children. Elkanah was a good man who loved God and was a dutiful husband and father. He was a polygamist, of course, and that was something which,

while an everyday fact in Israelite society in those days
(Deuteronomy 21:15–17), was out of line with God's revealed
will (Genesis 2:24). This was a source of problems in
Elkanah's family. But it was also an indicator of the generally
low spiritual condition of God's covenant people as a whole.
Compared with some of the priests, whose immorality was
legendary (2:22), Elkanah was a man of practical godliness.
He was, as each of us is more than we know, a child of his
time. But in the context of that era, he exemplified what was
best among God's people. This should remind us just how
easy it is for us to make concessions to the customs of our
culture at the expense of the principles of God's Word. We
have a lot less excuse than Elkanah for doing so, because
whereas he lived under the shadows of the law of Moses, we
live in the noonday sun of the full revelation of a completed
Scripture and a risen Saviour, the Lord Jesus Christ.

Clearly, the Lord had brought Elkanah to his situation 'for
such a time as this' (compare Esther 4:12–14). The internal
problems of his family, so closely related to the spiritual
condition of the nation, had brought him and his wives, as we
shall see, to the crossroads of history. The result was to be a
decisive development in God's plan of redemption for the
human race – the advent of the Davidic monarchy, with its
intimations of the coming of the messianic King, the Lord
Jesus Christ.

This glorious prospect was, however, very far from Hannah's mind at the beginning of our story. Her circumstances
were much more prosaic, and they were very painful, for
every day in life she was reminded, if only by the patter of tiny
feet, that she was childless, whereas Peninnah was not. It is
with this problem and her prayer that God would give her a
son that the account of a whole era in Israel's history begins.
And so, although the people involved were quite unaware of
it at the time, the initial step towards the establishment of
David's royal throne was the childlessness of a Levite's wife!

Hannah's problem [1:1–8]

Childlessness and a jealous 'sister-wife'[2] conspired to make
Hannah's life a misery. And never was that misery greater

than at the time of the family's annual visit to the tabernacle at Shiloh, when they went '**to worship and sacrifice to the Lord Almighty**' (1:3). How sad that Hannah's pain should be intensified, rather than alleviated, on the one occasion in the year when they worshipped in God's house! But such was the perversity of Peninnah that she chose that moment to vent her spleen on Hannah. Peninnah saw herself as in competition with Hannah for the affections of Elkanah. Jealous because Elkanah attempted to compensate for Hannah's childlessness with tokens of his love for her, Peninnah '**kept provoking her in order to irritate her**' (1:6). The NIV translation of verse 5 suggests that Elkanah gave a '**double portion**' of the meat of the sacrifice to Hannah and that this was the cause of Peninnah's wrath. This is probably misleading. A better rendering may be that of the RSV: '**He would give Hannah** *only* *one portion*, **because the Lord had closed her womb.**' The contrast, then, would be between the many portions – one per person – given to Peninnah and her children, and the single portion given to the childless Hannah. But, for all that her single portion only served to underscore her childlessness, Elkanah made sure that Hannah knew that he loved her very much. It was this that irked Peninnah no end. In consequence, she was exceedingly spiteful towards Hannah year after year: '**Whenever Hannah went up to the house of the Lord, her rival provoked her till she wept and would not eat**' (1:7).

Elkanah just could not cope with this situation, beyond attempting to comfort his grieving wife (1:8). It remained for Hannah herself to seek the Lord's help to bring to her the oil of joy for mourning and a garment of praise for the spirit of heaviness.

Hannah's prayer [1:9–16]

Hannah accepted that her childlessness was bound up with the Lord's providential ordering of her personal life (1:6). But she did not see that as a reason for any gratitude for her condition. It was, and remains, an affliction to be childless and it was her heart's desire to have a family of her own. Some Christians today will tell us that our response to such

a disability should be to 'praise the Lord anyway'. They
seem to think that a simple and final act of acceptance of the
trouble as God's will enables us to put it behind us and get
on with serving the Lord in other ways. It is as if such
acceptance exhausts the meaning and application of the
affliction for our lives. It is doubtful if Hannah's agony of
soul could have been assuaged by such a deceptively
attractive solution. That the Lord had, in his providence,
closed her womb was something she accepted – and without
reproaching him. But that fact did not suggest to her mere
resignation to her fate. On the contrary, it cast her on the
Lord as the only one who had the power to open her womb
and give her a child! It suggested that here was an opportunity for the Lord to be gracious and to demonstrate his
love and power towards one of his suffering children. There
is a fragrant normality about Hannah's turning to the Lord
for his help to overcome her problems. These are to be
regarded, quite properly, as the tests of life in the midst of a
fallen world. They call forth from us a prayerful dependence
upon the Lord and even the most importunate prayer for the
deepest desire of our heart. 'Is any one of you in trouble?'
asked James, 'He should pray' (James 5:13). Hannah did
not glibly 'praise the Lord anyway'. She knew whom she
believed. She therefore prayed her heart out, knowing that
the Lord could give her deliverance from her troubles. She
prayed for a son.

In the very brief account of her prayer, two features
command our attention and, indeed, can only encourage us
in our own personal devotion to the Lord.

1. *Hannah's exemplary godliness*
This was already evident in the way in which she had borne
the taunts of Peninnah. She was crushed by the unjust
treatment she received, but nowhere is there evidence of a
vengeful spirit. She took it patiently. And when she sought
the Lord, it was not for justice or the punishment of her
tormentor that she called, but simply for the healing of her
infertility (cf. 1:6–7). She had a very humble spirit in the
face of provocation.

When she turned to prayer, that quiet confiding spirit was
again to the fore: she poured out her soul to the Lord.

Although she was '**deeply troubled**' and '**in bitterness of soul**' (1:10, 15), there was no bitterness against God. She felt the deepest grief but she did not blame anyone for it, least of all the Lord. This is ever one of the great tests of a believing attitude to the Lord. How often our prayers can be mere vents for recrimination: 'Lord, why did you let this happen to me?' We so easily protest against the Lord's providence. It is as if we were sure we deserved better treatment and the Lord should have known better than to let bad things come into our lives! But Hannah, like all who truly love the Lord, knew her God and knew her own heart. She knew that this world is not heaven, but a fallen sin-sick place in which all of its inhabitants have a personal share in its imperfections and afflictions. As a believer, she knew that the Lord's purpose for her was one of blessing – even in and through her woes. She therefore waited upon the Lord with the sure conviction that her sorrows could not be charged to him, but that they could be brought to his throne of grace for help and healing. 'Personal suffering,' says John White, 'is never meaningless for the child of God. You may not know why you suffer, and your suffering may seem to you too painful to bear. Under such circumstances you must always bring your suffering to him and ask him to take it away.'[3] Hannah cried to the Lord in her trouble and, as we shall see, he delivered her from her distress (Psalm 107:6).

An interesting sidelight on Hannah's humility of mind is afforded by her exchange with Eli, the priest at Shiloh. Eli had very poor sight (4:15). As he observed Hannah praying, he saw her lips moving but heard no words: '**Hannah was praying in her heart...**' (1:13). He then jumped to the conclusion that she was drunk and rebuked her in no uncertain terms: '**How long will you keep on getting drunk? Get rid of your wine**' (1:14). Her gentle reply disabuses Eli of his uncharitable judgement and calls forth from him a formal priestly blessing – the only instance in Scripture of a priest blessing an individual (1:15–17).[4]

2. *Hannah's whole-hearted commitment*

We see this in her promise to dedicate her son to the service of God's house: '**And she made a vow, saying, "O Lord Almighty, if you will only look upon your servant's**

**misery and remember me, and not forget your servant
but give her a son, then I will give him to the Lord for all
the days of his life, and no razor will ever be used on his
head**" (1:11–12).

John Calvin calls this vow a 'vow of thanksgiving' and
likens it to Jacob's vow recorded in Genesis 28:18–22. In
that case, Jacob promises God a house and a tithe; here
Hannah promises the son that God would give. The question that imposes itself on our assessment of the vow is, of
course, 'Is this a model for us to imitate and if we do this,
how do we avoid the charge that we are bribing God?'

The taint of bribery must, of course, be rejected at the
outset. When Jesus was tempted (i.e., bribed) by Satan in
the desert, he was promised all sorts of things which Satan
had no right to offer and no power to deliver. Quoting
Deuteronomy 6:16 – 'Do not test the Lord your God' – Jesus
roundly rebuked the devil. The bribery was so obvious. In
Hannah's vow, however, there is no such chicanery – she
only promises to give to the Lord what he will give to her,
should he choose to answer her prayer with a 'Yes'. At every
point she had proved herself submissive to his will, whether
in years of childlessness or, as now, in asking for a son. The
whole climate is one of holy motives, hallowed desires and
humble submission. The notion that a vow such as Hannah's is by its very nature bargaining with God is simply
unfounded.

It must be admitted, however, that there are dangers in
making vows rashly – an example not to follow would be
that of Jephthah (Judges 11:30–40)[5] – and it will repay us to
look a little more closely at Hannah's vow before we set
ourselves to follow her example.

There is, for instance, a unique significance in Scripture
history to Hannah's vow, a fact which implies great care in
applying its lessons to our own practice. Here was a point in
redemptive history, no less, in which God was doing something vital to the next phase of his unfolding plan of
redemption for his people. Samuel would be a link in the
chain of salvation. Perhaps, too, his birth to the hitherto
childless Hannah would recall Sarah and Isaac (Genesis
17:15–19; 21:1–7) and remind them of the covenant promises of God. Here, then, was a special manifestation of the

power of God directed to the redemption of his people as a whole.

We might also notice that, as a son of a Levite, any child of Elkanah and Hannah was already devoted to the service of the tabernacle in the terms of the law of Moses. Hannah's vow was not remarkable for that particular point. Her son would inevitably serve as a Levite in God's house. What was distinctive about the vow was the promise that her son would serve in the tabernacle *from the earliest years* and that he would be a Nazirite *from the beginning*, even as a child. The Nazirite vow was an act of piety, normally for a set time of limited duration, for the purpose of deepened commitment and piety (Numbers 6:1–21; Acts 21:23–26). A life-long Nazirite vow was the mark of an extraordinary servant of the Lord. Samuel, like Samson before him, was to be committed to 'no razor ever be[ing] used on his head' (1:11).

This was a singular vow to be taking. Nevertheless, it was within Hannah's power to keep, given that the Lord provided a son. She could deliver her son to the priest at Shiloh and she could let his hair grow uncut and deny him the fruit of the grape. Of course, her son would have a mind of his own one day, but by then Hannah's part would be fulfilled as far as she had any responsibility or power to do anything about it. This reminds us that promises made to God are to be within realistic reach of our capacity to fulfil them. There is a realism to the strongest faith – a biblical realism that is guided by the canons of God's revealed will. This we see in Hannah's vow: she had her eye on God's law and her mind on the leading of God's Spirit.

We are encouraged by the Word of God to ask him for our heart's desire (e.g., Philippians 4:6). We are to pray in accordance with the Lord's known will. We are, on our part, never required to promise anything to the Lord beyond simple obedience to his revealed will in the Scriptures. If we are inclined to take a vow with respect to some particular action in the future, we should be asking ourselves some questions to be certain that what we are doing is right. Is the vow helpful to our spiritual life? Is it a proper expression of true godliness? Is it agreeable to the principles of the Scriptures? Is it an expression of gratitude to the Lord, or is it an attempt to bargain with him, as if he can be bribed into

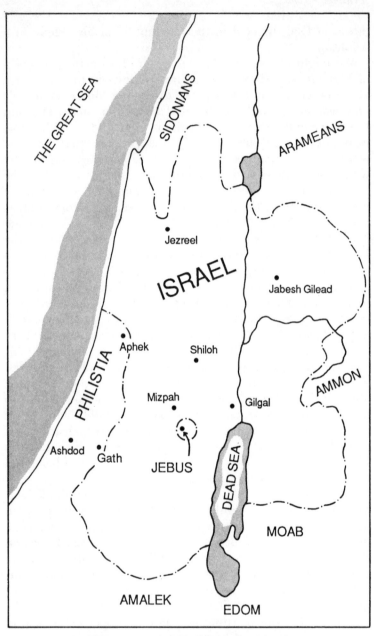

**Map 1 - Israel at the birth
of Samuel, c. 1100 B.C.**

blessing us? Can I reasonably expect, with the Lord's help, to fulfil the vow? Can I expect God's help to do so? When we pray, we stand on holy ground. Our prayer requests must be for what is pleasing to God. And our commitments likewise must breathe the righteousness of God. Hannah was full of grace when she prayed and promised. So must we be, when we come to God's throne of grace.

Hannah's peace and joy [1:17–20]

'Prayer is heart's-ease to a gracious soul,' said Matthew Henry three centuries ago. The blessing from Eli (1:17) signalled the coming of the peace of God into Hannah's soul. Peace always attends God's answers to prayer, because when God answers – whether 'yes' or 'no' – he speaks peace to us. He solves the problem and blesses us with the certainty of his good purpose for our lives. It is significant that it is in stillness that we can truly enjoy the knowledge of God (Psalm 46:10). Restlessness is an effect of sin (Isaiah 57:20). Hannah's response shows that her burden had been lifted. '**May your servant find favour in your eyes**' is a formal expression which, however, has a play on Hannah's name in it – the word 'favour' is the Hebrew *hen* – which highlights the role of the grace of God in her life. The proof of her restored spirits was that she '**ate something and her face was no longer downcast**' (1:18). Her son had not yet been conceived, far less born! But God had answered her prayer with an assurance of his love towards her. That is the fruit of all believing prayer. And because of this, God's people ought to be the most visibly joyous people in the world.

Hannah's life was changed for ever. The family returned home and in due course Hannah gave birth to her son, naming him '**Samuel, saying, "Because I asked the Lord for him"**' (1:19–20). Whatever the meaning of Samuel's name – and scholars have wrangled over this for years – the focus of it is the Lord himself. 'Samuel' most likely means 'heard of God' or 'name of God'. In any event, it is the Lord who is honoured as the giver of new life. God had taken a childless woman and made her a happy mother! (Psalm

113:9). In our day, children are too often seen as a burden rather than a joy, as a financial drain rather than a family's and a nation's true wealth. Hannah challenges the callous self-centredness that aborts millions of unborn babies every year. Hannah points us to the truth that children are God's heritage and a reward from the Lord (Psalm 127:3).

The Lord '**remembered**' Hannah and Hannah forgot the sorrow that had blighted her earlier life. At the personal level, this enshrines the liberating truth that the Lord never forgets his believing people. Do you feel bereft of the nearness of the Lord? Is there a burden or disability – perhaps childlessness, perhaps something else – that casts such a shadow across your life that the light of Christ seems remote and his blessing but a dream? Then, with Hannah, 'Cast your cares on the Lord and he will sustain you; he will never let the righteous fall' (Psalm 55:22).

Remember, also, that the appearance of Samuel brought the advent of the Lord Jesus Christ a step nearer. All the cares of all God's people were cast on him. He bore them in his own body. He suffered and died in the place of sinners so that healing and salvation might come to them. He still calls us to come to him that we might have rest, to believe on his name that we might have eternal life.

References

[1] R.W. Klein, *I Samuel*, (Waco, Texas: Word Books, 1983), p. 5. Ramathaim Zuphim is also called Ramah (1:19), but was probably not the Ramah of Benjamin with which Samuel was later associated.

[2] The Mormon term for wives of a polygamist.

[3] John White, *Daring to Draw Near*, (Downer's Grove, Illinois: IVP, 1977), p. 89.

[4] Robert P. Gordon, *1 & 2 Samuel – a commentary*, (Exeter: The Paternoster Press, 1986), p. 75.

[5] G.J. Keddie, *Even in Darkness*, (Welwyn: Evangelical Press, 1985), pp. 82–85.

2.

Answered prayer

Please read 1 Samuel 1:21 – 2:10

'I prayed for this child, and the Lord has granted me what I asked of him' (1 Samuel 1:27).

'The faithfulness of God,' writes A. W. Tozer, 'is a datum of sound theology but to the believer it becomes far more than that: it passes through the processes of the understanding and goes on to become nourishing food for the soul.'[1] God's answers to prayer not only minister to our real needs but they increase our love for him.

> 'I love the Lord, for he heard my voice;
>   he heard my cry for mercy.
> Because he turned his ear to me,
>   I will call on him as long as I live'
>
> (Psalm 116:1–2).

God's faithfulness calls forth deeper devotion and joyous certainty of his continuing goodness to us through all our years.

The presentation of Samuel [1:21–28]

Hannah became a happy mother, but she never forgot her promise to dedicate her son to the service of God's tabernacle at Shiloh. For reasons that are not altogether clear, Hannah decided not to take Samuel to Shiloh until he was

weaned and therefore ready to be left there under the
tutelage of Eli. Attendance at the tabernacle was a major
and even arduous expedition at the best of times. It
certainly would not have been easy for a nursing mother and
her infant child. Matthew Henry saw no more profound
reason than this for Hannah's decision and took occasion, in
the excellent practical manner of the seventeenth century,
to turn it into a point of encouragement for mothers of small
children everywhere: 'Those who are detained from public
ordinances, by the nursing and tending of little children,
may take comfort from this instance, and believe, that if
they do that duty in a right spirit, God will graciously accept
them therein; and though they tarry at home, they shall
divide the spoil.' And so, when the time came for Elkanah
and his family to go to Shiloh '**to offer the annual sacrifice
to the Lord**' and for Elkanah to fulfil some unspecified
'**vow, Hannah did not go**' (1:21–22). Elkanah agreed to
this, adding an invocation of the Lord's blessing: '**Only may
the Lord make good his word**' (1:23). A variant reading
has '**your vow**' instead of '**his word**'.[2] This would appear to
fit the flow of the passage, since the Lord had already
granted Hannah's wish for a son and it only remained for
Hannah to fulfil her promise.

Two or three years went by before Samuel was weaned. A
passing reference in the non-canonical Apocrypha suggests
that children were not weaned until they were three or four
years old (2 Maccabees 7:27). When that time came, '**She
took the boy with her, young as he was . . . and brought
him to the house of the Lord at Shiloh**' (1:24). After
presenting the appropriate sacrifices, Hannah took Samuel
to Eli and turned him over to the care of the priest in
fulfilment of her vow to the Lord. Her words, '**So now I give
him to the Lord**', contain an interesting word-play which,
according to D.F. Payne, expresses the theological meaning
of the whole transaction.[3] In three verses, variants of the
Hebrew *sha-al* ('ask' and 'give') are used. These are:
'**Because I *asked* the Lord for him**' (1:20); '**The Lord has
granted me *what I asked of* him**' (1:27); and '**So now I
give him . . . he shall be *given over* to the Lord**' (1:28).
The root *sha-al* resembles Samuel's name ('*Shemu-el*'), while
the usage in 1:28 (*sha-ul*, meaning 'given' or 'lent') is

identical to the name of Israel's first king, Saul (*Sha-ul*). The idea then is that Samuel is the true national leader – the 'true *Sha-ul*' – as over against the Saul the people would want as their king in days to come.

At a more prosaic level, the spectacle of a mother handing over her three-year-old son to the care of a priest seems very hard to take. The element of personal sacrifice on Hannah's part is so obvious that it requires no comment. What raises modern eyebrows is the cost to Samuel, who was, after all, deprived of a normal family upbringing. Was it not the responsibility of Hannah, as a mother, to keep her child at home until he had grown up and was able to assume his responsibilities as a Levite for himself? The answer to this question is surely to be found in the uniqueness of Samuel. Hannah was not raised up to provide a moral example for mothers in all succeeding ages as to the upbringing of children. No one is called to be another Hannah. Hannah's experience was unique. Her son was to be unique. And whatever lessons are to be gleaned from God's dealings with them, we must be careful to distinguish what is timeless from what was exclusively for that moment in the unfolding history of God's plan of redemption. God had his special consolations and care for both Hannah and Samuel, in spite of the otherwise 'unnatural' separation of mother and child. And every element in this whole process dovetailed into his purposes not only for Israel, but for the future course of redemptive history.

A song of thanksgiving [2:1–10]

The underlying uniqueness of the birth of Samuel finds its most eloquent expression in what Geerhardus Vos has called the 'prayer-song' of Hannah.[4] It is a prayer in the form of a poem or a song. Keil and Delitzsch call it a 'psalm', for it is, indeed, a Scripture song – a 'spiritual song' (i.e., a Holy Spirit-given (inspired) song) as in Ephesians 5:19 and Colossians 3:16.[5] But it is more than that, because it is a prototype of the Magnificat (Luke 1:46–55), in which Mary praised God for the child she was soon to bring into the world.[6] The Magnificat and also Zacharias' Benedictus

(Luke 1:68–79) are virtually identical in content to the Song of Hannah, although a millennium comes between them! And this places in even finer focus the redemptive significance of the latter – Hannah, moved by the Spirit of God, uttered a song of praise that was prophetic and messianic! From Samuel it looked ahead to the Lord Jesus Christ. Hannah and her song are not mere echoes of a past long gone – a story to warm the emotions after the fashion of magazine fiction. Hannah directs us to her Redeemer. And, as we listen to her, we hear the voice of Jesus.

1. Praise to the Lord (2:1)

Hannah's joy was unconfined. But her praise did not dwell on the gift that God had given her. Her praise was for the *Giver* of the gift. She rejoiced, 'not in Samuel, but in the Lord. She overlook[ed] the gift and praise[ed] the Giver' (Matthew Henry). From within her heart, she rejoiced in the Lord, for her '**horn**' was '**lifted high**'. The horn is that of the ox and is a symbol of strength (Deuteronomy 33:17; Psalm 75:5). God had overthrown her weakness in giving her a son. Consequently her mouth gave testimony to her delight in this deliverance. She '**boasts**' over her enemies (NIV), but the more accurate rendering of the AV is to be preferred, '**my mouth is enlarged over my enemies**,' for it is of God's goodness she speaks and no mere boast in the humbling of the opposition. The 'enlarging' of the mouth refers to the positive content of spiritual blessedness. Because she has been blessed so much, her mouth must open wider to give thanks to the Lord. And this in turn speaks of the experience of the Lord's people as a whole. What was true of Hannah can be, will be, must be true for all believers in every age.

2. The celebration of God for who he is (2:2–3)

The body of the song (2:2–8) is an exalted tribute to the character of God and to his mighty acts. He is first praised for who he is in himself. Hannah sings of the divine attributes. She looks at who God is before she considers what he has done. She thinks on her God. She meditates purely and simply on him as he has revealed himself. What we think about God is, as A. W. Tozer perceptively observed, 'the most important thing about us'.[7] The reason for this is obvious enough. The natural thing for a person to do is to construct his own idea of God and to the extent that this comes forth from an ignorant and darkened heart, so it will produce an idea of God that is not only different from the true character of God but is even a blasphemous distortion of his self-revealed glory. When God manifested himself to Moses at the burning bush – and this was only a shadow compared to what God revealed of himself to Moses on Mount Sinai – it was with the most intense awe and reverence that the patriarch was obliged to draw near to hear the word of the Lord. It was still 'only' (if we may use the term reverently) a theophany or visible representation of himself, and in symbolic form. It remained true that no one could see God and live (Exodus 33:20). God has revealed himself. His Word defines and directs our idea of who he is and how he is to be thought of and worshipped. And the other side of that is that what we actually do think about God tells a great deal about where we are spiritually. Someone, for example, who can talk about God as 'the man upstairs' – and we hear this very frequently, even from public figures on national television – cannot know him or, indeed, care in the slightest for him. Such a notion is sheer blasphemy and betrays a complete lack of interest in what God says about himself and a contemptuously trivial attitude to God and his claims upon the lives of his creatures. As always, the touchstone is God's self-revelation in his Word, the Bible. If we are to know the true God, we must know him as he has revealed himself in the Scriptures. It is 'to the law and to the testimony' that we must go. And if our imaginations or the speculations of churches, theologians, visionaries and artists do not speak 'according to this word, they have no light. . . !' (Isaiah 8:20).

Hannah had a high view of God, because she had a scriptural understanding of who he is. And the depth of her personal knowledge of God was commensurate with her readiness to embrace God's revealed view of himself. Everything in her believing experience only served, at one and the same time, to intensify both her awareness of his *otherness* as the altogether holy God who is to be reverenced and feared and her awareness of his *nearness* as the heavenly Father who

loves the people he has saved by grace through faith and
now fellowships with them as his children by adoption. The
tension between God's otherness and his nearness is resolved in the dynamic of saving faith. The believer knows
the real distance between the sinner and a holy God. Yet the
exercises of a faith that worships and adores that holy God
are the very means by which the Lord draws near and
ministers even within the human heart by his Spirit.

Hannah praised God for four attributes in particular: his
holiness, his omnipotence, his omniscience and his justice.

a. God is *holy*. '**There is no one holy like the Lord; there is
no one besides you. . .**' (2:2). He is holy because he is the
absolutely independent and self-sufficient God – the one
besides whom there is no one, the one from whom all
goodness and truth flow. 'Holiness is simply the moral
reflection of the glory of the one absolute God.'[8] (Compare
Isaiah 6:3.)

b. God is *all-powerful*. '**There is no rock like our God**' (2:2).
The Song of Moses is recalled here: 'For their rock is not
like our Rock, as even our enemies concede' (Deuteronomy
32:31; also vv. 4, 15). He is the Rock in which his people can
always trust, because he cannot be overthrown.

c. God is *all-knowing*. '**Do not keep talking so proudly or let
your mouth speak such arrogance, for the Lord is a God
who knows. . .**' (2:3). He knows the end from the beginning.
He is the searcher of our hearts and minds (Isaiah 46:10;
Hebrews 4:12).

d. God is *just*. His perfect knowledge and holiness issue in
perfect justice in all his ways. '**By him deeds are weighed**'
(2:3). The classic example of this is, of course, Daniel 5:27,
where Belshazzar was told, 'You have been weighed on the
scales and found wanting' (compare Proverbs 16:2; 21:2;
24:12).

3.   *The celebration of God for his mighty acts [2:4–8]*
Because he is who he is, he rules his creation in terms of his
kingdom government. His actions are expressive of his
attributes. There is holiness, power, wisdom and justice in
them all. For this reason, the wicked should tremble and be

afraid of the judgements of God, whereas the righteous need have no fear but may have a sure confidence in the Lord. Hannah therefore goes on to exult in the way in which God delivers his people and establishes his righteousness upon the earth.

Three examples of God's mighty acts are set forth in terms of a just reversal of circumstances.

a. **'The bows of the warriors are broken, but those who stumbled are armed with strength'** (2:4). The breaking of the bows refers not to the literal destruction of the weapons themselves, but to the breaking of the men in their hearts. Except for Jeremiah 51:56, all usages of the Hebrew *hatat* (to be broken or dismayed), refer to the person's spirit. It is a spiritual breaking that is meant (compare Jeremiah 10:2; 49:37). God will break wicked people. But, in contrast, he will lift up his poor and vulnerable ones. 'Blessed are the poor in spirit, for theirs is the kingdom of heaven,' said Jesus (Matthew 5:3).

b. **'Those who were full hire themselves out for food, but those who were hungry hunger no more'** (2:5). The godless rich will be dispossessed and the Lord's hungry and oppressed will be filled with good things. The wicked will even become a ransom for the righteous (Proverbs 21:18). The positive rewards of sin are transient; the wages of sin is eternal death (Romans 6:23).

c. **'She who was barren has borne seven children, but she who has had many sons pines away'** (2:5). 'Seven' is the symbolic number of the blessing of the God of the covenant (compare Ruth 4:15). Hannah was to have six children including Samuel (2:21). The pining away of the one who has had many sons, but has now lost them, is a reflection of the essential meaning of childlessness. It means the end of a posterity: 'Her sun will set while it is still day' (Jeremiah 15:9). For the Lord's people, covenant blessing means blessing in the line of the generations of believers. God's family has a future. And this, of course, includes all believers, whether single or married, childless or with families, because his family is a family of faith (Mark 3:35; 10:29, 30).

The point in these three examples is not to teach a doctrine of mechanical reversal of fortunes. If people think that being poor in this world will be rewarded with the riches of heaven, they are sadly mistaken. Poverty is not a virtue, any more than wealth is a sin. The real question is a person's relationship to the Lord. We must learn with the apostle Paul 'to be content whatever the circumstances' (Philippians 4:11). But for God's people there will be the healing of all that may have afflicted them in the course of their lives.

Three reasons for God's mighty acts are added in parallel with the foregoing examples. It is God who does these things – who (a) **'brings death and makes alive'**; (b) **'sends poverty and wealth'**, and (c) **'raises the poor from the dust. . .'** (2:6–8).

> 'No one from the east or the west
>   or from the desert can exalt a man.
> But it is God who judges:
>   He brings one down, he exalts another'
>
> (Psalm 75:6–7).

He can do this because he is the creator and upholder of the world (2:8).[9]

4.   *A prophecy of the coming of God's kingdom [2:9–10]*
These verses 'rise to a prophetic glance at the consummation of the kingdom of God'.[10] The key is the promise of a king. **'He will give strength to his king and exalt the horn of his anointed'** (2:10).[11] The king in view is the Davidic king. God would give him strength. And so we read of David in Psalm 89:20–21:

> 'I have found David my servant;
>   with my sacred oil I have anointed him.
> My hand will sustain him;
>   surely my arm will stengthen him.'

Then, in the Garden of Gethsemane, we see Jesus, the King of kings, receiving the ministry of the angels of God: 'An angel from heaven appeared to him and strengthened him'

(Luke 22:43). Ultimately, Jesus is the King to whom the word of prophecy points. How clearly Hannah understood this we are not told. But it is sure that she anticipated God's king and kingdom in the spirit of prophecy.

For the New Testament believer, there is a powerful practical thrust. We are called to Christ, to acknowledge him as the messianic King, and to give thanks with heart, voice and life for all his love towards us. We are called to live the life of his kingdom, the characteristics of which flow from the character of Jesus, its King. The promise is to all the generations of God's believing children from Hannah and before her right down to the present day and beyond, even to the great day when Christ returns to consummate his kingdom. The Lord will surely '**guard the feet of his saints**' (2:9). And he will as certainly overthrow the wicked and '**judge the ends of the earth**' (2:10). The Lord Jesus Christ has come. He has saved his people and given each one the gift of eternal life. He has been faithful to his promise. He has answered the prayers of his people abundantly. He has been our constant and faithful guide and companion. He has been the bread of life to us day by day. How great is his faithfulness!

Hannah gave thanks for answered prayer. We are called to reflect on how the Lord has dealt with us. Will you say, with godly Hannah,

> 'My heart exults in the Lord
> My horn is exalted in the Lord.
> My mouth speaks boldly against my enemies,
> Because I rejoice in thy salvation'?

> (2:1 NASB).

References

[1] A.W. Tozer, *The Knowledge of the Holy*, (Bromley, England: Send the Light Trust, 1961), p.86.

[2] R.P. Gordon, *1 & 2 Samuel*, p. 77.

[3] D.F. Payne, *Samuel*, (Philadelphia: Westminster Press, 1982), p. 12.

[4] G. Vos, *Biblical Theology*, (Grand Rapids: W.B. Eerdmans, 1948), p. 329.

[5] C.F. Keil and F. Delitzsch, (*The Books of Samuel*, Grand Rapids: W.B. Eerdmans), p. 29.

[6] R.P. Gordon, p. 78.

[7] A.W. Tozer, p. 10.

[8] C.F. Keil and F. Delitzsch, p. 31.

[9] *Ibid.*, p. 33.

[10] *Ibid.*, p. 34.

[11] This statement is regarded by 'critical' scholarship to be 'impossible for Hannah' on the grounds that her son, Samuel, later 'held earthly kingship to be a rejection of Yahweh's kingship'. An editor is said to have taken these words from a later setting – probably during the monarchy but before the exile – and ascribed them to Hannah in order to support the monarchic *status quo* (See R.W. Klein, pp. 14–15). Such a viewpoint rests on the presupposition that the text as it stands is not a genuine account of the events it purports to record, that it was inconceivable that Hannah should be the vehicle of a prophetic revelation from God, that anything that seems prophetic had to have been written after the event and that the divine inspiration, infallibility and inerrancy of the Scriptures are an impossibility (See Keil and Delitzsch, pp. 29–30, for a fine statement of the issues involved).

3.
The fall of the house of Eli

Please read 1 Samuel 2:11–36 and 4:12–22

'Therefore the Lord, the God of Israel, declares: "I promised that your house and your father's house would minister before me for ever." But now the Lord declares: "Far be it from me! Those who honour me I will honour, but those who despise me will be disdained"' (1 Samuel 2:30).

There is not a Christian parent alive who does not earnestly desire his children to follow him in the faith and believe on the Lord Jesus Christ as their own Saviour and Lord. As the writer of Proverbs says,

> 'The father of a righteous man has great joy;
>   he who has a wise son delights in him.
> May your father and mother be glad;
>   may she who gave you birth rejoice'
>   (Proverbs 23:24–25).

'Happy was the famous Eliot, the apostle to the native Americans,' wrote George Lawson, 'who could say, that God had given him six children, of whom three were with Christ, and the other three were in Christ.'[1] On the other hand, says the same writer, 'Unhappy is the parent who beholds his children walking in the way of destruction, and deaf to that voice which recalls them.'

The children of believers are peculiarly privileged. 'Sons are a heritage from the Lord,' says the psalmist, 'children a reward from him' (Psalm 127:3). The children of believers, says the apostle Paul, 'are holy' (1 Corinthians 7:14). They are, unlike unbelievers and their children, within the sphere of the covenant community, in both the home and the church. Like Timothy, they are taught the Scriptures 'from infancy' (2 Timothy 3:15). They are taught to pray to God, as to a heavenly Father. And they are taken to the public worship of God, to sing praise, to join in prayer and to hear the preaching of the Word. They are prayed for by the whole people of God and they are urged to embrace the promises of God personally, through coming to Jesus Christ in faith and receiving him as Saviour and Lord. And without presuming on the sovereignty of God in salvation or any other aspect of his covenant promises, we expect blessing for our children as much as we expect blessing for ourselves as confessing Christians. We not only want them to embrace Christ, we look for them to embrace Christ! And we do so with a confidence that is not of ourselves, but rests upon the nature of the gospel of Christ and the promises of God in Christ as set forth in the Word of God. No Christian parent expects his child to reject the gospel and commit himself to unbelief in one of its forms. He may be afraid of this happening. He will pray and work to the end that it does not. But when it comes to his expectations, he expects great things from God, because it is in the very nature of God to do great things for his people.

It is therefore always felt to be a wonderful blessing when a child is born into a believing home, and still more, when that child comes to profess faith and follow the Lord. And it is as deeply felt to be a tragedy – and an abnormality, a breach of normal Christian expectations – when a child of believing parents turns away decisively from the Lord, sets his face against Jerusalem and places his feet upon the road to a lost eternity. There is a particular sadness about the rejection of privileges, especially the privileges of the gospel and the covenant community, the church. This was the awful sin of the Jews of Jesus' day and it was soon to cast its shadow over the New Testament church (Matthew 23; Hebrews 6; 2 Peter 2; compare 2 John 4).

We have already seen, in the unfolding of the events recorded in 1 Samuel, the joy of Hannah in the birth of her son and in his dedication to the service of God's house at

Shiloh. In a divinely inspired, prophetic song of the kingdom of God and the Lord's Anointed, she praised the Lord for all his goodness (2:1–10). She saw nothing but the blessings of God's everlasting covenant. And she expected that her three-year-old son, Samuel, would be blessed and be a blessing in terms of all the promises that God had made to his people and to her, as a child of God. And we know that Samuel did, by the grace of God, become a mighty servant of the Lord and fulfil the prayerful desires of his godly mother for his service to Yahweh.

In the passage that follows we are presented with a tragic contrast (2:11–36). From the sublime heights of Hannah's prophetic utterance we are plunged into the grim and degraded realities of the actual spiritual state of God's people, in this case exemplified by the wretched behaviour of the sons of Eli, Hophni and Phinehas. Here was the case of a godly father with wicked sons. Here was the situation into which Samuel was called and over against which he would exercise his prophetic ministry from God. Here was a covenant community with unbelieving priests, inviting the judgement of God and desperately in need of spiritual revival.

Contrasts within the covenant community [2:11–26]

Israel was the church of the Old Testament. It was the covenant community of God upon earth. It consisted of all those, together with their families, who were bound in covenant to be God's people, the sign of which was circumcision. This covenant was monergistic; that is to say, God made the covenant out of his absolute – and, therefore, unilateral – sovereign purpose of love. Although, in the Old Testament, this covenant was administered by God in terms of a theocratic national entity (Israel), its central focus was not racial purity *per se*, but the religious covenant relationship itself. In actual fact, relatively little of the blood of Abraham was in the covenanted 'seed of Abraham' (Genesis 14:14; 17:10–14). James Jordan has pointed out that 'Although only 70 from the loins of Jacob went down into Egypt, so many servants went along that they had to be

given the whole land of Goshen in which to live.'[2] Everything in the life of God's people was conditioned by God's
covenant. The whole of life was a matter of responding
faithfully to that covenant and submitting every aspect of
life to the rule of Yahweh – the covenant God, the Father-
God, the Redeemer of his people.

This is, of course, exactly what the life of the New
Covenant/Testament Christian is about. It is to be regretted
that modern Christians are more adept at deciding what is
not carried over from the Old Testament to the New, than
they are willing to accept what *is* clearly of positive application for today. Here, then, is the starting-point for a
positive grasp of the meaning and application of the teaching of the Old Testament: namely, the centrality of the
covenant in the dealings of God with the human race.

Sin, then, is not a matter of mere ignorance, presumably
resolvable through instruction and exhortation. Sin is
covenant-breaking and sinners are covenant-breakers. This
has its particular meaning, of course, in the context of the
covenant community. And the seriousness of the transgression is that much more aggravated, precisely because it
is the breach of known duty and prior commitment.

There is a threefold contrast arising from the account of
the latter days of the priesthood of Eli at Shiloh. Firstly, the
degenerate priesthood of Eli's sons is contrasted with the
emerging revived priesthood of Samuel. Secondly, there is
an implied contrast between lax parental nurture and godly
family life. Thirdly, there is a theological dimension involving the fact of election and reprobation within the external
administration of the covenant, i.e., within the covenant
community, the church.

1. Covenant-breaking clerics (11:18)

The Old Testament church was not itself apostate. There
were godly priests and devout people (2:24, 27). As usual,
downgrade movements – whether political, ethical or religious – are movements of the upper classes. Ordinary folk
tend to be more conservative than the leadership classes,
who like to use their position of power and influence to
maximum personal advantage. The chief priest and judge of
Israel, Eli, was a godly man but he was old and was losing

control of the situation. His sons, Hophni and Phinehas, were '**wicked men**' who '**had no regard for the Lord**' (2:12). As they were the heirs apparent to their father, their influence could be assumed to be disastrous to the welfare of God's people. They did not know the Lord.

Their rotten attitude was exemplified by the way they plundered the meat of the sacrifices brought by the Lord's people. According to God's law, the priests were allowed particular portions of the animals offered for these various sacrifices.[3] The sons of Eli were guilty on at least two points of transgressing these laws (Leviticus 1–7, especially Leviticus 7:31–36).

a.   The first was that they used a '**three-pronged fork**' to extract from the pan (in which the meat was being boiled) '**whatever the fork brought up**' (2:13–14). They therefore disregarded the precise restrictions on what they could and could not take for themselves. In general, then, they set aside God's law and did what they wanted to do (2:13–14).

b.   The most blatant manifestation of their irreverence for the things of God was that '**Even before the fat was burned, the servant of the priest would come and say to the man who was sacrificing, "Give the priest some meat to roast; he won't accept boiled meat from you, but only raw."**' And he was prepared to take it by force, if the worshipper insisted on the burning of the fat first (2:15–16). The fat, you see, was reserved for God. To eat it was forbidden by the law and the penalty for doing so was death (Leviticus 7:22–25). The function of this law was to indicate in a most tangible way the nature of holiness: on the one hand, the holiness of God, to whom this portion of the sacrifice was to be exclusively dedicated; and, on the other hand, the separation of the covenant people to the Lord, sealed by obedience to God's Word.[4]

The contrast between the sons of Eli and the son of Hannah is then plainly stated: '**The sin of the young men was very great in the Lord's sight, for they were treating the Lord's offering with contempt.**' Samuel, on the other hand, '**was ministering before the Lord**' (2:17–18). Mention is made of his wearing a priestly garment – '**a linen ephod**'. R. P. Gordon notes that 'There is no talk of lower age limits for priestly service in this story where grown men have failed (cf. Numbers 8:24–26; 1 Chronicles 23:24–32).'[5] The unique nature of Samuel's calling is thereby emphasized. The lifelong Nazirite was a lifelong priest. And with every passing year, Samuel was growing in grace. What an irony – and yet a wonderful consolation from God – that Eli should see Samuel flourish under his tutelage in the twilight of his days, when his own children had turned out to be such worthless characters!

2.   The breakdown of the family (2:19–25)

It is no accident that the faithfulness of Hannah and her husband and the growth and happiness of their family life are mentioned side by side with the apostasy of Hophni and Phinehas and the weakness of their father. Godly families are absolutely essential to the social fabric of nations. They are also a vital component of a flourishing church. The history of Israel was itself a proof to God's people, if proof were needed, that God 'caused his covenant to develop in the line of successive generations'.[6] Like every other aspect of daily life, the family was subject to the lordship of Yahweh, the covenant God, God had, and always has, a proprietary interest in the family. His people have very definite responsibilities towards their children, to the end that they might also embrace God as their Lord and be a powerful witness in their own generation. This was no mystery to the children of Israel (Genesis 3:15; 9:9; 17:7) and it is every bit as clear in its New Testament fulness to us today (Acts 2:39; Galatians 3:7–9; John 15:1–2 [cf. Psalm 80:8–16; Isaiah 5:1–7]). The family is to be an arena in which personal godliness is promoted and the glory of God is manifested in personal relationships that are rooted in commitment to the Lord (Ephesians 5:21–24; Colossians 3:1–21; 1 Timothy 5:8; 2 Timothy 3:15; Titus 2:4–5; 1 Peter 3:1–7).

Hannah's family life exemplified these claims and blessings of the Lord. Even though she had given Samuel into the care of Eli, to serve in the tabernacle at Shiloh, she continued to be as much of a mother to him as these unique circumstances allowed (2:19). And the Lord honoured her and blessed her so that she was to be surrounded by little 'olive shoots' in the persons of three sons and two daughters (2:20–21; Psalm 128:3). This was a family as it ought to be. This was the fruit of God's everlasting covenant as it applied to the life together of a believing husband and wife in Israel (Psalm 68:6; 127:3–5; 128:3).

This appears not to have been the case with Eli and his sons. We are told nothing about their earlier home life. What is clear is that all parental authority had been lost. Complaints had come to Eli about the immorality of his sons: '**How they slept with the women who served at the entrance to the Tent of Meeting**' (2:22). The background to this may be, as D. F. Payne has noted, 'the fact that at Canaanite shrines there were ritual prostitutes'. Payne further suggests that 'It may be that Eli's sons were importing pagan as well as immoral practices to Shiloh.'[7] This was a public scandal (2:23–24). But more than that, it was total rebellion against God and so aggravated an offence as to imply the most fearful consequences: 'But if a man sins against the Lord, who will intercede for him?' (2:25). Hophni and Phinehas were priests. They interceded for the sins of others. Who would intercede for them, when they so flagrantly violated the law of the Lord?

Eli rebuked them, but they ignored him completely. This is a common experience of parents and hardly a ground for censure, far less judgement. Where, then, did Eli fail? The answer to that is also to be found in the Word of God. In Deuteronomy 21:18–21, provision was made whereby the parents of a profligate son who refused persistently the discipline of his father and mother were to bring him to the civil authorities ('the elders at the gate of his town') for judgement. This could involve the death penalty: 'You must purge the evil from among you,' said the Lord. 'All Israel will hear of it and be afraid.' It should be remembered that small children at home were not in view in this proscription. It concerned older sons in the context of an extended family in which parental responsibility was operative irrespective of what we call 'the age of consent'. Eli's relationship to Hophni and Phinehas fell into this category exactly. And Eli's sin was in doing no more than expressing his displeasure. In God's eyes, it was not enough to enter a dissent. He had to do more. He had to move heaven and earth to call them to account and purge away the evils for which they were responsible – evils which were blighting the worship of God at Shiloh and therefore eating away at the national, covenant integrity of the life of God's people. But Eli did nothing and the effect of that, in practice, was to honour his sons more than the Lord (2:29; 3:13).

One wonders what kind of discipline Eli had exercised over his sons in their formative years. We are not told. What is plainly implied is our responsibility before the Lord – both parents and children. There must be a loving discipline in the home (Proverbs 19:18; 23:13–14; Colossians 3:21). And it must be answered by a loving obedience (Proverbs 15:5; Colossians 3:20).

3. Election and reprobation (2:25–26)

God's covenant with Israel was not a guarantee that all the children born to Hebrew parents would grow up to be committed believers in the Lord. And it was similarly true that the godliest of parents could have wicked children. There was – and there remains – nothing automatic about the grace of God. As to his sovereign will, the election of sinners to salvation is unconditional and his covenant promises are therefore unconditional. He *will* save his people from their sins. '*All* that the Father gives me,' declared Jesus, 'will come to me. . . I shall lose *none* of *all that he has given me*, but raise them up at the last day' (John 6:37, 39). This is put into effect, however, in the dynamic arena of human response to the gospel call to repent and believe. Therefore Jesus added, 'Whoever *comes to me* I will never drive away' (John 6:37). Coming to the Lord is the essential requirement for enjoying the benefits of the covenant promises of God. It is an evidence, rather than a condition, of the sovereign hand of God in saving the sinner. But in the personal experience of that sinner, there is a turning to the Lord which is at once free and yet also the work of God the Holy Spirit. The external evidence of the inward change and commitment has always been a credible profession of faith – that is, a profession of faith in Christ *in words*, together with a *consistent life* that evidences the sincerity of that profession.

The Bible, however, teaches what we may call 'the doctrine of hypocrisy'. People lie – to God, to the church and sometimes to themselves. And, however much the church tests the credibility of those who profess to be believers, the truth is that our discernment is very fallible. Only God looks on the heart. The covenant community is always afflicted with the need for the disciplinary sifting and testing of both backsliders and hypocritical professors of faith. This was true in Israel and it is true in the church of the New Testament. It will remain true until the Lord returns. Indeed, some of the worst enemies of God's people will be those who arise from within their own ranks – disorder, division, heresies and antichrists all arise from within the covenant community (1 Corinthians 11:18–22; James 4:1; John 2:18–19).

Here is the key to understanding the case of Hophni and Phinehas, except that we are told the deeper purpose of God for that depraved pair: they '**did not listen to their father's rebuke, for it was the Lord's will to put them to death**' (2:23). We are given a glimpse of the other side of God's secret will – his purpose to condemn the reprobate lost. Again, we cannot read the heart. We see human wickedness but cannot tell what God's purpose is towards its per-petrators. After all, he saves sinners. Every believer knows he was lost and wicked, when the Lord saved him. But with Hophni and Phinehas, God drew back the veil and showed us his otherwise secret will. He meant to put these fellows to death. And there can be no doubt that a lost eternity is in view. Hophni and Phinehas were reprobates – not in the everyday sense of the incorrigible rascal for whom we feel a sneaking affection, but in the biblical and theological sense of the *adokimos*, the irrevocably committed sinner who is reprobate before God (Romans 1:28; 2 Corinthians 13:5–7; 2 Timothy 3:8; Titus 1:16).

Why does God reveal this? At one level, it is to highlight the work of grace he was doing in bringing Samuel and reformation to the covenant people of God. But at the personal level, it is to show us that all the privileges of the covenant promises of God will avail nothing if we refuse to commit ourselves to the Lord. Hophni, Phinehas and Sam-uel were all Levites and covenant children. They were born into the church of their time. They were born to the blessed privileges of the covenant community. They were expected, according to the promises of the God of all grace, to come to mature faith and obedience and minister before the Lord in his house. As to the external administration of the covenant, the same promises and privileges were given to all three. But two were reprobates and one was of the elect.

The challenge is clear. Covenant privileges do not automatically guarantee salvation. Circumcision did not save. Neither does baptism, whether of an infant or of an adult. Profession of faith is worthless and church membership a charade if these are not accompanied by the evidence of a changed life. We are justified by faith alone, but not that faith which is alone. Each one must know the Lord in his own heart. That is the question for you, right now!

Promise and performance [2:27–36]

God's promises are not blank cheques. It isn't enough just to write in your name and rest in blithe presumption of the Lord's favour. Covenant obligations are attached to covenant promises. Eli's sons had failed and the reckoning was at hand.

1. Blessings rejected (2:27–29)
A prophet was sent to Eli to confront him with God's controversy with the performance of his family in the service of the tabernacle. He reminded Eli of all that God had done for his **'father's house'** (2:27–28). The reference was to Aaron and to God's promise that the Aaronic priesthood would continue in terms of 'a lasting ordinance' (Exodus 29:9). Eli was of the line of Ithamar, the fourth son of Aaron.[8] Eli and his sons were priests according to that promise. Why then, asked the Lord, did they so abuse that trust and scorn God's appointed sacrifice? Eli's complicity in this error was one of toleration rather than participation, but it was complicity nevertheless, for he had honoured his sons more than the Lord by letting them go unchecked (2:29).

2. Sentence pronounced (2:30–36)
The conjunction of promise and performance within the sphere of God's covenant was sealed in the words of the

anonymous man of God: '**Those who honour me I will honour, but those who despise me will be disdained**' (2:30). God's covenant dealings with men and women interact dynamically with human response to the claims of obedience. The priesthood would be taken from the line of Eli. This would not happen immediately (2:31). But Eli's descendants would die in the prime of life (2:33).

The sign that this was happening would be the death, in the same day, of Hophni and Phinehas (2:34). Thereafter the descendants of Eli would be obliged to depend upon the largesse of the revived priesthood which would supplant them (2:36). The line of Eli did indeed continue in the persons of Ahijah, Ahimelech and Abiathar. When Abiathar was deposed, Zadok became the sole high priest and the line of Eleazar became permanently established (1 Kings 2:27).[9]

This was a fearful judgement. But in it there is for us a reaffirmation of the promises of God and a challenge to all who will hear what he is saying. God will honour all those who honour him! And there is all the greater power and incentive to heed that word and claim the promise now that the priesthood of the Old Testament has been superseded by the fulness of the New Covenant in Jesus Christ, the once-for-all 'high priest' (Hebrews 8:10–13; 9:11–15). The one everlasting covenant of God has been republished with all the clarity of the gospel of Jesus Christ. He commands our faith and our love. And he commands our obedience. All the privileges of a Christian home and a Christian church fellowship, profoundly redolent as they are of the promises of God, point us earnestly to Christ, that we might embrace him as our Saviour in repentance and faith.

In the 1924 Olympic Games in Paris, the Scottish athlete Eric Liddell took the gold medal in the 400 metres in world record time. Athletics historian John W. Keddie records that 'Back in the British quarters [a hotel] on the morning of the final a British team masseur passed a little note to Liddell, who said he would open it at the Stadium. The note read: "In the old book it says, He that honours me I will honour. Wishing you the best of success always." The quotation was from 1 Samuel 2, verse 30. By Liddell's own testimony that act and that note had a profound effect on

the outcome of the race.'[10] Liddell had been one of the
favourites for the 100 metres, but had declined to run when
he heard, long before the games, that the heats were to be
run on the Lord's Day. As a Christian – he would later be a
missionary in China – he believed that honouring the Lord
meant denying himself the opportunity to excel in what
was, until that point, his best event.

The Lord is faithful: those that honour him he will
honour.

References

[1] G. Lawson, *Sermons on the Family* (c. 1800), p. 219. The Rev. Dr George
Lawson (1749–1820) was an eminent Scottish pastor and professor of the
Secession Church. John Eliot (1604–1690), the 'Apostle to the Indians',
was one of the towering figures in the development of the New England
colonies. He was responsible for the first Bible printed in America (in
Algonkian, not English!) and also the first book for congregational praise
(*The Bay Psalm Book*, 1640).

[2] James B. Jordan. 'Christian Zionism and Messianic Judaism',
Appendix B in David Chilton, *The Days of Vengeance*, (Fort Worth, Texas:
Dominion Press, 1987), pp. 613–614.

[3] Gleason L. Archer, *A Survey of Old Testament Introduction*, (Chicago:
Moody Press, 1964), p. 232.

[4] Rousas J. Rushdoony, *The Institutes of Biblical Law*, (Nutley, N.J.: Craig
Press, 1973), pp. 83–88.

[5] R. P. Gordon, p. 82.

[6] Herman Hoeksema, *Believers and their Seed*, (Grand Rapids: Reformed
Free Publ. Assoc., 1971), p. 85.

[7] D. F. Payne, p. 18.

[8] We know this in a roundabout way. Ahimelech was 'a descendant of
Ithamar' (1 Chronicles 24:3). Ahimelech's father was Ahitub, the son of
Phinehas, who was, of course, the son of Eli (1 Samuel 22:9; 14:3).

[9] C. F. Keil and F. Delitzsch, p. 39.

[10] John W. Keddie, *Scottish Athletics*, (Glasgow: Scottish Amateur Athletic
Association, 1982), p. 56.

4.
God's spokesman

Please read 1 Samuel 3:1–4:1

'Then Samuel said, "Speak, for your servant is listening."... *The Lord was with Samuel as he grew up, and he let none of his words fall to the ground'* (1 Samuel 3:10, 19).

'The child is father of the man,' said the poet, John Milton. Parents can see the steady emergence of the characteristics of adulthood in their children, even from a very early age. And however great the changes in these young lives may be, the personality of the child is readily discernible in that of the mature individual. We know this is true for ourselves. We look at the photographs of long-departed infancy and see, in the twinkle of an eye or the set of the mouth, the attitudes and traits of middle age. We may have come a long way, but we are the same people. The child was indeed the father of the now grown man.

The Christian sees more than naked physical or mental development. His eye of faith discerns the hand of God in all these things. One of the most amazing revelations of the greatest change that the human heart can experience – being born again by the Holy Spirit (regeneration, John 3:3–8) and coming to Christ in faith (conversion, Acts 16:31) – is to realize that the Lord was dealing with us throughout the whole course of our lives and, indeed, had a purpose for us from before the creation of the world (Ephesians 1:4). God has revealed himself as the God who deals with us in terms of his everlasting covenant in Christ. He fixed his love, in eternity, upon those he purposed to save, in time. And even when we were oblivious to his loving purpose and his providential care, he was steadfastly fulfilling his plan for our lives. The keystone of this truth is the fact that 'While we were still sinners, Christ died for us' (Romans 5:8).

The same hand of God is so clearly evident in the development of the young Samuel. We have already seen the events surrounding his birth and dedication (1:1–28). In the Song of Hannah, we were afforded a prophetic glimpse of the kingdom of the Lord's anointed and thereby given to suspect that Samuel was to have a key position in the unfolding of that kingdom (2:1–10). Then the contrasts between Samuel, the godly seed, and Hophni and Phinehas, the reprobate sons of Eli, were set forth and we heard God's pronouncement of doom upon them and upon the whole house of Eli (2:11–36). In the third chapter, the next phase of the rise of Samuel is unfolded. The years had gone by. It is probable that Hannah's other children were born during this time (see 2:21). Samuel was perhaps twelve years of age. Hophni and Phinehas continued to heap discredit on God's house and add to the mountain of provocations that was to crash down upon them in God's good time (see 4:12–22). And at this point – before the deluge of divine chastisement upon Israel and Eli's house – God acted to install Samuel as a true prophet of the Lord. Samuel became God's spokesman.

The passage falls very naturally into three sections, each one reflecting an aspect of the way in which God calls his people to his service. First of all, the Lord reveals himself to Samuel (3:1–9); secondly, he gives Samuel his first prophetic message – about the fall of Eli's house (3:10–18); and thirdly, Samuel is recognized by God's people as a true prophet of the Lord (3:19 – 4:1).

The call of God [3:1–9]

The narrative is straightforward. Samuel and Eli ministered in the tabernacle day by day. They also slept there, probably in booths at the side of the main enclosure (3:1–3). We are reminded in these verses of the progressive incapacity of

Eli: not only were his eyes '**becoming so weak that he could
barely see**,' but there is more than a hint of his decline as a
man of God, for '**In those days the word of the Lord was
rare; there were not many visions**.'

It was late at night. The great seven-branched lampstand,
the Menorah, which was lit at evening and allowed to burn
out by morning (Exodus 27:21; Leviticus 24:3), still burned
within the Holy Place.

A voice came out of the night – presumably from the
direction of the Most Holy Place and the ark of the
covenant, for there it was that God's presence was manifested (3:4). Samuel thought it must be Eli and went to the
old priest, who told him to go back to sleep. Twice more –
three times in all – this was repeated until it dawned on Eli
that it was God who was calling. And so, '**Eli told Samuel,
"Go and lie down, and if he calls you, say, 'Speak, Lord,
for your servant is listening'"**' (3:9). At that point Samuel
was ready to hear the Lord's voice.

1. The word of the Lord was rare

It is specifically noted in the text that there was a dearth of
prophecy at that time: '**The word of the Lord was rare;
there were not many visions**' (3:1). This was an indication
of the spiritual declension of the time. It also points up a
principle that equally applies to our own day: namely, that
apostasy in the church is accompanied by a famine of the
Word of God. God withdrew his light from the wicked
priests at Shiloh. And the same thing has happened in
modern churches which have turned from God's Word to
the empty residue of a century or more of critical scholarship and the hollow self-deceit of Christless doctrine and
ethics. Now, as then, there is no shortage of 'religion' and
certainly no shortage of clergymen! It is the revealed truth
of God that is conspicuous by its absence from the theology,
the preaching and, not least, the lives of clergy and people
alike. As in the days of the boy Samuel, the so-called
Christian West is afflicted by a famine of the Word and the
need of revival is nowhere more obvious than in the
crumbling churches of a degenerate main-line Prot-
estantism. Lachlan Mackenzie, that rugged preacher of the
Scottish Highlands, once preached at the ordination of a

new minister in Applecross, in the West Highlands. His sermon was on 'The Call to the Ministry'. In it he declared, 'If people go to perdition in these days it is not for want of ministers. The clergy are likely to become soon as plentiful as the locusts in Egypt, and which of them is the greater plague of the two, time and the experience of the Church will discover.' Nearly two hundred years on, the evil fruits are too apparent to require much comment. There has rarely been a day when there was not a greater need for men to be raised up to declare God's Word to the most worried generation the world has known. God knew the need of Israel and he sent Samuel. He knows our needs and has, in Christ, given the church the outpouring of the Holy Spirit with the mandate to preach Christ to the ends of the earth until he shall have complete dominion over all his enemies (Psalm 110; Hebrews 1:13).

2.   *The readiness of Samuel to hear the call of God*

Samuel was a child of the covenant. The Lord was with him from the very beginning of his life. There is a sweetness about the spirit with which he answers the successive calls from the Lord. Each time he goes to Eli, ready to do his bidding. Matthew Henry says of these calls, 'The call which Divine grace designs to make effectual shall be repeated until it is so, till we come at the call.' Samuel answered with a willing enough spirit.

He did not recognize that it was the Lord calling him because he had not, up to that point, directly experienced the revelation of God's Word. This is the meaning of the word: '**Now Samuel did not yet know the Lord: the word of the Lord had not yet been revealed to him**' (3:7). To say he did not yet know the Lord does not mean, in this context, that Samuel was an unbeliever. What it refers to is the fact that up to this moment, Samuel had not been given that special *prophetic knowledge of God* which is fundamental to the prophetic gift. Had he already been called and gifted in this way, he would not have made the mistake of thinking it was Eli. R. P. Gordon rightly notes that 'It is Samuel's inexperience which delays his response to the divine caller.'[2] He loved the Lord but he was not yet able to recognize his voice.

The gifts for serving God [3:10–18]

When the Lord called Samuel for a fourth time, the boy was armed with the answer that Eli had given to him. It would seem that, on this occasion, God came to Samuel in a more distinct way: '**The Lord came and stood there, calling as at other times, "Samuel! Samuel!"**' (3:10). This is one of these verses in Scripture that sometimes can tell us more about the commentator than the commentator can tell us about the text. Klein, in his First Samuel volume in the putatively 'evangelical'[3] *Word Biblical Commentary* series, follows the redaction-criticism approach and sees it as a dream experience – and one attributed to Samuel centuries later by the 'deuteronomist historian'. Gordon keeps us guessing with a vague prevarication that suggests Samuel's experience with the voice was more than a dream. He never quite comes out and says as much in plain English. Payne, on the other hand, asserts that Eli 'was able to bear witness that Samuel heard the call of God' and that God's fourth call to Samuel was accompanied by 'a vision of God'.[4] The text clearly emphasizes the objective reality of God's call to Samuel. Samuel replied as audibly and objectively as the Lord had called him: '**Speak, for your servant is listening**' (3:10).

God then told Samuel the substance of the prophecy which, years before, he had declared by a man of God to Eli (3:11–14; cf. 2:27–36). This was, of course, news to Samuel. And it surely hit him with some force, for there was the implication that this was to be the first prophetic declaration of his career as God's spokesman.

Samuel went back to his bed and when he got up in the morning he went about his regular chore of opening the doors of the house of the Lord (3:15). For obvious reasons, Samuel was afraid to tell Eli what the Lord had told him (3:15). But Eli adjured Samuel to tell all, emphasizing the order with the characteristic Hebrew oath: '**May God deal with you, be it ever so severely . . .**' (3:16–17; cf. 1 Kings 22:16; Matthew 26:63). Once told the truth – it was, in fact, the confirmation of the earlier prophecy of the unnamed 'man of God' – Eli sadly uttered words which have found a place in many a believer's heart, when he recognized the chastisement of the Lord: '**He is the Lord; let him do what is good in his eyes**' (3:18). Eli submitted to the Lord's verdict. William Garden Blaikie's assessment of Eli hits the mark: 'Eli was memorable for the passive virtues. He could bear much, though he could dare little.'[5] Samuel had fulfilled his first prophetic assignment.

This incident is replete with points of application relevant to each one of us today and to the way in which we serve the Lord in the church.

1. Spiritual gifts precede office

In God's service, the necessary gifts are given by the Lord before entrance into the office to which they are directed. Samuel was prepared for his prophetic task and office. He received the gifts and began to exercise them: then he was publicly recognized as a prophet. What was true of the priestly and prophetic offices of the Old Testament is true of the offices in the New Testament: 'No one takes this honour upon himself; he must be called by God, just as Aaron was' (Hebrews 5:4). And God never calls a man without also giving the necessary gifts. Men who seek influence rather than service tend to seek the ministry as a position or as a platform, rather than an office of God-called servanthood. Churches sometimes will call a man to be a pastor, even though there is scant evidence of genuine pastoral gifts. We hear far too often of the desire of a congregation to 'get a minister', as if having a body in the pulpit was equivalent to an effective ministerial settlement. The same principle applies to the plurality of elders and deacons in any given congregation. Whenever our eyes shift away from the biblical emphasis upon the discerning of spiritual gifts (as in 1 Timothy 3 and Titus 1), the tendency is for the order to be reversed. Men are put in office first and then expected in some way to discover and exercise the gifts later, if at all. Small wonder then, that instead of prophets we have 'churchmen' and instead of elders we have committee men (cf. 1 Timothy 5:22).

2. Gentleness in the service of God

It is interesting that God never commanded Samuel to go to Eli. To be sure, it was implicit in the revelation itself that Eli should hear the message. It was obviously not for Samuel's private edification. But the conveying of the prophecy was, to a degree, left to Samuel's judgement. It was taken out of his hands by Eli's insistence on hearing all that the Lord had said. But Samuel did not rush off and immediately blurt out his message to Eli. He slept on it and he pondered it. And in the meantime he went about his normal business. Of course, Samuel was very young and he was apprehensive about the inevitable confrontation with Eli, should he broach the subject. And yet, there is surely an element of humility in his restraint. 'It would be less offensive,' said Matthew Henry, 'and therefore more useful to Eli, when he saw that Samuel was not puffed up with it, nor forward to vent it, until Eli forced it from him.' There was a holy caution about Samuel's response. He was humbled by God's call and was most solemnly affected by the prophecy that God had given to him. This provides a fragrant contrast with the media-image of a prophet as a harsh fire-raising visionary who positively revels in his messages of doom. A true prophet preaches with tears in his eyes, especially if his message is a difficult one. The faithful preacher of the Word can only preach as 'a dying man to dying men'. Why? Because love for God is his motive and a compassionate knowledge of the human predicament is part of the fabric of his own person and experience, tempered by an awareness of the mercy of the Lord which has covered his own sins. As Jesus lamented for reprobate Jerusalem, who would not turn from their ways, so all God's true servants have heavy hearts as they proclaim the terrors of the law. And they rejoice all the more in the gospel of sovereign, free and saving grace in Jesus Christ and in those who come to Christ in repentance and faith.

3. *Proclaiming a difficult message*
Samuel's first prophecy was arguably as hard a message as any he was given in the later course of a ministry of difficult messages. It dramatically points up an ever-present element in all ministry for the Lord – the fact that the rebuke of sin is always integral to the message of redemption. The gospel message is essentially a very hard message both to preach and to hear, because it is a call to sinners to confess their

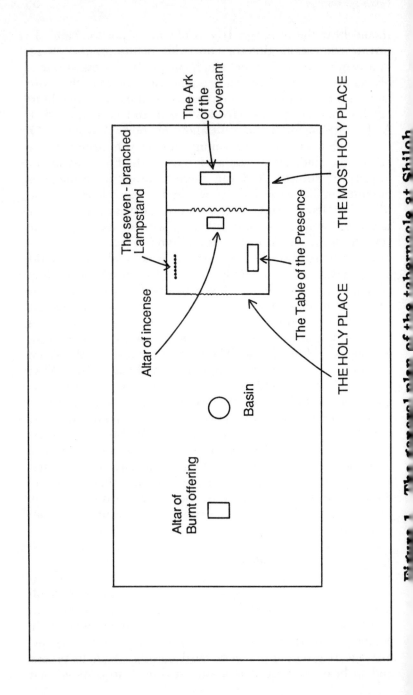

Figure 1 The general plan of the tabernacle at Shiloh

helplessness to save themselves and turn in repentance and faith to the Lord Jesus Christ for salvation through his substitutionary atonement for sin. And however winsomely and positively the benefits of the gospel are presented, it is impossible to avoid the 'offence of the cross' when Christ is faithfully proclaimed (Galatians 5:11). There are, of course, plenty of 'different' gospels that offer a less humbling redemption through our own self-generated good works and good thoughts (Galatians 1:6). But where Christ is proclaimed, we are confronted in the depth of our rebellious hearts with the necessity of unconditional surrender to his will and unreserved dependence upon his grace. We are obliged to renounce all our best thoughts and efforts and confess our 'righteousnesses' to be as 'filthy rags' (Isaiah 64:6 AV). And it is not as if it is necessary to belabour these points and deliver endless discourses on the terrors of the law, in order to confront people with the offence of the cross. No New Testament preacher is called to be a negativistic 'prophet of doom' who, like the character beloved of newspaper cartoonists, traipses up and down the high street resplendent in sandwich-boards emblazoned in lurid apocalyptic scarlet with the message: 'Prepare to meet your God – the end is at hand!' Christ *himself* is a stone that causes men to stumble and a rock that makes them fall (Isaiah 8:14; 1 Peter 2:8). Proclaiming Jesus as Saviour means preaching the cross. And that is the hardest message for someone who is spiritually dead in sin. Yet it is the most positive message in the world, for it cuts through all of our spiritual need and calls us to embrace Christ and, in him, to be reconciled to God our heavenly Father.

We are reminded, too, that speaking for God is no easier for the preacher than it is for the hearers. Just as the Lord takes no pleasure in the death of the wicked, so his servants do not enjoy calling men and women to account before God. It is never easy for a man, who is himself a weak sinner, though a saved one, to speak the words of the Lord. How can a sinner rebuke sin in others? How can an unrighteous man call for righteousness in others? Only with his eyes on Christ. Only with a love for people in his heart. Only with a candid awareness of his own debt to the mercy of the Lord Jesus Christ, his Redeemer.

Recognized by the Lord's people [3:19–21]

The years continued to pass. The awful judgement on the
house of Eli was deferred and Samuel continued to serve
the Lord at Shiloh under the tutelage of Eli. Three things
happened, however, which sealed Samuel's emergence as
God's spokesman and brought him to prominence and
maturity as the prophet of Israel.

1.   The Lord was with Samuel (3:19)
Samuel grew up physically and spiritually. All the earlier
aspirations of his mother, Hannah, and the promise of a life
devoted to the Lord from the beginning came to wonderful
fruition in the young man. He continued in the prophetic
ministry and the seal of that was that God '**let none of his
words fall to the ground**'. His prophecies were fulfilled. His
ministry 'rang true'. The Word of God attested to itself as
truth throughout the ministry of his servant. This is a
principle that stands for ever in the work and witness of the
followers of God. Personal holiness and the truth of the Word
are palpably evident in the life of true believers and are a most
powerful tool of evangelism.(Matthew 5:16: John 17:23).

2.   Samuel was publicly attested as a prophet (3:20)
The Lord's people discerned the work of God in Samuel.
They recognized his gifts and they honoured him as a true
prophet of the Lord. This too enshrines a universal principle: namely, that God's people recognize his messengers.
At a more basic level, perhaps, the point is that believers
recognize each other. There is a kind of spiritual instinct –
a fellow-feeling of shared faith – which draws believers to
one another. We can feel as if we have known one another
all our lives, even though we only met the other day.

3.   God blessed the people with his Word (3:21)
The famine of the Word – the rarity of God's self-revelation –
was relieved because '**The Lord continued to appear at
Shiloh, and there he revealed himself to Samuel through
his word**.' The worst excesses of Hophni and Phinehas, if not
yet a thing of the past, were eclipsed by the revival wrought
through Samuel's ministry. Shiloh was once more the lamp of

Israel and the godly could rejoice in the exaltation of divine truth and holiness in the very ministrations of the house of God. Whenever the church of God experiences the breath of the Holy Spirit, the whole tone of community life is tangibly raised. Like the coming of spring after the dreariness of winter, the sense of blessing from God fills the heart and transforms the daily course of life.

Let us pray for God to raise up his spokesmen for today. Let us pray for the filling of the Holy Spirit for each and every believer. Let us learn the work of God in Samuel's life and ministry, to look to the Lord for his blessing every day. Let us listen to what the Lord has said in his Word, the Bible and, with hearts devoted to the Lord Jesus Christ in love, go forward in joyous obedience to claim the promises of his everlasting covenant.

References

[1] C. F. Keil and F. Delitzsch, pp. 48–49, give a clear account of the arrangements in the tabernacle with relation to Samuel and his hearing of the voice of God.

[2] R. P. Gordon, p. 89.

[3] The dust-jacket proclaims the *Word Biblical Commentary*, in which Klein's *I Samuel* is the tenth volume, to be 'a showcase of the best in *evangelical critical* scholarship for a new generation'. 'Evangelical critical' is a seductive paradox. The 'critical' is *higher* critical and accepts the current redactionist theories which see 1 Samuel as a 'deuteronomist' history completed, from a wide variety of sources, just before, or even after, the Exile. Divine inspiration sinks without trace in an ocean of speculative scholarship. This is reflected frequently in the treatment of those passages which most explicitly involve the supernatural. Thus Klein sees 2:10 as 'impossible for Hannah' (see chapter 3, note 11). Likewise, God's calling of Samuel is never stated to be an objective historical event. It is, in accord with anti-supernatural modern scholarship, an 'auditory message dream theophany' (Klein, p. 31). The give-away is the word 'dream'. Like a convoy whose speed is determined by that of the slowest ship, the meaning of this statement is determined by that subjective inwardized notion – 'dream'. Did God really speak to Samuel? Was it in a dream? The text does not suggest that to be the case! As Keil and Delitzsch correctly observe, the words 'The Lord came and stood there' show 'that the revelation of God was an objectively real affair, and not a mere dream of Samuel's' (p. 49). Not even R. P. Gordon (p. 89) can bring himself to make such a clear statement, although he hints at his convictions by means of a curiously contrived comparison of

3:10 with the vision of Eliphaz in Job 4:12–16 – and that is surely a long way for a short cut!

[4] D. F. Payne, p. 23.

[5] W. G. Blaikie, *The First Book of Samuel*, (London: 1888), p. 57, quoted by R. P. Gordon, p. 90.

5.
The glory has departed!

Please read 1 Samuel 4:1–22

'She said, "The glory has departed from Israel, for the ark of God has been captured"' (1 Samuel 4:22).

The Philistines have long been a byword for uncultured heathenism, although today you are only likely to hear the word used, with mock hauteur, of people who are unenthusiastic about grand opera and unusual blends of tea. This is certainly unfair to the real Philistines for, although notorious pagans, they were neither uncultured nor something to joke about. These 'sea peoples', as they were also called, came from Crete and the Aegean, the biblical Caphtor, and settled on the coast near Gaza around 1175 B.C. – that is, during the judgeship of Deborah.[1] They were, in fact, superior to the Israelites in many departments and, consequently, were very formidable foes. Militarily, technologically and administratively they were, pound for pound, one of the most efficient nation states in the Eastern Mediterranean. They were the 'mighty mouse' of the region, willing to challenge, albeit without success, even the might of the Egypt of Rameses III.[2] As the vigorous and ambitious tenants of a rather narrow strip of the coastal regions of Palestine, the Philistines naturally saw the potential for increasing their territory by annexing part of the Israelite-occupied interior. Their restless expansionism therefore afforded a perennial challenge to the territorial integrity and national sovereignty of God's covenant people. And, for a century or two, the Philistines were a foil to Israel's faith.

They were – to use the phrase applied to Attila the Hun in
relation to the decadent Western Roman Empire of the fifth
century A.D. – the 'scourge of God', raised up to chastise
the backslidings of the Lord's people. For Israel, they would
always represent the serrated edge of the powers of
darkness and the looming spectre of the wrath of God
against their sins.

Israel's relationship with the Philistines was a barometer
of their relationship with God. When they experienced
defeat, they saw it as the withdrawal of divine favour. They
therefore asked the right questions when faced with a
set-back. They did not, however, always come up with the
correct answer.

Right question: wrong answer [4:1–4]

The Philistines were always nibbling away at Israel's territory and had been attempting to gain control over the
nation since their appearance during the period of the
judges. On this occasion, they had crossed the frontier and
camped at a place called Aphek. The Israelites responded
by assembling nearby at a place which, twenty years later,
would be called Ebenezer – literally, 'stone of helping' –
after the Battle of Mizpah (1 Samuel 7:12).

Sad to say, there was no helping Israel in this battle – the
First Battle of Aphek. Israel was defeated with the loss of
4,000 men (4:2). There was no Philistine pursuit – an
indication that it had also been a costly day for them – and
the Israelites were given a respite to prepare for a second
battle. At a council of war, the elders assessed the defeat in
the most solemn of terms: '**Why did the Lord bring defeat
upon us today before the Philistines?**' (4:3). Their answer
was to order that the ark of the covenant be brought from
Shiloh, on the supposition that its presence with the army
would save them from the hands of the Philistines (4:3). The
ark was then brought to the camp and the writer notes two
significant facts: firstly that God was '**enthroned between
the cherubim**' of the ark, and secondly, that the ark was
accompanied by the wicked sons of Eli, Hophni and
Phinehas (4:4).

1. We should first recognize that the elders of Israel asked
the right question after their defeat in battle. This teaches us
the proper question to ask in the face of any personal or
communal set-back. '**Why did the Lord bring defeat upon
us today. . .?**' was a question which recognized the sovereignty of God in the events of history and which sought the
reason for his permitting his people to experience failure. It
presupposed that, humanly speaking, they had thought
themselves reasonably adequate to the task, but had failed
because the Lord had withdrawn his favour and help. Defeat
implied that the Lord had a controversy with his people and
was intent on teaching them through discipline – or, as we
might say, 'the school of hard knocks'.

This has to be the obvious – and obviously right – question
for anyone who believes that God is sovereign. Our personal
problems all beg this question. Why has the Lord allowed
this to happen to me? What is his deeper purpose? Why has
he closed this door? Why has he dealt this particular blow to
my plans and ambitions? What is he teaching me about
himself, his law, myself, my relationship to him . . . my sins?
It is easy enough to be thankful for the sunshine, but it is
something else again when rain spoils the picnic. When
problems arise, faith is tested and shown to be the real
thing. . . or not! In dark experiences, the light shines
brighter and the triumph of faith is all the sweeter. To search
our hearts, minds and consciences and ask the question of
the Israelite elders is not morbid introspection but the
advancement of true self-knowledge with the goal of personal
victory in Jesus Christ. There will certainly be sins to be
identified and repented of, but there will also be the
discovery of fresh avenues in God's everlasting way to life.
God did not bring defeat to Israel in order for them to wallow
in the sins of the past and the miseries of some unchangeably
overcast future! He called them to face the consequences of
their sin so that they might change their ways and enjoy the
escalation of divine blessing into a future bright with the
redeeming love of their Father-God!

2. Asking the right question does not, alas, guarantee that
the correct answer will be forthcoming. The elders of Israel
got to the starting-gate all right, but then charged off in the

wrong direction! Their answer to the problem of the Lord's
absence from the battle-line – the presumed reason for their
defeat – was to send men to Shiloh and bodily bring him up
to the camp! Of course, it was the ark that they fetched from
Shiloh. But was the Lord not present with the ark? Had he
not manifested himself between the cherubim throughout
the centuries since the wanderings in Sinai? This seemed
logical to them. Bring the ark and God would be there as
well!

If it was logic, it was the logic of superstition. The fallacy
in their reasoning was that God's presence was so inseparably bound up with the ark in a mechanical kind of way that
he would be bound to come with it and, it was to be hoped,
exert a decisive influence against the Philistines. The ark, of
course, was never meant to be used as a talisman. Even
more importantly, the Lord never revealed himself as a
localized tribal deity who, like some glorified genie in a
bottle, could be summoned up by ritual action and incan-
tation. The elders of Israel should have known better. The
ark was a focus of covenant worship and covenant faith, not
a relic to be venerated, or manipulated, in order to extract
its presumed efficacious properties. The tabernacle and its
furniture, including the ark, taught lessons about the Lord
and about salvation through the symbolism of the struc-
tures, the layout and the procedures of priestly sacrifice and
service. These were designed to pass away, because they
were always to be regarded as pointing to spiritual realities
and future fulfilment. Superstition comes naturally; living
faith is born of God's Spirit. The symbols of Israel's faith
were being used as if they were magic keys to unlock the
storehouse of God's power. Years later, the psalmist would
record for us God's comment on this sad passage in Israel's
history:

> 'But they put God to the test
>   and rebelled against the Most High;
>   they did not keep his statutes.
> Like their fathers they were disloyal and faithless,
>   as unreliable as a faulty bow.
> They angered him with their high places;
>   they aroused his jealousy with their idols.

When God heard them, he was very angry;
   he rejected Israel completely.
He abandoned the tabernacle of Shiloh,
   the tent he had set up among men.
He sent the ark of his might into captivity,
   his splendour into the hands of the enemy.
He gave his people over to the sword;
   he was very angry with his inheritance'
                        (Psalm 78:56–62).

Instead of seeing why God was angry with them, instead of confessing their sins and shedding tears of repentance, instead of seeking the Lord's help according to his way, they resorted to the blasphemy of using the ark as a talisman.

The scourge of God [4:5–11]

The arrival of the ark of the covenant elicited a tremendous roar of excitement and anticipation from the Israelite army. The ground shook and the Philistines heard the shouting. When they discovered the reason for the uproar, they were afraid. They interpreted the coming of the ark as signifying exactly what the Israelites hoped it would mean – the coming of God into the camp! As real pagans, they had a healthy respect for the unknown gods of other nations, which they could easily imagine to be as strong as Dagon, their own god. Never before had they faced an army that had brought a god into its camp. So they felt themselves to be in trouble, for they had heard of Israel's history and the exodus from Egypt (4:6–8). They resolved, however, to face this situation with the grim determination to do or die that has characterized men in every age whose backs were to the wall. Charged to '**Be men, and fight!**' they stood fast in their lines and awaited the Israelite onslaught (4:9).

The Second Battle of Aphek was a disastrous defeat for Israel. '**The slaughter was very great; Israel lost thirty thousand foot soldiers. The ark of God was captured, and Eli's two sons, Hophni and Phinehas, died**' (4:10–11). Israel's superstition had been laid in the dust. The Philistines had been the instrument of God's judgement on his

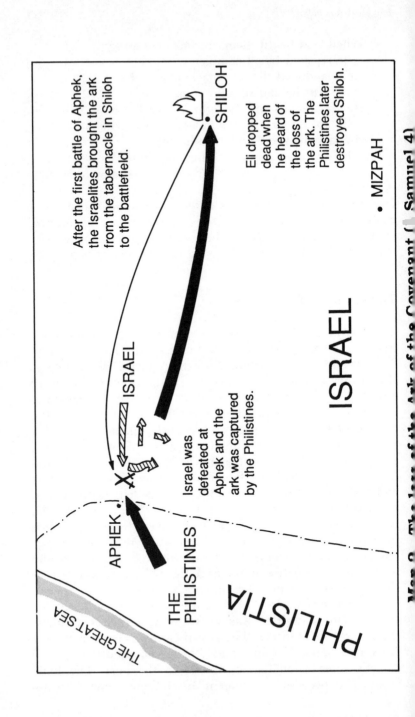

Map 2. The loss of the Ark of the Covenant (1 Samuel 4)

own people's apostasy and his last word on their 'creative' use of the ark.

Epitaph for a nation [4:12–22]

The remainder of the chapter narrows the focus to the house of Eli. Already the prophecy against Eli's house had been partly fulfilled in the death of his wicked sons (2:27–36; 3:11–14). Eli had feared the worst. He knew that the ark should never have been moved without the express command of God (cf. Deuteronomy 12:5, 11). When the news was brought to Eli and he realized that not only was Israel defeated, but his sons were dead and the ark had been taken, he fainted away and, falling back, broke his neck and died. The shock was too much for that sad but godly old man. He had judged Israel for forty years only to see the utter prostration of the nation under the heel of the Philistines and for no other reason than their backsliding from God (4:12–18).

The news had a similarly devastating effect on Eli's daughter-in-law, the unnamed wife of Phinehas. She had been expecting a baby. The shock of the news from Aphek caused her to go into labour, to give birth to her child and, sadly, to die in childbirth. Before she died, she gave the baby boy a name, 'Ichabod', that was to be the epitaph for Israel. 'Ichabod' means literally 'no glory'. It can be taken as a question, 'Where is the glory?' or as an answer, 'The glory has departed.'

The glory (Hebrew *kabod*) referred to 'the awesome splendour of God's invisible presence'.[3] **'The glory has departed from Israel, for the ark of God has been captured'** (4:22). It must have seemed to many in Israel that the Lord had abolished his covenant with his people when he took away from them the earthly throne of his glory. And yet, to the godly, who knew that God did not dwell in temples made with hands, the answer could never be that God's glory had permanently gone down the road to Gaza to be humiliated before the fish-god of the Philistines. Sober reflection on the Word of God would not only bring the realization that Israel deserved to be chastised for her apostasy from God, but also the awareness that, however much the Philistines had unwittingly been used as the instruments of that chastisement, they had also to answer for themselves and would find in due course that it is a fearful thing to fall into the hands of the living God. The inspired historian, writing years after the event, knew that, within a generation, God revived and restored his people and crushed the Philistines so that they would never again exercise power over Israel as they had in the past. The Philistines would not have to wait long, as we shall see in the succeeding chapter, for the first instalment in that process. The God of Israel was not to be denied – not by the wavering devotion of his covenant people and certainly not by the blind arrogance of the heathen nations. Behind the darkest clouds, the sun still shines. God would bless his people in ever greater measure in the fulness of his appointed time.

The experience of the New Testament church and of modern Christians echoes that of Israel, which was the church of the Old Testament. The Lord has frequently exposed his people to humbling experiences, not excluding their shame before a watching world. But there is always a purpose of love in these chastisements, so that God's erring children may be restored to a full experience of his nearer presence. Our guarantee is that Christ stands for all of history amidst the golden lampstands, those symbols of his light in the world, the church (Revelation 1:12–13). He will not leave us or forsake us and he assures us, 'Surely I am with you always, to the very end of the age' (Matthew 28:20).

References

[1] K. A. Kitchen, *Ancient Orient and Old Testament*, (Chicago: IVP, 1966), pp. 80–81. References to smaller settlements of the same people are found in Genesis 26:1, 14. See also Amos 9:7; Jeremiah 47:4.

[2] R. K. Harrison, *Old Testament Times*, (Grand Rapids: Eerdmans, 1970), p. 181.

[3] D.F. Payne, p. 28.

6.

The return of the ark

Please read 1 Samuel 5:1–7:1

'Who can stand in the presence of the Lord, this holy God? To whom will the ark go up from here?' (1 Samuel 6:20).

There has always been an arrogant symbolism in the use to which nations put the trophies of victorious wars. The 'stone of Scone', upon which the kings of Scotland were crowned – supposedly Jacob's pillow from Bethel – was incorporated by the English into their Coronation Chair in Westminster Abbey after its seizure by Edward I in the thirteenth century. A German field-gun stands sentinel in a park in Boalsburg, Pennsylvania, before a memorial to men whose lives were snuffed out by its shells in the Argonne battles of 1918. The Victoria Cross, Britain's highest award for gallantry for over a century, has been cast from the bronze of Russian cannon captured in the Crimean War. For all the superficial civilization of such usages, the heart of the matter in each case is naked triumphalism in the face of the fallen foe. This is perpetuated 'for ever' in military pageantry and war memorials, no doubt in the hope that they will inspire future victories over tomorrow's adversaries, should the need arise. 'We won the war,' is the invariable message of these sermons in stone or gun-metal.

When the Philistines marched home after their victories in the two battles of Aphek, they carried the captured ark of the covenant – arguably the greatest trophy ever taken in any war in history. Here was the very throne of God and the symbolic heart of Israel's faith in the hands of the worshippers of the fish-god, Dagon! The Philistines took the ark to Ashdod and '**carried [it] into Dagon's temple and set it beside Dagon**' (5:1–2).

What followed is surely one of the most bizarre episodes in all of Scripture history. Yet it teaches the most basic of truths. Behind the somewhat strange details, we discover God teaching both the Philistines and the Israelites some lessons in the first two commandments of the Decalogue: 'You shall have no other gods before me' and 'You shall not make for yourself an idol. . . ' (Exodus 20:3–4). The theme of 5:1–7:1 is that of God's judgement upon idolatry or, more generally, false worship. In a dramatic reversal of his policy at Aphek, God makes the ark the focus of judgements that are very specifically targeted upon the sins of both his covenant people and their temporarily victorious enemies.

Judgement – the ark among the Philistines [5:3-6:12]

1. The narrative records the history of the ark of the covenant in the hands of the Philistines and shows how the hand of the Lord reached out in wrath in order to recover the ark and to teach the Philistines that it is a fearful thing to fall into the hands of the living God.

The first of three phases in the unfolding of this narrative recounts the consequences of the depositing of the ark in the temple of Dagon (5:1–5). Twice, by the miraculous intervention of God's power, Dagon was made to fall flat on his face before the ark of God. On the second of these occasions, the idol's '**head and hands had been broken off and were lying on the threshold**' – an eerie anticipation of the fate of that other Philistine hero, Goliath (5:4; cf. 17:51).

The second phase saw the people stricken with '**devastation**' and '**tumours**' (5:6–12). That the former refers to crops and produce is indicated by the subsequent offering of gold rats to placate God's wrath. The 'tumours' have been variously interpreted as the symbols of haemorrhoids and bubonic plague. The pathology is irrelevant: the discomfort certainly was not! The people of Ashdod did not mistake the message: '**The ark of the god of Israel must not stay here with us, because his hand is heavy upon us and upon**

Dagon our god' (5:7). So they insisted that it be moved and it was taken to Gath. The same thing happened there. The ark was then sent to Ekron but the result was more death, disease and panic. And the desperate plea was that their rulers **'send the ark of the god of Israel away'** (5:11). The ark of God, like the Trojan horse, turned out to be a truly lethal acquisition!

In the third phase of their melancholy experience with the ark, the Philistines devised a plan to test whether or not the ark was the source of the trouble which they had been experiencing (6:1–9). They really knew that the God of Israel was responsible, but they had won the ark in battle and did not want to give it up. They hoped that their test might let them keep the ark. They first came up with a guilt-offering consisting of '**five gold tumours and five gold rats, according to the number of the Philistine rulers**' (6:4). Their priests recalled that the Egyptians had let the Israelites leave after God had brought plagues and death on Egypt and they counselled the people not to harden their hearts as Pharaoh had. Notwithstanding these strong words, they decided to put the matter to the test by putting the ark on a new cart, together with a chest containing the guilt-offering, and hitching this to two cows that had calved and never been yoked. This assemblage would be sent on its way and watched. If it went up to Israelite territory, they would know that the Lord had brought their disasters on them – if not, they would reckon these afflictions to have come on them by chance (6:7–9). It is significant that the cart was new and the cows previously unyoked. Like the guilt-offerings, these were of sacrificial quality – both cows and cart had not been put to a profane use. The fact that the cows had calves, which had been taken from them, meant that their natural instinct would be to go back to their offspring. Should they go up to Israel – away from the calves – this would confirm that the God of Israel was behind all their woes.

They did not have long to wait for the result. Without ado, the cows **'went straight up towards Beth Shemesh'** (6:12). The ark had gone home.

2. The lessons of their experience were not entirely lost on the Philistines, although it cannot be said that they were

more warmly disposed to follow the God of Israel than they
had ever been. They perhaps had a healthier respect for
God than before, but were no less hostile to him. In this,
they furnish us with a spectacular lesson in the nature of the
spiritual darkness that unbelief really is. Over-arching that,
of course, is the fact of God's ultimate triumph over all who
oppose him.

The nature of unbelief
Sin is any and all rebellion against God and his revealed
will, as set down in his Word, the Bible. Unbelief is the
condition of those who reject God. Error is the expression of
unbelief in action. Error, as opposed to truth, is the point at
which sin strikes at God.

1. The perfect comment on God's dealings with the
Philistines over the ark is in Romans 1:18–19 where we read,
'The wrath of God is being revealed from heaven against all
the godlessness and wickedness of men who suppress the
truth by their wickedness, since what may be known about
God is plain to them, because God has made it plain to
them.' Unbelief, when faced by the facts, suppresses them
in sheer unrighteousness! The Philistines are a prime
example of this spiritually blind opposition to truth. Notice
how they handled the ark. They knew the history of Israel
(4:8; 6:6), but it did not stop them expressing contempt for
God by placing the ark at the foot of Dagon as a tribute to
the fish-god's supposed superiority. When God knocked
Dagon down, they did not get the message. And when
Dagon was then decapitated and his head deposited on the
threshold of the temple, far from seeing the utter impotence
of their vaunted 'deity', they made the spot where Dagon
lost his head into a holy place! (5:5). The dogs returned to
their vomit! The facts said one thing, but the heart-
commitment of the Philistines required them to say the
opposite. In their unbelief they suppressed the truth – that
is to say, they reinterpreted the truth in terms which
continued to bolster the basic presuppositions of their
system of belief. That which proved it to be a worthless
delusion (Dagon's head on the threshold) was made to add
to the corpus of their faith in Dagon (a new ritual obser-

vance relating to a new holy place)! Unbelief recognizes the truth only in reversion from it – even when it stares truth in the face! The principle of sin – that of enmity to God (Romans 8:7) and aversion to truth (John 3:19) – is so powerful that it enslaves the mind and stamps its prejudices on every rational process. Facts that challenge these prejudices are reinterpreted in favour of the latter and both mind and conscience turn the truth of God into a lie (Romans 1:25).

2. Unbelief tries to evade the wrath of God without turning to him in his way. Seven months of misery – in Scripture, the number seven is symbolic of completeness – convinced the Philistines that they had had enough pain on account of the ark. They were not convinced that they should turn to God and honour him. Instead they decided to get rid of the ark and thereby, they hoped, induce God to leave them alone. 'Carnal hearts', remarked Matthew Henry, 'when they smart under the judgements of God, would rather, if it were possible, put him far from them, than enter into covenant and communion with him and make him their friend.' They are like the people of Gadara, who, after the loss of their pigs, asked Jesus to depart from them (Luke 8:37). The method by which the Philistines sought to alleviate the judgements of God also gives insight into the tragedy of their unbelief. It is true that they made an effort to appease the wrath of God. It is true that they had a sense of God's 'eternal power and divine nature' (Romans 1:20). But at no point did they trouble to ask how God ought to be worshipped or how his wrath should have been appeased. If they did not know already about the rituals of Israel's worship, it would have been easy enough to find out from any Israelite priest. But they did not. Why? Because they thought they could approach God in their own way. They were not about to surrender either their autonomy or their religious system!

This is characteristic of all unbelieving response to God's dealings. This remains true whether the person concerned is a Buddhist, a Jew, a nominal Christian or a Marxist. Unbelief in all its forms is self-justifying religion. Any attempt to please God – or whatever 'god' is in view – is

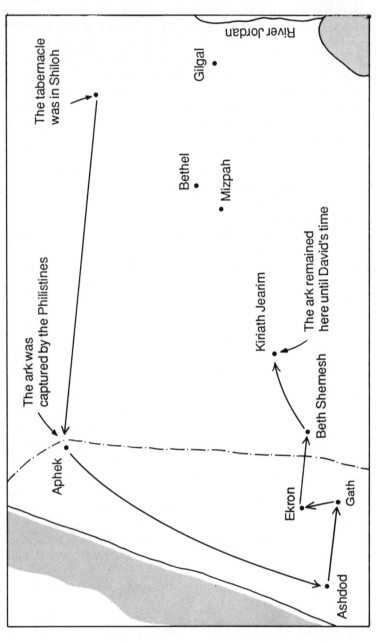

Map 3 - The movements of the Ark of the Covenant

inevitably an exercise in pleasing self, i.e. seeking justification and peace of mind without any change of heart in terms of the claims of the one living and true God. Unbelief will try anything – false religions, muttered incantations, transcendental meditation – but the truth of God. So instead of a genuine atonement for sin through the shedding of blood, the Philistines come up with a pay-off in grotesque gold trinkets; instead of the sacrifices of a broken spirit and a contrite heart they unashamedly cling to their pagan superstitions and hope that God will go away! (See Hebrews 9:22; Psalm 51:17.)

The ultimate triumph of God

The destruction of Dagon and the plagues of rats and tumours stand on the pages of the Word of God as lasting tokens that God can, does and will vindicate his holy name before sinful humanity. His judgements are constantly being revealed in the world (Revelation 15:4). One day all these will come together in the victorious consummation of his kingdom. Grasping this truth and constantly looking for victory in Christ is a great encouragement in the face of so much apparent, though temporary, success on the part of human wickedness (cf. Psalm 73). Our faith can only be lifted by the contemplation of the triumph of Christ.

The anticipation of the Lord's victory must also stir up within believers a great compassion for the lost, who, like the Philistines, stand in peril of the endless death of a lost eternity in hell. They appear neither to see their predicament nor to be interested in the way of salvation. It is axiomatic, of course, that no one can want to be saved from that which he, as yet, perceives to be no problem. False religion is like the mirage to a man who is not thirsty – a fascinating and lovely sight. The gospel of Christ only becomes a spring in the desert to the person who, in desperate thirst, has reached out to the mirage and found it to be an arid deception. God's judgements are his first words to lost and hell-deserving sinners to stop, to change and to turn from personal idols to serve the living and true God. But they must hear more – far more. They must hear of Christ and of his love and his power to save. And they must hear and see that love in his ambassadors, who plead for

him with sinners, that they might come to him in evangelical repentance and saving faith.

Chastisement – the ark in Israel again [6:13–21]

1. The cart bearing the ark of the covenant trundled into
Beth Shemesh, in Israel, and in the presence of the lords of
the Philistines, the villagers welcomed the ark's return with
rejoicing and the offering of sacrifices. The accounting of
the number of gold tumours and gold rats seems to suggest
that there were more than the five of the latter originally
proposed by the Philistine priests, although it may be
another way of expressing the five domains of the Philistine
lords in such a way as to make explicit mention of the whole
nation (6:17–18, cf. 5:4).

No sooner had the ark found a resting-place by the large
rock in the field of Joshua of Beth Shemesh (6:18b) than
some of the men of Beth Shemesh looked into the ark, in
manifest contravention of the law of God (Numbers 4:5–6,
15–20). Seventy men perished as a result of this irregularity
– a reminder that if sin knows no frontiers, neither does the
wrath of an offended God. Recognizing their sin and fearful
of further woes, the people of Beth Shemesh sent messengers to Kiriath Jearim asking that village to provide a
home for the ark.

2. If God's judgements on the Philistines' handling of the
ark indicated his anger with his enemies, his dealings with
his covenant people in Beth Shemesh reminded them that
he remained a God who required obedience and not mere
sacrifice. God served notice on his people that there was
nothing automatic about his grace. The return of the ark did
not mean instant blessing for all Israelites irrespective of
their attitude of heart towards the Lord and their practical
response to the Lord's will. Some today might well say,
'Was it not harsh and arbitrary' ('cruel and unusual punishment' in modern parlance) 'to kill seventy men for
looking into a box containing interesting and historic
objects relating to the nation's heritage? After all,' they
might say, 'the ark was only a fancy box with carved angels

on the top!' Put in such casual terms, the holiest objects can be turned into peep-shows without a second thought! Thoughtless curiosity is a hair's breadth from reverent decorum. For example, we would consider it a disgrace to exhume the corpses of dead relatives, but we think nothing of going to a museum and viewing the corpses of other people's relatives – albeit mummified ancient Egyptians! One man's desecration is another man's cultural enlightenment!

What was at issue with respect to the ark was not the box *per se*, but the majesty of the law of God. It was not a mere assemblage of acacia wood and gold (see Exodus 37:1–16) that was mishandled by the men of Beth Shemesh. It was nothing less than the truth of God which they abused and the very perfection of the Lord's righteousness necessitated a demonstration of his corrective discipline. An exactly analogous circumstance arose in the New Testament church at Corinth over the abuse of the Lord's Supper and because of that many people were sick and some died (1 Corinthians 11:17–34). To peer into the ark as if it were merely a curio – or even a priceless national treasure – was to ignore completely the ark's true meaning and so trample on the Lord himself. The ark was God's throne upon earth. It was the point in space and time at which the covenant God, Yahweh, met with his covenant people and received their worship. Like the burning bush in the desert, it was designated 'holy ground' because the presence of the Lord was there. To treat the ark as an object of curiosity was to ignore all of this. It was as if the Lord's will and purpose were irrelevant. It was to mock God. The death of the men of Beth Shemesh declared in no uncertain terms: 'Do not be deceived: God cannot be mocked' (Galatians 6:7). It is no accident that the Lord did not permit the ark to survive into the age of museums. That which declared his glory and represented his covenant salvation was not to be gawped at as a bizarre relic of a bygone age.

The response of the people of Beth Shemesh to the Lord's dealings was both mournful and fearful. Unlike the Philistines, they recognized the majesty and dignity of God and gave indications of genuine repentance: '**Who can stand in the presence of the Lord, this holy God?**' (6:20). They

were afraid of the ark's presence and would not feel safe
until it was well away from them. They immediately took
steps to get rid of the ark. Their repentance should,
perhaps, have issued in such a spirit of reconciliation to the
Lord that they could have handled the ark with reverence
and holy confidence according to God's law. But they lacked
that confidence and could not see themselves as the cus-
todians of the ark after such signal failure to keep God's law.
This is understandable but it falls short of the intended
scope of the restoration to which the believer may be
brought by true gospel repentance. Let no Christian,
overtaken in a fault, but brought to a repentant spirit and
reconciled fellowship with the Lord, say that the Lord
cannot use him again in his service. Says Matthew Henry,
'May the Lord give us a spirit of humble fear, filial love, and
heavenly hope, that we may be preserved from errors, and
profit by the salvation of his gospel.'

A new beginning [7:1]

The blessing passed from Beth Shemesh to Kiriath Jearim.
The men of that village came up to carry the ark away. The
reverence of the whole procedure is evident from what
followed: '**They took it to Abinadab's house on the hill,
and consecrated Eleazar his son to guard the ark of the
Lord**.' This may or may not have been a priestly
appointment but it appears that for the succeeding decades
the ark was effectively in suspended animation as far as the
worship of the tabernacle was concerned. It seems likely
that this temporary arrangement prevailed pending a
'declaration of the divine will . . . respecting its removal into
the tabernacle'.[1] The judgement which the loss of the ark
constituted cast a long shadow and the worship of Israel was
to be deprived of this central symbol of God's covenant love
for his people until David moved it from Kiriath Jearim to
Jerusalem many years later (2 Samuel 6). Nevertheless, it
was the beginning of spiritual revival for Israel. The ark's
return heralded the continuing faithfulness of the Lord to
the everlasting covenant he had made with his people
(Genesis 17:13).

The call of God's free grace resounds across the chronicles of human history and sets its challenges before all who will listen:

> 'Come, let us bow down in worship,
>   let us kneel before the Lord our Maker;
> for he is our God
>   and we are the people of his pasture,
>   the flock under his care.
> Today, if you hear his voice,
>   do not harden your hearts as you did at Meribah,
>   as you did that day at Massah in the desert,
> where your fathers tested and tried me,
>   though they had seen what I did'
>   (Psalm 95:6–8, cf. Hebrews 4:7)

References

[1] C. F. Keil and F. Delitzsch, pp. 69–70.

7.
With God's help

Please read 1 Samuel 7:2–17

'*Then Samuel took a stone and set it up between Mizpah and Shen. He named it Ebenezer, saying, "Thus far has the Lord helped us"*' (1 Samuel 7:12).

Despite the return of the ark and its intimations of the future blessing of God, Israel was a nation in deep, deep trouble. For some twenty years[1] – '**a long time**', says the historian with obvious weariness (7:2) – Israel languished under the oppression of the Philistines and the depression of spiritual declension. The tabernacle struggled on under the descendants of Eli but the fact that the ark sat, inactive, year after year, in the house of Abinadab only served to emphasize how far the people of God had fallen.

With remarkable economy of expression, the writer surveys these two trying decades and the great transition at the end which saw the overthrow of the old ways and the spiritual revival of the nation. When the text says that '**All the people of Israel mourned and sought after the Lord**,' it is indicating the culmination of a process of national humbling. Israel learned very slowly. Until they were afflicted they went astray (Psalm 119:67). But trouble concentrated their minds and, bit by bit, they came to see that God was their only hope. The ministry of Samuel during these years would have had its leavening effect in bringing this national spiritual crisis to the boil. This was, as Edersheim observes, 'only preparatory. It was Samuel's work to direct to a happy issue the change which had already begun. His earnest message to all Israel now was: "If with all your hearts you are now returning to Jehovah," – implying in the expression that repentance was primarily of the heart, and by the form of the Hebrew verb, that that return had indeed commenced and was going on – "put away the strange gods (Baalim, ver. 4), and the Ashtaroth, and make firm your hearts toward Jehovah" – in opposition to the former vacillation and indecision – "and serve him alone." To Israel so returning with their whole heart, and repenting alike by the removal of their sin, and by exercising lively faith, Jehovah would, as of old, prove a Saviour – in the present instance from the Philistines' (7:1–3).[2]

The day came when the Israelites as a whole '**put away their Baals and Ashtoreths, and served the Lord only**' (7:4). This had happened spontaneously in ones and twos and a village here and a village there, as the Spirit of God had convinced the people of their sin. The scene was then set for one of these great gatherings of God's people in which they would renew their covenant with God in a solemn convocation before the Lord. In this way, as Gordon remarks, they would 'fulfil the third element in the scheme of apostasy-oppression-repentance-deliverance which is outlined for the period of the Judges (Judges 2:11–23) and which is, to a degree, exemplified in this chapter.'[3] Deliverance was at hand!

Repentance at Mizpah [7:5–6]

Samuel called the entire nation to assemble at Mizpah, some eight miles north of modern Jerusalem. Israel frequently gathered there for the purposes of both worship and war (Judges 20:1; 21:1, 5, 8; 1 Samuel 10:17). On this occasion there was no thought of war, although a battle was its immediate result. Samuel's purpose was to seal the piecemeal spiritual revival, in which '**the Israelites**' (7:4) had *individually* put away the false gods of the Canaanite religion, with a national act of covenanting in which the whole body theocratic-politic of '**Israel**' (7:5) *corporately* engaged in repentance for sin and recommitment to the Lord. It was attended by the pouring out of water, fasting, confession and then the intercessory prayer of Samuel, who presided as the 'judge' of Israel.[4]

1. Pouring out water before the Lord
The first of the two actions associated with Israel's confession of sin consisted in drawing and pouring out water. This was a symbolic act. It outwardly represented something true about inward spiritual experience. And what did it mean? Other passages give us more than a clue. In Psalm 22:14, the distress of Christ is prophetically described by the psalmist: 'I am poured out like water, and all my bones are out of joint.' The pleadings of God's people are described in Lamentations 2:19 in terms of the pouring out of their heart 'like water' in the presence of the Lord. A similar idea is expressed in 2 Samuel 14:14: 'Like water spilled on the ground, which cannot be recovered, so we must die.' Clearly, the water poured out was a symbol of heart-felt distress. It was a comment on both the temporal and spiritual condition of the nation. They were saying, 'We are like this water poured out on the ground – lost to all usefulness on account of our sins. And as we pour it out, so we pour out our hearts, in recognition of our need of cleansing and restoration before you, our God.' The water was not being used productively, as in the irrigation of crops. It was being wasted by being poured out indiscriminately. Israel was saying, 'We have wasted ourselves and our privileges as your covenant people, O God!' It was symbolic, then, of chastened hearts who were now ready to seek renewal by the redeeming power of God.

This is a world away from some of the cherished notions of many modern strains of teaching about Christian experience. The self-image and self-improvement school of thought, with its emphasis on 'positive thinking' and 'how to' be a better Christian,[5] would regard such self-abasement as negative and unhelpful. Repentance is 'out' and renewal is 'in' – where renewal is understood to be the realization of one's own inner potential, developed, of course, through 'faith'. The beginning of such renewal is to forget the past and tell yourself to feel great because God loves you! Stop feeling defeated; stop mourning over mistakes; begin to do great things for God! It goes without saying that such teaching is bound to be popular in a world of sinners. Why? Because sin, as such, is treated as little more than a microbe that has afflicted us from outside and kept us back from realizing our best potential. It is also presented as something we can cure – with a little help from the power of positive thinking plus a dash of God and a sprinkling of inspirational quotations from the Bible and assorted luminaries, ancient and modern. In its worst form, this kind of thinking tells people: 'You can be whatever you want to be: just believe in yourself.'[6]

The Word of God, however, has a pervasively relentless emphasis upon the sinfulness of sin and nowhere encourages sinners to believe that they can pull themselves up by their own bootstraps and commend themselves to God by their own unaided efforts. Consequently, the idea that 'We can be what we want to be' is conspicuously absent from the teaching of the Scriptures. Scripture tells us that what 'we want to be' is our problem, because, by nature, it is the exact opposite of what God wants us to be. What we *need*, therefore, is a new heart, reborn by the Holy Spirit and, flowing from that, a new life, expressed in repentance for sin and saving faith in Christ as the only Redeemer of sinners. Such repentance and faith presuppose the deepest awareness of our prior lostness and condemnation before our holy God. New life in Christ does not begin with a sense of our self-worth and an enlarged vision of our self-generated capacity for good deeds acceptable to God. It begins with a palpable helplessness and a sense of utter destitution, produced by the Holy Spirit to the end that we might come to Christ and experience the fulness of his salvation – and, in doing so, realize, not our existing innate potential, but rather his imputed and implanted divine power which makes *his strength* perfect in *our weakness*. The heart of the matter is not what we will do to help ourselves – far less what we will do for God – but rather what God sovereignly, freely and graciously needs to do for us, in order that we might be saved from the consequences of our own sin-sick folly! It is certainly humbling to come to the end of our personal resources and realize in the depths of our heart that we have hitherto been a stench in the nostrils of God. But how else can true contrition be experienced? It is

impossible to confess sin with a happy and exalted spirit, as
if offending God were not grievous failure worthy of eternal
condemnation. To see our sin for what it is means to look
into hell and justify the anger of God against all rebellion
against his law. In that light, an emphasis upon 'self-image'
and 'self-worth' is so much pious narcissism. The answer to
our sad and justifiably depressed state is not to persuade
ourselves about how much we are worth or how much we
should love ourselves, but to look to God, in Jesus Christ,
who did the only loving that can translate into salvation and
new, redeemed life in reconciled fellowship with God.
'Humble yourselves, therefore, under God's mighty hand,
that he may lift you up in due time' (1 Peter 5:6). The point
is that the only way to experience genuine usefulness and
value before God – to know by experience in the exercise of
faith that we are worth many sparrows (Matthew 10:31) –
necessitates our turning in utter denial of sin and self to the
Lord Jesus Christ. All sin calls for repentance on our part
and it can only be after true repentance that the joy of
forgiveness and newness of life floods into the heart and
refreshes the soul. In the normal Christian experience of the
joy of salvation, a person might feel a sense of 'self-worth',
in the happiness of knowing the love of God and realizing
that it was through the blood of Christ that he or she had
been brought to saving faith. It may be enquired, however,
whether a believer who is rejoicing in God's work of grace in
his life and is joyously caught up in union and communion
with Christ will be absorbed to any extent in anything that
may be prefixed by 'self'. When your eyes are fixed on your
Saviour, you can have eyes for no one and nothing else.
Outside of Christ, we are nothing in ourselves. But, in
Christ, we are more than conquerors through him who loved
us. Christ is the 'worth' of believers; he is their 'image'; and
he is their 'esteem' – their glory. 'Self' is lost in knowing
him. But he who loses 'self' has truly found himself – in
Jesus Christ.

2. Fasting

Fasting, curiously perhaps for a people bound to a very
elaborate system of dietary regulations, was nowhere pre-
scribed in the Mosaic law. The nearest thing in the law to

fasting was the rather undefined requirement of self-denial on the Day of Atonement (Leviticus 16:29). Yet, as Fairbairn notes, 'We have abundant evidence of fasts having been observed from time to time by the covenant people when anything called for special humiliation and grief.'[7] These could be anything from individual and occasional fasts, as in the case of David (2 Samuel 12:21) or even the wicked Ahab (1 Kings 21:27), to those which were corporate and cyclical (Zechariah 8:19). They could involve total abstinence from food for one day (Judges 20:23, 26) or a restricted diet over a period of weeks (Daniel 10:2). In every instance it was as an aid to concentrate the mind upon the crisis at hand.

Israel fasted at Mizpah. This was altogether in accord with the spirit of true humiliation before the Lord. Fasting, as a symbolic act of privation, not only removed practical obstacles to their worship of God (meals) but signified an element of chastening which their sins so clearly deserved.

Taken together, the pouring out of water and the self-denial of food represented what they subsequently 'explained and confirmed by their verbal confession'.[8] With solemn candour they confessed, '**We have sinned against the Lord**' (7:6).

Deliverance at Ebenezer [7:7–12]

The Philistine intelligence service evidently had its eye on the Mizpah convocation and what they saw indicated the advisability of a pre-emptive strike. Accordingly, '**the rulers of the Philistines came up to attack them**' and, with Israel unprepared for war, they succeeded in spreading fear among the people of God (7:7).

Fear and a determination to fight are natural enough companions in time of war. Israel was resolved to resist the Philistine onslaught. Little did they know that their oppressors were delivering themselves into the hands of the Lord! They called upon Samuel to continue '**crying out to the Lord**' that he might rescue them from their enemies (7:8). Samuel offered a lamb as a burnt offering and cried out to the Lord on Israel's behalf, '**and the Lord answered him**' (7:9).

That answer came in a tremendous thunderstorm, which '**threw**' the Philistines '**into such a panic that they were**

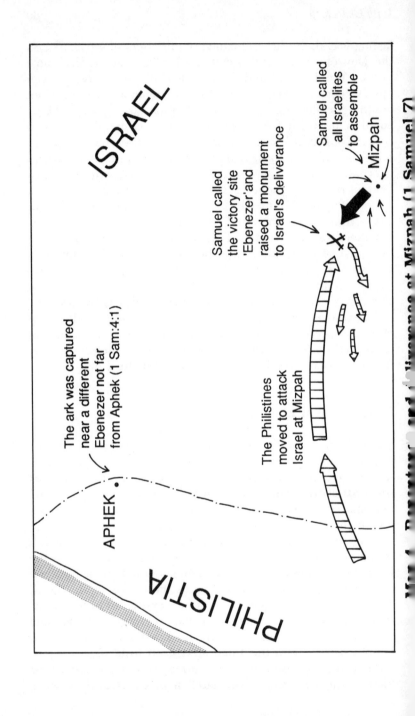

Map 4: Repentance and deliverance at Mizpah (1 Samuel 7)

routed before the Israelites,' who pursued them and exacted a fearful toll before the day was done (7:10–11). The victory complete, Samuel raised a monument on the site and called it 'a stone of helping' (Hebrew, *eben-ha-ezer*), thereby giving the battle the name by which it has since been remembered – the Battle of Ebenezer. In a solemn benediction on this most signal intervention of God, Samuel summed up both the meaning of the victory and the gratitude of the true people of God: **'Thus far has the Lord helped us**' (7:12).

1. An eight-day old lamb
Samuel took **'a suckling lamb**' and offered it as a burnt offering (7:9). In accordance with the law, this would be at least eight days old (Exodus 22:30; Leviticus 22:27). Two points ought to be noted.

The first concerns the offering itself. 'The sacrifice was the substratum for prayer.'[9] The psalmist says, 'If I had cherished sin in my heart, the Lord would not have listened' (Psalm 66:18). The sin had to be put away. The burnt offering signified just that – it indicated both the putting away of sin and the consecration of the sinner to new life in the Lord. It thus lent wings to the prophet's intercessory prayer.

The second point concerns the age of the sacrificial lamb. It had to be an eight-day-old lamb. In Scripture, seven signifies completion and eight is symbolic of a new beginning – a second number one, a fresh start. This pattern recurs throughout the Bible, pointing in every case to an aspect of salvation, including 'newness, redemption, sanctification and rest'.[10] For example, Noah's family (eight people), were saved from the judgement of the flood. Circumcision, the Old Testament sign of covenant membership and spiritual rebirth, was to be administered to boys on the eighth day after birth. Many Old Testament rituals and events were observed in connection with 'the eighth day' and, consistently, a pattern of renewal was involved.[11] It is no accident, therefore, that the resurrection of the Lord Jesus Christ took place on the first day of the week – actually the eighth day of the week of his death. This, as Chilton observes, is why this day 'becomes the replacement

Sabbath for the New Creation' – the Lord's Day, the modern
Sunday, the day of resurrection and new life.[12] Accordingly,
the sacrifice offered by Samuel on behalf of Israel must be
seen in the context of the significance of the eighth day. It
pointed to new life and a new beginning with the Lord.

2. Ebenezer

Monuments are designed to tell succeeding generations
something about their heritage from the past. I recall
discovering, as a child, a strange stone that stands in a niche
in a wall near where I grew up in Edinburgh. I had no idea
what it was. Why was this dirty stone sitting in that
forgotten corner of a busy street? The answer was that, in
the fateful summer of 1513, King James IV of Scotland
planted his standard in that stone – the Bore Stone – and
mustered his army for the invasion of England and the
disastrous defeat of Flodden Field. History lives when you
know what the stones mean! And what might be a forgotten
corner becomes a scene of imagination – the army terrible
with banners marching off to distant death!

The monuments raised by the Lord's people were de-
signed to fulfil a similar, though more profound, function –
to bear witness to the mighty acts of God. Jacob's dream at
Bethel (Genesis 28:18–19); the crossing of the Jordan
(Joshua 4:20–24) and the covenant renewal at Shechem
(Joshua 24:26) were all to serve as a sign among God's
people so that, 'In the future, when your children ask you,
"What do these stones mean?" tell them that the flow of the
Jordan was cut off before the ark of the covenant of the
Lord. . . These stones are to be a memorial to the people of
Israel for ever' (Joshua 4:6–7). The idea of these memorials
was that they be a standing witness to what God had done in
the past for his people, and to what he would yet do in time
to come.

Samuel's stone was called 'a stone of helping' and gave its
name to the place where God had given Israel the victory. It
stood as a testimony to the grace of God towards Israel:
'Thus far has the Lord helped us.' Centuries later, the
apostle Paul was to use similar language when he testified
before King Agrippa: 'But I have had God's help to this very
day, and so I stand here and testify to small and great alike

(Acts 26:22). In spiritual terms, Paul was raising a personal 'Ebenezer' – a witness in his heart and in his personal testimony that the Lord had been with him up to that point in his life. And this is the testimony of God's chidren in all ages. Our 'Ebenezers' stand as milestones along our pilgrim path: 'Hitherto has the Lord helped us!'

The peace of God [7:13–17]

Peace and national security came to Israel and endured, for the most part, during the time of Samuel's judgeship. The fourth part of the cycle so characteristic of the period of the judges had come to fruition: there had been apostasy, oppression, repentance and, finally, deliverance. Even so, Israel's condition left much to be desired. Shiloh remained deserted; the ark was marooned in Kiriath Jearim; and even the worship of the tabernacle itself, under the doomed priesthood of Eli, recedes into the background. Few would have known that Israel was on the threshold of a long and painful period of transition and revival which would issue in her transformation from a republic ruled by judges to a monarchy, whose king, in the person of David, was to point them to the promise of the messianic King.

Samuel was to be the key figure in God's gracious purposes for his people. Year after year, he ministered among the people and paved the way for that deeper revival to follow under David. How gracious is our God! He saves and preserves sinners even against our inclinations and our provocations. He reaches into our weaknesses with the overtures of redeeming love and calls us to a closer walk with him. He sent his only-begotten Son, the Lord Jesus Christ, to save sinners such as we are. May you know Jesus as your Saviour and have an 'Ebenezer' in your heart which constantly testifies that 'thus far, the Lord has helped' you.

References

[1] Verse 2 cannot define the entire period in which the ark remained in Kiriath Jearim, in spite of what our English translations imply. That period must have been more than forty years, as it encompassed the careers of both the adult Samuel and Saul (cf. Acts 13:21). Keil & Delitzsch, p. 71, bring out

the true sense of the passage as follows: 'And it came to pass, when the days multiplied from the time that the ark remained at Kiriath Jearim, and grew to twenty years, and the whole house of Israel mourned after Jehovah, that Samuel said, etc.' In other words, there are twenty years between 7:1 and 7:3.

² A. Edersheim, *Bible History: Old Testament*, (Wilmington, Delaware: AP&A, nd) p. 258.

³ R. P. Gordon, p. 106.

⁴ The NIV inexplicably renders this as 'leader' and thereby somewhat obscures the continuity of Samuel with the judges of Israel, of whom he was the last. The judges were, to be sure, leaders, but the concept of judgeship involved far more than conventional ideas of leadership. The judges fulfilled a prophetic-priestly-kingly function of mediating between God and Israel in order to bring about the restoration of a relationship of blessing and favour.

⁵ Robert Schuller, of Crystal Cathedral, Garden Grove, California, and electronic church fame, following his co-denominationalist Norman Vincent Peale (*The Power of Positive Thinking*), is undoubtedly the most visible and influential exponent of this teaching today. Their influence is seen in the plethora of Christian self-improvement materials available today.

⁶ This is little more than the heresy of Pelagianism dressed up in modern psychological language. It says that man is born morally neutral, free from guilt and pollution except that he is surrounded by the bad example of others who have learned to do bad things. 'Sin' is, therefore, not a fallen condition or wicked desires and tendencies in our spiritual make-up; it is this or that act of will to do something hurtful or negative. Sin is not a human *condition*, only a human *problem*. We do not need to sin, said Pelagius (the fourth-century British theologian who formulated this viewpoint). We can choose to sin or not, according to the actions of our free will. We do not need God's grace to do good, although it could only help. This heresy denies the truth at every point.

⁷ P. Fairbairn D.D., Editor, *The Imperial Standard Bible Encyclopedia*, (Grand Rapids: Zondervan, [1891], 1957) Volume 2, p. 278 (Article on 'Fast, Fasting'). It is worth pointing out that the non-ascetic tradition of the Old Testament continues in the New Testament, in inevitable contrast with the Pharisees' love of ceremonial fasting. Our Lord, for the most part, paid little attention to the practice, even disparaging its role in the life of the Jews (Matthew 6:17). His own fast, at the outset of his ministry, does suggest that 'At special seasons and emergencies the total or partial abstinence from food may be practised with advantage by believers.' 'But,' Fairbairn concludes, 'to institute periodical times for doing so, or to connect peculiar privileges or hopes with any amount of simple abstinence, is entirely alien to the spirit of the gospel; nor can it ever be done, without the greatest danger of fostering the spirit of self-righteousness.'

⁸ C. F. Keil and F. Delitzsch, p. 73.

⁹ *Ibid.*, p. 74.

¹⁰ F. N. Lee, *The Covenantal Sabbath*, (London: L.D.O.S., c. 1972), p. 13ff.

[11] See Exodus 22:30 (dedication of the first-born); Leviticus 9:1 (inauguration of the Aaronic ministry); Leviticus 14:23; 15:29 and Numbers 6:10 (ceremonial uncleanness); Leviticus 22:27 (sin-offering). See also 2 Chronicles 7:9 (Solomon's dedication of the temple).

[12] D. Chilton, *The Days of Vengeance*, (Fort Worth: Dominion Press, 1987), p. 347.

8.
The attractions of tyranny

Please read 1 Samuel 8:1–22

'When that day comes, you will cry out for relief from the king you have chosen, and the Lord will not answer you in that day' (1 Samuel 8:18).

Malcolm Muggeridge once observed that when people are faced with the alternatives of anarchy and tyranny they will always opt for the latter. And it matters not whether that tyranny is of the 'left' or of the 'right'. Any 'law and order' is more attractive than none at all. There is within the mass of humanity a sense of insecurity that yearns for strong leadership that will say, 'Do this!' and 'Do that!' Many people actually want the security of being told how to live their lives. Others, whose personal preference would be otherwise, soon tolerate and even welcome totalitarian government when it appears to sweep away anarchy and lawlessness in society. Germany, smarting from the humiliation of the inaptly named 'Peace' of Versailles and crushed by the social disintegration of the Weimar Republic, welcomed Fascism and Adolf Hitler, because they offered stability and the restoration of national pride, even if it was at the price of the persecution and murder of Jews, homosexuals and outspoken clergymen. Nearer our own time, the atheist philosopher Bertrand Russell said that he would rather 'be red than dead'.[1]

Self-interest and survival are powerful motives for the abandonment of principles. To survive with a degree of order, many Germans simply closed their minds to the murder of Jews and, indeed, to their own enslavement to the Nazi State. And worse still, free men, chasing a socialist utopia, could welcome Communism as the answer to the world's inequalities, as so many did in the first half of the twentieth century. Even professed Christians, like the then Dean of Canterbury, Hewlett Johnson – aptly nicknamed the 'Red Dean' – could unblushingly declare that Joseph Stalin was doing the work of the kingdom of God![2]

Why does this kind of phenomenon arise again and again in human history? What is the attraction of tyranny? I believe that the events recorded in 1 Samuel 8 point us to an answer. The situation in Israel at the time of the period of the judges was anarchic: 'In those days Israel had no king; everyone did as he saw fit' (Judges 17:6; 21:25). When there were godly judges, there was peace in the land. It is significant, too, that when Gideon was judge, the people wanted to make him king and he refused in terms which saw hereditary monarchy as inimical to the rule of the Lord (Judges 8:23). This suggests that the growing desire for the monarchy was related to declining devotion to the rule of God through the institutions of the Hebrew republic, with its judges and its priests. And this, as we shall see, was indeed the nub of the problem.

The voice of the people [8:1–9]

It is a sad irony that the appetite for a hereditary monarchy was probably whetted by the prophet Samuel himself. In his old age, he established his own *ad hoc* dynasty of judges by appointing his sons, Joel and Abijah, as judges. This irregular procedure might have been forgiven, had they been good men. But they were a wicked pair and '**turned aside after dishonest gain and accepted bribes and perverted justice**' (8:1–3). The best of men can raise the worst of sons. The parallel with Samuel's predecessor, Eli, and his apostate sons, Hophni and Phinehas, is unmistakable.

The effect of this was to bring the '**elders of Israel**' to Samuel's doorstep in Ramah with a request for the appointment of a king (8:4–5). It is evident that they spoke for the people as a whole (cf. 8:7). They expressed a national desire for change.

1. *The argument of the elders* was twofold. The first was that
Samuel had become too old. The second was that his sons
were not walking in his ways (8:5). Clearly, their concern
was with the succession of political power. Samuel would
not live for ever, and it made them shudder to think of Joel
and Abijah assuming the reins of government. This seems
to be a very reasonable concern. But such a judgement was
utterly superficial. Why? Because there is no indication that
the Lord or his promises – or his will, as they should have
first sought it through the prophet – ever figured in their
assessment of the needs of Israel. Matthew Henry wisely
observed that 'The Israelites were more displeased at the
injury to their temporal interests, than by all the dishonour
done to God...There had been many fairer occasions to ask
for a king. Discontent, fondness for change, and a desire of
outward splendour, are natural to man; they follow him
from the cradle to the grave, unless subdued by Divine
grace. No change can cure this, the same dissatisfaction
with the present situation, whatever it may be, is felt – the
comfort of some other is ignorantly imagined.' Where was
God's kingdom in all their reasoning? The answer is:
nowhere! They wanted a king of their own!

Their conclusion confirms the secular tenor of their
thinking: '**Now appoint a king to lead us, such as all the
other nations have**' (8:5). This was foreseen in the law of
the king given in the book of Deuteronomy (17:14–20).
God's answer was not to rule out a king altogether, but to
specify that he was to be the Lord's choice and, in his
behaviour, the Lord's man. Perhaps the elders felt they were
acting in accord with Deuteronomy 17. The Lord's response
suggests otherwise and casts serious doubt upon their
motives.

Were they, for example, justified in proposing the
appointment of a king as the logical answer to Samuel's age
and sons? Surely not! Why could they not turn to the Lord
and pray for godly judges to be raised up in the future,
precisely as he had done in the past? Had God ceased to
sanction their present system of theocratic rule? Had God
called, through his prophets, for the establishment of a
monarchy? No! It was an unhallowed thirst for change,
clothed in the language of piety and laced with the poison of

worldly wisdom, that lent wings to their request! They were not content to be faithful to God and wait upon him. Their eyes were on the other nations. Were they not modern, effectively organized states? Were they not magnificently led by their kings? Should not the people of God – because they are God's nation – surpass all these heathen peoples for the splendour of their national life and the panoply of their power?

2. *Samuel's response* was negative. '**This displeased Samuel; so he prayed to the Lord**' (8:6). We would expect anyone in Samuel's position to feel a sense of personal rejection in these circumstances. They were telling him he was not needed as much as a king! The prophet was, however, possessed of great spiritual discernment and knew there were far deeper issues at stake than his personal feelings. His displeasure, therefore, took him to the Lord in prayer – and provides us all with an example as to how to respond to any provocation. I believe that Samuel saw what the elders of Israel could not or would not face up to: that they were putting glamour before God. Their request for a king was, in fact, a reflection upon their attitude to God! Israel, once again, was turning away from the Lord.

3. *God's answer* to Samuel's prayer was not long in coming (8:7–9). And what a solemn and instructive answer it was! There are three principal elements to be noticed.

First of all, and surprisingly, *the Lord granted Israel her request.* He told Samuel, '**Listen to all that the people are saying to you**' (8:7).

Then, in the second place, *the Lord made it clear that their request was a rejection of his sovereignty.* He assured Samuel, '**It is not you they have rejected, but they have rejected me as their king**' (8:7). This was only what they had been doing all along – from the day the Lord delivered them from Egypt (8:8). This was, no doubt, a consolation for Samuel in his feelings of personal rejection, but far more profound is the fact that when God allowed Israel her king, it came as a concession and not as a gift.[3] Neither could it be construed that God was a democrat who meekly went along with the will of the people, as if the voice of the people was in effect the voice of God.

Thirdly, *the Lord gave a warning* about the mistake that Israel was making. He told Samuel, '**Now listen to them; but warn them solemnly and let them know what the king who will reign over them will do**' (8:9). As the Lord allowed Jonah to get his way and take ship for Tarshish when he ought to have gone to Nineveh, so Israel was given her king. And the purpose was the same: to administer humbling lessons and, more than that, to bring true blessing out of the ashes of misguided dreams.

The voice of God [3:10–18]

The prophet Samuel faithfully communicated the Lord's warning to Israel. Interestingly, they are called '**the people who were asking him for a king**' (8:10). R. P. Gordon points out that there is a word-play here that would not be lost on Hebrew readers. The word '**asking**' (Hebrew, *so'alim*) is from the verb *sa'al*, which is assumed to be the base of the name of King Saul (*sa'ul* – 'requested').[4] What follows is an account of a typical despotic monarchy (8:11–17). All the details of the kind of oppression they would soon experience are there – drawn, no doubt, from the well-enough known practice of the kingdoms of the Near East. What we need to notice is the Lord's purpose in telling them all this.

1. First of all, the Lord wanted Israel to think twice about what they were getting into. It was true that God had told them that they would eventually have a king (Deuteronomy 17). But he had also emphasized that it was *his* will that was to bring this about. It was not Israel's prerogative to decide when the prophecy would be fulfilled. But they could not wait. They knew what *they* wanted. 'All right,' said the Lord, 'you want a king . . . then count the cost!' And that cost would be great, for all that there would be certain benefits as well. Whatever a king would give to the nation, it is certain that he would take much more. The king would take their sons, their daughters, their vineyards, their grain, their servants, their flocks and, in the end, themselves. They would be enslaved by despotic tyrants. As things turned out, they did not have to wait long – it was just such

enslavement that precipitated the division of Israel upon the death of Solomon! (1 Kings 12:1–20).

2. In the second place, the Lord witnessed to his freedom from reproach in the matter. He entered his dissent in writing, as it were, and thereby asserted his innocence of the evil consequences of their decision: '**When that day comes, you will cry out for relief from the king you have chosen, and the Lord will not answer you in that day**' (8:18). This was not vindictiveness on God's part. It was only stating the just consequence of deliberately going against the known will of the Lord. When we go our own way, we forfeit the consolation of answered prayer and have to face alone the evil fruit of our sin. We cannot 'have our cake' and 'eat it.' The Lord will never underwrite our rebellion against his will.

This unutterably solemn warning must give us pause, when we contemplate any course of action that we know is contrary to God's Word. It is true that he will always save his believing people from their sins. It is certain that he will receive the returning backslider. But even for Christians who have insisted on their own way as over against God's will, there will be emptiness of soul and the heavens will seem like brass to their prayers, before repentance and renewed faith restore to them the joy of the Lord.

'In my anger I gave you a king' [8:19–22]

Confronted by a clear choice between God's precept and her own desire, Israel insisted on her own way. They must have a king! And so, with a heavy heart, Samuel turned again to the Lord to seek his will. Then, in words which echoed his earlier words (8:7), the Lord commissioned Samuel to give Israel her king: '**Listen to them and give them a king**' (8:22). The Lord let Israel cross her Rubicon and change her national life for ever.

In one sense, the Israelite monarchy was to cast a long sad shadow over the subsequent history of God's people. Three hundred years later, God would write his epitaph for that institution through the prophet Hosea: 'So in my anger I gave you a king, and in my wrath I took him away' (Hosea 13:11). The king they wanted, you see, was the wrong king. In the end, the kings let them down and their removal was a signal of the wrath of God against the evil which had consumed the nation.

But in another sense, the monarchy – particularly in the person of David – was designed to foreshadow the coming of that other King, the Lord Jesus Christ. Jesus is the true King. Jesus is the King of kings and Lord of lords. He is the King who saves his people from their sins. He is with them to the end of the world. He is the Redeemer of God's elect. His yoke is easy and his burden is light. He washes away the burdens of sin and its consequences. He gives eternal life to all who call upon his name in repentance and faith.

Let us not resist the Word of the Lord. His revealed will is for our happiness. God's plan for our lives will never be as glamorous as the way of the world – but it is more beautiful and it will stand the test of both time and eternity. When Jesus, in the Sermon on the Mount, told us not to worry about our life – as to what we would eat or drink, or wear – he reminded us that while the world does these things, we have a heavenly Father who knows our needs and cares for us every day. How then are we to live? He answers, 'Seek first his kingdom and his righteousness, and all these things will be given to you as well' (Matthew 6:33).

God has given us a King. He died upon the cross to bear our sin. He rose from the dead to reign in resurrection power and glory. Let us rejoice in him.

References

[1] Interviewed on the American CBS TV programme *The Second Battle of Britain* (March 1976), Muggeridge was asked if the freedom-loving British people would acquiesce to Communism, were it to seize power. He replied that they would adapt quite readily, since they had no real moral fibre or sense of purpose.

[2] Dr Hewlett Johnson was Dean of Canterbury between the two World wars and an inveterate supporter of Marxist causes.

[3] R. P. Gordon, p. 110.

[4] R. P. Gordon, p. 110.

PART II:
Saul - the
people's king

9.
The man who would be king

Please read 1 Samuel 9:1 – 10:27

'About this time tomorrow I will send you a man from the land of Benjamin. Anoint him leader over my people Israel; he will deliver my people from the hand of the Philistines. I have looked upon my people, for their cry has reached me' (1 Samuel 9:16).

The decision to give Israel a king having been made, it only remained for the man to be appointed. But how would such a choice be made? This was a new venture and in the nature of a concession on the part of God and his prophet-judge, Samuel. How would Samuel, having asserted his own authority in sending them to their homes (8:22), provide for a transition of power to someone whose office would be less than to his liking?

These questions are answered in a lengthy, even leisurely, passage covering four chapters (9:1 – 12:25). We are told how Saul was identified as the future king of Israel (9:1 – 10:16); how he was publicly inaugurated (10:17–27); how he was tested in battle (11:1–11); and finally, how he was confirmed as monarch 'in the presence of the Lord' (11:12 – 12:25). This last event included Samuel's valedictory address in which, as the last of the judges, he solemnly made way for Saul to assume the reins of power.

In this study we shall look at the first phase of this great transition point in Israel's history – the identification and inauguration of Saul as Israel's king (9:1 – 10:25). The passage records a few very momentous days in the life of Saul, the son of Kish, and shows how God, in his providence, brings his purposes to fruition even when the leading character is wholly unsuspecting.

The identification of Israel's king [9:1–10:16]

It was not exactly 'log cabin to White House'[1] for Saul, but to go looking for donkeys and instead find a kingdom was remarkable enough. Saul was the scion of well-respected Benjamite stock (9:1). To have a genealogy at all confers a certain distinction, even in modern times; only the aristocracy can catalogue their ancestry in the centuries before public records were instituted. People generally want to know where they came from. They also like to know something about the family origins of their leaders. Men from nowhere do not seem generally to inspire confidence in the minds of their potential subjects. Saul's pedigree was beyond reproach and Saul himself looked just right for the part. He was '**an impressive young man. . .a head taller than any of the others**' (9:2). It is a fact of life that physical size and beauty are always impressive. In fairy tales, the princes have to be handsome and the damsels in distress of matchless beauty! Saul was every inch a king. He fulfilled all the canons of popular expectation in a monarch! (cf. 16:7). This was the young man who went out to look for his father's donkeys and so set foot on the road to the throne.

1. A wild-goose chase (9:3–4)
The fundamental uncertainty of human existence gives a brilliant lustre to the providence of God. Insignificant events herald God's almighty acts. Something commonplace leads to a decisive turning-point in life. Isaac went for an evening walk in the field to meditate – and met his future wife, Rebecca! (Genesis 24:63–5). Sleepless David got up from his bed and took a stroll on the palace roof. There he espied Bathsheba and set in motion a chain of events leading to adultery and murder (2 Samuel 11:2). And in the present case, Kish's straying donkeys were to be the means of bringing Saul to a meeting with the prophet Samuel. Saul's search through the hills of Ephraim and Benjamin was meant to be a 'wild-goose chase', for its true purpose was to give Israel her king!

2. Encounter with the prophet (9:5–25)

Saul and his companion failed to find the lost animals and Saul, concerned that his father might begin to worry about them, decided to head for home. But it 'just so happened' that they were approaching Ramah ('**this town**,' 9:6) and the servant thought it worth consulting '**a man of God**' who lived there. He might show them where to find the donkeys. Two obstacles to this projected consultation presented themselves immediately. The first was the necessity of a gift for the seer (1 Kings 14:3). But the servant 'happened to have' a suitable silver coin on him (9:7–10). The second problem was actually making contact with the prophet. But this too was easily resolved, for it 'just so happened' that they met some girls outside the town who directed them to Samuel. And he was just coming out of town as Saul and his servant arrived at the town gate (9:11–14). This and that may 'just so happen' in our experience, but to call it 'lucky' is simply to deny the sovereign hand of God in all the details of our lives. He who marks the fall of the sparrow has a more abiding interest in the lives of his beloved children! The wandering donkeys, the fruitless search in the hills, the quarter shekel and the girls on the road were all within the ambit of the absolute sovereignty of God. We will never know what a day will bring forth, but God knows the end from the beginning! (Proverbs 27:1; Isaiah 46:10). And he who does all things after the counsel of his own will always works these things together for the blessing of his people (Romans 8:28; Ephesians 1:11).

A brief parenthesis, in 9:15–16, records a special revelation from God to Samuel the day before. In it God had revealed that in twenty-four hours he would meet '**a man from . . . Benjamin**', whom he should anoint as the leader who would deliver Israel from the Philistines. The language used echoes Exodus 3:7, 9: '**I have looked upon my people, for their cry has reached me.**' Then, it had been the Egyptians who oppressed God's people; now, the Philistines were, so to speak, the new Egyptians, whose designs against the people of God again threatened their very existence and therefore necessitated a mighty intervention of divine power.

Picking up the thread of the narrative, the historian records a further revelation from God to Samuel just as he caught sight of Saul. '**This is the man**,' said the Lord, '**. . . he will**

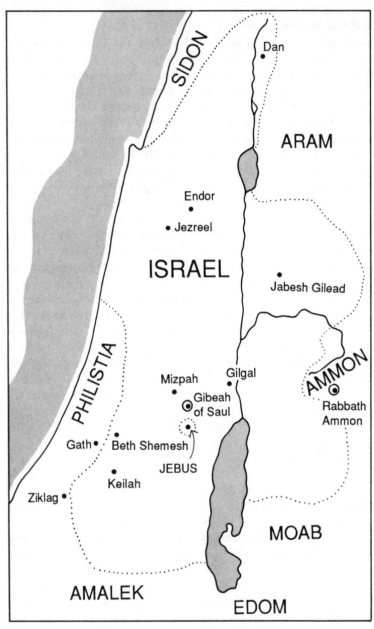

**Map 5 - The kingdom of
Saul, c. 1050 B.C.**

govern my people' (9:17). Samuel was also given to understand that the donkeys Saul had been looking for had been found. He used this information both to introduce himself to Saul and to tell him that he was indeed a prophet of God. He then took the first step in Saul's preparation for kingship. Having invited him to the sacrifice and promised a full explanation the next morning, Samuel asked Saul a most portentous, if slightly enigmatic, rhetorical question: '**And to whom is all the desire of Israel turned, if not to you and all your father's family?**' (9:20). This could only be understood as referring to Israel's recent request for a king. Saul responded with appropriate self-effacement: was he not, after all, only a Benjamite, '**from the smallest tribe of Israel**'? (9:21). At the feast following the sacrifice, however, he found himself to be the guest of honour and, as such, he received the choicest portion of the meat (9:22–24). Afterwards Saul and his companion went home with Samuel, where they sat on the roof of the house and 'visited' (as the Americans say) until the advance of darkness and weariness sent them to their beds.

3. A private anointing (9:26–10:13)
The next day Samuel contrived to be alone with Saul to give him '**a message from God**' (9:27). He then solemnly anointed Saul with oil and declared him to be the Lord's choice as Israel's ruler (10:1). This would be confirmed, in the first instance, by three signs: first, he would meet two men near Rachel's tomb who would tell him that the donkeys had been found; secondly, he would meet three men at '**the great tree of Tabor**' on their way to Bethel; and, finally, he would meet a company of prophets near '**Gibeah of God**' and the Spirit of God would come upon him in power and he would, thereafter, be ready to serve the Lord, for God would be with him (10:2–7).

a. The act of anointing was associated in the Near East with vassalage.[2] Vassal kings were anointed to signify that their authority was derivative from the king to whom they owed allegiance, such as the Egyptian Pharaoh. When God anointed Saul to be king, the act itself defined the limits of his monarchical authority. God was the true King, while

Saul was his earthly vicegerent. The anointing of the monarchs of Christendom and their crowning by the agents of the church carried a similar significance. Queen Elizabeth II was anointed at her coronation in June 1953. Like her celebrated ancestor, King James VI of Scotland, she was thereby denoted, in Andrew Melville's robustly lucid definition, 'God's sillie vassal'.[3] This sounds a great deal more disrespectful today than it actually was in 1596, for 'sillie' then meant 'helpless' rather than the modern 'foolish'. The point is a vital one, however, and what Melville went on to say stands as a word from God to all rulers and governments: 'Therefore, Sir, as divers times before I have told you, so now again I must tell you, there are two kings and two kingdoms in Scotland: there is King James, the lord of this commonwealth, and there is Christ Jesus, the King of the Church, whose subject James the Sixth is, and of whose kingdom he is not a King, nor a lord, nor a head, but a member.' Professor John Macleod was not understating the case when he observed that 'It took grit to beard kings who aspired to be tyrants!'[4] The Lord says, 'By me kings reign and rulers make laws that are just' (Proverbs 8:15). In Saul's case, this limitation of powers received an immediate and specific application in the requirement that he go to Gilgal and wait seven days for Samuel to come and sacrifice burnt offerings and fellowship offerings (10:8). This was a test that Saul would fail on a later occasion (13:7–15). There was, as Gordon neatly observes, 'a tree of knowledge in Saul's Eden (cf. Gen. 2:16f.)'.[5]

b. Anointing by God also signified the endowment of the Spirit of God to equip the king for the task before him. As the Spirit had come with power upon the judges of Israel, so he came upon Saul (10:9–16). '**God changed Saul's heart ...**' and '**The Spirit of God came upon him in power**' (10:9–10). Saul joined in the prophesying of the prophets he had met at Gibeah and this so amazed those who knew him that they asked, '**Is Saul also among the prophets?**' (10:11). The prophesying in view was probably ecstatic utterance of some kind (and in the language of the people). This was completely out of character for Saul and therefore indicated to the people that a great change had come over him – one induced by the Spirit of God. The expression 'Is Saul also among the prophets?' became a byword for such a dramatic and unexpected change in behaviour and perhaps also for a change in gifts.[6]

Whatever the change in Saul, it is clear from his subsequent spiritual regress that it was not a true regeneration of the heart. He was not a true believer, although that was not at all evident at the time of his anointing. He may have, in Old Testament terms, 'tasted the heavenly gift . . . shared in the Holy Spirit . . . tasted the goodness of the Word of God and the powers of the coming age' (Hebrews 6:4–5), but it went no deeper and, later, the Spirit of God would depart from him and deprive him of such gifts as had been given to him to equip him for kingship (16:13–14). There is no ground for believing that Saul was 'a regenerate man living a carnal life' or that he was 'a man who knew God but did not pattern his life after God's will'.[7]

There are only two lines of evidence that indicate a saving relationship with the Lord. One is what we *say*; the other, what we *do*. And what we do is itself the evidence and confirmation that what we say is true. In the end, it is obedience to the Lord, albeit in the context of spiritual struggle, that tests the credibility and, indeed, the reality of any faith that we might profess. At points along the road of the Christian life, the issue may appear to hang in the balance. We can see-saw a great deal between faith and unbelief, between gospel holiness and downright wickedness. But, sooner or later, the fruit of our true spiritual condition will manifest itself in a decisive manner.

The evidence may not yet be complete for you and me, but it certainly is for Saul. His life was, in the end, an unmitigated disaster. He did his country some good, to be sure. But so have most tyrants. The truth is that his career ended, for Israel, in the misery with which it was punctuated almost from the start. And his personal life and relationship with God was a downward spiral of sin and rebellion.

The warning this affords modern men and women is not to be watered down by vain hopes that people who once seemed to be converted, but have since given their lives over to sin, are really saved. This may be comforting to friends and loved ones, but it is an illusion. And it is a dangerous illusion, especially for the so-called 'carnal believer' himself. James Hogg, in his classic novel of the sinfulness of sin, *The Private Memoirs and Confessions of a Justified Sinner*, showed how seductive an abstract view of salvation can be.[8] In the story, a mysterious character named Gil-martin, whom we soon see is Satan, corrupts young Robert Wringhim into a life of wickedness, while assuring him that sins will not affect his salvation, since he is one of God's elect. Hogg, himself a convinced Calvinist, was not attacking the doctrine of election, but rather expounding the subtle snare of abstracting it, as a ground of the assurance of being saved, from the full-orbed emphasis of Scripture on the necessity of a holy life as the evidence of truly being saved by grace. How do we know we are of the elect of God? Only by the evidence of faithful confession of Christ and a holy life. We are saved by grace through faith *alone*, but not that 'faith' which is alone (i.e., devoid of works). James said that 'faith . . . not accompanied by action' is dead – it is not true faith in Christ. Jesus therefore was at pains to impress upon the disciples that love for him as their Lord meant keeping his commands (James 2:17; John 14:15).

4. The secret king (10:14–16)
Saul's later defects were yet in the unknown future. We must not let the hindsight afforded by our reading of the whole of 1 Samuel blind us to Saul's early promise. He was handsome, accomplished and likeable. He was going to be a popular choice for king. As yet, this was still a secret and when his uncle asked about his time with Samuel, Saul said nothing of his anointing. There is no reason to believe that this was anything other than an honest humility on Saul's part. The Spirit of God led him to keep his own counsel. He was to be the secret king of Israel until that moment when the Lord chose to reveal him to the world.

Inauguration at Mizpah [10:17–27]

Saul's anointing remained a secret until Samuel's convocation at Mizpah, where, some time before, the revival of Israel had been solemnly sealed and the Philistine oppression overthrown in battle (7:5–8, 10, 15–16).

Samuel's 'key-note address' took the form of a rebuke of Israel's desire for a king (10:17–19). This repeated, in substance, the earlier admonition (8:10–18) and underscored the fact that Israel's enthusiasm for a king cast an aspersion on the Lord as their Redeemer. They, in effect, had rejected God when he was the very one who had saved them so many times in the past. At the same time, the request was being granted and for the purpose of selecting a king, they were commanded to present themselves before the Lord by their tribes and clans. This sombre introduction was clearly designed to prepare Israel for the great fall that awaited them, as a result of their thirst for a monarch. God was registering his dissent. Just as in modern rules of order for business meetings a member purges his conscience from complicity in the decision from which he dissents, so the Lord was distancing himself from Israel's decision.

The election of a king followed immediately (10:20–24). A system of lots was used. In this way, human decision was deemed to be eliminated and the choice became a matter of God's sovereignty exercised through the lot. '**The lot is cast into the lap, but its every decision is from the Lord**' (Proverbs 16:33).[9] Saul was chosen and, after he had been found '**hidden . . . among the baggage**', he was presented to the people and acclaimed as their king. As he stood there, a head taller than everyone else, Samuel sealed his elevation in words of fulsome approbation: '**Do you see the man the Lord has chosen? There is no one like him among all the people.**' And the people replied with a roar: '**Long live the king!**' (10:24).

A *written constitution* was then prepared by Samuel and deposited '**before the Lord**', that is, in the tabernacle (10:25). Then he dismissed the people to their homes. Saul, too, went to his home in Gibeah '**accompanied by valiant men whose hearts God had touched**'. The people supported him, except for '**some troublemakers**'. But Saul kept his own counsel (10:26–27).

Law and the king

Israel's monarchy was constitutional from its inception. The God-given '**regulations of the kingship**' were 'an important brake on the development of absolute power'.[10] Absolutism is, in principle, an injustice and an offence against God's law. It is *law*, informed by the principles of revealed truth and executed by the civil power as that ordained by God to be a terror to evil-doers, which is to govern the affairs of men and nations, neither the will of absolute dictators or oligarchs, whether of left or right, whether patrician or proletarian, nor the fifty-one per cent vote of a supposedly sovereign electorate!

At a personal level, the abiding precept is that all privileges carry with them commensurate responsibilities. The servants of the Lord have great and precious promises. But we have a calling to the fellowship of the work of the gospel. And the Lord says to us, 'If you love me, you will keep my commandments.'

References

[1] The romanticized summary of Abraham Lincoln's rise to the presidency of the United States.

[2] D. F. Payne, p. 50.

[3] E. Whitley, *The Two Kingdoms*, (Edinburgh: Scottish Reformation Society, 1977), p. 26. King James VI became King James I of England on the death of Elizabeth I (1603), and was the same King James whose name is connected, especially in the USA, with the Authorized Version of the Bible (1611).

[4] J. Macleod, *Scottish Theology in relation to Church History* (Edinburgh: Banner of Truth, 1974 [1943]), pp. 46–47.

[5] R. P. Gordon, p. 118.

[6] The obscure and much debated question in 10:12 evidently explains why this became a proverbial statement – that is, it would if we knew what it really meant. It *may be* that the man who asked, '**And who is their father?**', was saying that, as we know that the fathers of the company of prophets were not prophets themselves and that their gift, therefore, was not hereditary, so we should not be surprised that Saul is given the same gift 'out of the blue' and without any hereditary background in prophecy.

[7] J. C. Laney, *First and Second Samuel*, (Chicago: Moody Press, 1982), p. 40. This slender commentary is the most usable and most soundly biblical of modern expositions of the books of Samuel.

[8] James Hogg, *The Private Memoirs and Confessions of a Justified Sinner* (Oxford: Oxford University Press, 1981 [1824]). Hogg (1777– 1835), also known as 'the Ettrick Shepherd', wrote many novels touching on Christian themes.

[9] Compare Leviticus 16:7–10; Joshua 7:14; 14:2; Jonah 1:7; Acts 1:26. With the outpouring of the Holy Spirit at Pentecost, lots became obsolete. See Romans 8:14; Galatians 5:18.

[10] D. F. Payne, p. 53.

10.
Changing times

Please read 1 Samuel 11:1–12:25

'As for me, far be it from me that I should sin against the Lord by failing to pray for you. And I will teach you the way that is good and right. But be sure to fear the Lord and serve him faithfully with all your heart; consider what great things he has done for you. Yet if you persist in doing evil, both you and your king will be swept away' (1 Samuel 12:24–25).

It was not for nothing that the Spirit of God had come upon Saul in power. Saul knew that one swallow doesn't make a summer. He had been acclaimed as king by the people but had yet to command their allegiance through proven competence. To be a real king, he would have to exercise the leadership that should characterize one to the manner born and fulfil the practical expectations that the people had of their king (8:6, 20). It showed remarkable political maturity in a young man to keep a low profile after such a heady advancement to national prominence. Saul wisely affected no regal airs and graces. Apart from a modest retinue of 'valiant men whose hearts God had touched', he lived as he had before, as a farmer of some substance (10:26; 11:5). And in the face of the critics and troublemakers, he maintained a discreet silence.

Although he was the king, Saul lived in the manner of the judges and, indeed, apart from his title and its longer-term implications, he was, in all practicality, the new judge of Israel. The difference was, however, that Saul was in a transitional mode, as was the nation of Israel itself. These changes would come, but in God's good time. In this respect, Saul's policy must not be seen as a mere stratagem to woo the willing support of the people. Rather, it grew out of the awareness that 'Jehovah had chosen him ruler over his people without any seeking on his part' and, therefore, 'he would wait for higher instructions to act, before he entered upon the government.'[1] Perhaps, in any case, he did not quite know what to do. He did not have long to wait before the opportunity and challenge arose that would seal the establishment of his rule and the end of the era of the judges.

Tested in battle [11:1–11]

The Ammonites were a Transjordanic people descended from Lot's involuntary incest with his younger daughter (Genesis 19:30–38). These sordid origins were matched in iniquity by the subsequent history of that nation. They appear to have anticipated Adolf Hitler's demonic policy of 'the final solution' to the 'problem' of the Hebrews by adopting a policy of slavery and then genocide to clear them from the east side of the Jordan and enlarge the Ammonite kingdom (cf. Amos 1:13–15).

1. The siege of Jabesh Gilead (11:1–5)

Gilead was the land east of the Jordan and north of the Jabbok which was occupied by the Israelite tribes of Gad and Manasseh. This had always been a vulnerable salient bordered by potentially hostile territory. The Ammonites had been nibbling at it for years and once, in the time of Jephthah, had mounted a major attempt to annex the region (Judges 11:4–33). The current Ammonite monarch, Nahash, decided to try again, so he laid siege to the regional capital, Jabesh Gilead. The beleaguered inhabitants offered to make a treaty – literally, 'to cut a covenant' (Genesis 15:9–11, 17–18) – in which they would acknowledge the suzerainty of Nahash. That bloodthirsty despot had, however, 'no aspirations to being a humane conqueror'.[2] He demanded, as the condition of such a treaty, that the right eye of every inhabitant be gouged out. This done, a population of one-eyed serfs would be a standing disgrace to the Israel that was impotent to save them!

The elders of Jabesh appealed for a seven-day truce, in which they might seek help from Israel. If relief were not forthcoming in that time, they would surrender and cast themselves upon the mercy of Nahash. The Ammonite king granted the request, perhaps out of contempt for Israelite effectiveness but perhaps also with an eye to the greater costs of an assault on the city (11:3).

Messengers were sent to Gibeah, to Saul, and the peril of Jabesh Gilead was laid before the fledgling king (11:4–5).

2. The muster of Israel (11:6–8)

Saul responded as had the judges Othniel, Gideon, Jephthah and Samson before him (Judges 3:10; 6:34; 11:29; 14:19). 'The Spirit of God came upon him in power, and he burned with anger' (11:6). Then in a symbolic act reminiscent of the cutting up of the murdered woman in Judges 19:29, Saul sent pieces of dismembered oxen throughout Israel as a summons to war against Ammon. The name of Samuel was invoked. And as a result, '**The terror of the Lord fell on the people, and they turned out as one man**.' The 'terror' of the Lord was not primarily the fear of punishment but 'a fear inspired by Jehovah'. In Saul's energetic appeal the people discerned the power of Jehovah, which inspired them with fear, and impelled them to immediate obedience.'[3] The host of Israel, 330,000 strong,[4] assembled at Bezek, within striking distance of Jabesh.

Saul had acted with authority. He had secured united action from the people and had successfully stood the initial test of his new-found office.

3. The relief of Jabesh Gilead (11:9–11)

The people in Jabesh were justifiably elated to learn of their imminent deliverance. So much so that they cockily sent word to the Ammonites that they would surrender on the morrow. This disinformation doubtless served to encourage their adversaries to 'count their chickens before they were hatched'!

Early next morning, during the last watch of the night (2–6 a.m.), Saul threw his army in three divisions against the Ammonite camp, crushed the enemy and raised the siege. At one stroke, Saul had demonstrated his competence as a soldier and silenced his detractors.

Reaffirmation of the monarchy [11:12–15]

Others remembered the malignants who had muttered against Saul's investiture as king. As is so typical of the excesses that follow in the train of victory, a clamour arose for the death of these men. But Saul, to his credit, forbade this monstrous vindictiveness on the ground that '**the Lord [had] rescued Israel**' that day – the same basis on which his own men would, years later, prevent him from putting his own son to death (11:12–13; see 14:45). At this early stage in his career, Saul saw that 'The best way of eliminating enemies is to turn them into allies.'[5] He would not always be so magnanimous (see 22:6–23).

Samuel, meanwhile, took occasion from this victory to call the people to Gilgal for a ceremony reaffirming Saul as the anointed King of Israel. Gilgal was to be a place of destiny for Saul, where what was confirmed on this day would later be solemnly revoked by the word of the Lord (13:7–15; 15:12–33). But on this occasion there was joy and a new beginning; the confirmation of high hopes and the fulfilment of early promise in the new king. '**So all the people went to Gilgal and confirmed Saul as king in the presence of the Lord. There they sacrificed fellowship offerings before the Lord, and Saul and all the Israelites held a great celebration.**' King Saul was firmly established on his throne.

Valediction for the Hebrew republic [12:1–25]

It was the end of an age and no one was more aware of it than the prophet Samuel. He was the last of the judges and stood between the past and the future – a pivotal figure whose shadow would be cast across the land for many a year yet, but who was, nevertheless, yesterday's man. And the Lord laid on his heart the words that would stand as an interpretive milestone along the path of the history of God's people, both reminding them of the past and pointing them to the future.

Samuel's speech was almost conversational. He interacted with the people, calling for an audible response from time to time. At the same time, the address does contain the elements of a covenant. It includes a *preamble*, in which Samuel establishes his credentials as the Lord's spokesman (12:1–5), a *historical prologue* which reviews the Lord's dealings with his people up to that point (12:6–12), *ethical stipulations* setting forth their obligations to the Lord (12:14), *sanctions* outlining the consequences of disobedience (12:15) and although this is out of its customary third place in the sequence, a *succession arrangement* which points to the provisions for the covenant in the future (12:13). Such analysis may owe more to the conventional wisdom of modern scholarship than to Samuel's own conception of what he was saying to Israel.[6] In any event, God's covenant with his people is inevitably at the heart of Samuel's speech. Even if there was no formal covenant renewal, as such, on this occasion, the entire event has a covenant purpose. All of Israel's life was rooted in God's covenant.

The specific focus, however, is Samuel's farewell to Israel as the last judge. But we should note that it was not farewell to Samuel as the prophet of Israel. He continued to wield tremendous influence into the future, not least in the anointing of David to be king in succession to Saul. It was, rather, Samuel's farewell to the period of the judges. He marked the passing of the Hebrew republic and set the conditions for the blessing of the new monarchy. It was his valedictory address for an epoch which was gone. The times, they were a-changing! And they had changed – for ever!

1. The integrity of God's prophet (12:1–5)

Samuel prefaced his great valedictory address by a declaration of his integrity as the judge of Israel. In majestic simplicity, he reviewed his public life.

Firstly, he had transferred power to their king as they had requested. He had, in other words, been a faithful servant of the Lord's people. He had not clung to his position as judge in a self-centred way. He had served them from his youth (12:1–2).

Secondly, he had judged Israel with unimpeachable integrity. Calling for testimony against himself, the prophet asked, '**in the presence of the Lord and his anointed**' (i.e., before the heavenly King and his earthly vicegerent, Saul), if he had robbed, cheated or oppressed anyone. Had he ever taken a bribe to subvert justice? If so, he would make restitution (12:3).

The people responded with a sincere acclamation of his innocence of any injustice and, in their uncomprehending way, made a devastating comment on their own behaviour. '**The Lord is witness against you**,' said Samuel, '**and his anointed is witness this day, that you have not found anything in my hand**' (12:4–5). This implied that there was no substantial ground for their dissatisfaction with Samuel's administration and 'consequently no well-founded reason for their request for a king'.[7]

2. The history of God's dealings with Israel (12:6–12)

This was now driven home explicitly by a review of the '**evidence . . . as to all the righteous acts performed by the Lord**' for them and their fathers (12:6–11). He had delivered them again and again – from the consequences of their own sin, be it noted (12:9) – when they had cried to him in repentance and renewed faith (12:10–11). Then, in connection with the latest crisis, as Nahash descended upon Jabesh Gilead, they insisted on a king to lead them, when the Lord was their King already! They had, as we know, asked for and received their king before Nahash had invaded Gilead, but Samuel highlighted that event because it was the proof of Israel's retreat from the lordship of God and of their determination to have a king like the other nations.

3. The future way of blessing under the monarchy (12:13–15)

They had their king. But God is gracious. They had been delivered from the Ammonites through the instrumentality of King Saul. If they loved and served God – both people and king – then they would enjoy the blessing of the Lord.

But if they rebelled, they would incur the anger of God, as had their fathers.

4. The authentication of the prophetic word (12:16–18)

The crack of doom was immediately heard in '**thunder and rain**' – in the middle of the dry season! In Israel, it rained in winter, with the 'latter rain' in the spring followed by dry weather up to and past the May-June wheat harvest. This was a miraculous manifestation of God's anger against Israel, sealing the terms of the prophet's admonition to the people regarding the blessing of God in the future. It was, as George Whitefield once said in reference to a peal of thunder during a sermon in Boston, 'the voice of the Almighty as he passed by in his anger'.[8]

5. Confession of sin and final exhortation (12:19–25)

The people were truly humbled before the power and the holiness of God and made confession of their sin, asking Samuel to intercede for them before the Lord (12:19).

Samuel responded with impassioned exhortations that they serve the Lord with their whole heart. And in the midst of these, he gave two promises: one from the Lord and one of his own. The Lord, he said, 'for the sake of his great name' would '**not reject his people, because [he] was pleased to make [them] his own**' (12:22). As for himself, Samuel would not sin against God by '**failing to pray for**' them. Furthermore, he would continue to teach them '**the way that is good and right**' (12:23). Finally, he warned them that the consequences of persisting in evil would be the end of both king and people (12:25).

The claims of God

One of the ever-present perplexities of the Christian life is discerning the difference between what we *want* for our own selfish reasons and what we *should desire* for the true blessing of our whole life, physical and spiritual, and for the honour of our Saviour and the glory of God. It might seem that this would be an easy assignment, but the truth is that our motives are often very mixed and even blatant self-

centredness can be overlaid with pious language and self-
serving rationalizations. We persuade ourselves that we
need this or that, even when it is clear, on any plain reading
of God's Word, that he would not agree with us.

Israel, to use the language of popular psychology, felt that
'their needs were not being met' by God's arrangements for
their national government, the judges. They 'needed' a king
like other nations. They persuaded themselves, even in the
face of the Word of God through the prophet Samuel, that
monarchy was indispensable for their collective security
and happiness. 'Need' conquered all. 'Need' became the
justification of unhallowed desire. 'Need' became the
imperative above God. 'Need' became a god! Israel (and we
sinners in the act of chasing our sins) were like the small
boy, maybe nine years old, who stopped me in the street in
Berwick-on-Tweed. 'Hey, mister,' he said, holding out a
grubby hand in which sat a rather lonely penny, 'can ye get
me a Woodbine in thon shop ower there?' When I, in
declining his request, asked him why he wanted a cigarette
at his age, he replied, 'Aw, mister, Ah need wan, Ah cannae
give them up!' Ask a silly question and you get the obvious
answer! Whatever has enslaved us becomes a need. Need
sounds better, even to a seared conscience, than sheer
self-destructive bondage ever could. This is basic to the
character of all rejection of God's will.

Assessing Israel's desire for a king is made more compli-
cated by the fact that God had promised a king through
Moses (Deuteronomy 17:14–20). God, of course, would
determine the time of such an appointment. But Israel
'jumped the gun'! They decided that God was wrong to
withhold fulfilment of the promise and they were right to
insist on it now! Their argument was wholly pragmatic, of
course: 'We have to be practical. It will make us successful
and grand, like other nations. The economy will improve
and the standard of living will rise for all of our people. We
will be respected in the counsels of the nations. We will be a
nation of which anyone would be proud to be a citizen. And
– we almost forgot – God will be glorified before the world!
Others may listen more carefully to his Word in future!'

But God saw this as so much will-worship. They were
simply not content to trust him. They were not willing to

face up to the fact that their problems as a nation flowed from their own folly rather than any defect in their God-given system of government. They implicitly blamed God for their own inadequacies and invented a solution which they explicitly maintained was superior to the claims of God! It took a supernatural storm and a wind of the Spirit from the prophet's mouth to bring them to their knees and admit their sin!

In the midst of these changing times and, not least, the fickle movements of sinful hearts, it is the unchangeable and unchanging God who stands sure and steadfast, the anchor of the soul who trusts in him! The answer to Israel's need was holiness to the Lord, not political theory and a change of regime! And holiness is only possible where God's Word is heard and obeyed. Only the Word and the Lord of that Word provide a way of happiness and prosperity, then as now. Hence, the overture of God's love and free grace comes to every repentant sinner and redeems the years that the locusts have eaten: '**Do not be afraid. . .you have done all this evil; yet do not turn away from the Lord, but serve the Lord with all your heart**' (12:20).

References

[1] C.F. Keil and F. Delitzsch, p. 110.

[2] R.P. Gordon, p. 123.

[3] C.F. Keil and F. Delitzsch, p. 112.

[4] The figure of 330,000 is not too high when it is considered that this was a muster – a *levée en masse* – of the whole of Israel's able-bodied manhood.

[5] D.F. Payne, p. 56.

[6] Other scholars see a different structure altogether. R.W. Klein, for example, sees it as a 'legal process' in which Israel is accused of sin and finally threatened with exile (12:25) in case of persistent disobedience. But then, Klein thinks Samuel's speech was probably written after the Exile (i.e., 500+ years later), to provide an interpretation of the downfall of kingdom of Judah!

[7] C.F. Keil and F. Delitzsch, p. 116.

[8] A. Dallimore, *George Whitefield*, (London: Banner of Truth, 1970), Vol. 1, p. 543.

11.
No time to wait for God!

Please read 1 Samuel 13:1–14

'So I felt compelled to offer the burnt offerings' (1 Samuel 13:12).

Every businessman knows that a large part of the success of his enterprise depends on an intangible element called 'good will'. He also knows how easily it can be blown away, perhaps by his own folly, but sometimes even by forces beyond his control. In my student days in Aberdeen – the 'Granite City' in Scotland's north-east corner – I witnessed a startling example of how the loss of good will can destroy a thriving business. A typhoid epidemic broke out, hundreds of people became ill and several of them died. The cause of the problem was traced to a single large can of corned beef, the contents of which had been sold, sliced, over the delicatessen counter. It was later revealed that the offending tin had been purchased from British Army surplus supplies. These had originally come from Argentina, where, it was thought, this tin had somehow been contaminated with the typhoid bacillus. The loss of public confidence in that supermarket was overwhelming. It was avoided 'like the plague' by the Aberdeen shoppers and, starved of trade, it too became a casualty of the epidemic it had unwittingly unleashed upon its unsuspecting customers.

Confidence that took a generation to build up can evaporate in the twinkling of an eye with just one mistake! One little match in the wrong place can burn down a thousand trees! The irony of history is that so often the great tragedies turn on an action that seemed insignificant in itself – or even went unnoticed at the time!

We see a similar phenomenon in the experience of God's people. Saul became King of Israel and began his reign with a degree of promise. He succeeded in relieving besieged Jabesh Gilead (11:1–11) and his popularity climbed to heights that would never be exceeded. He was every inch a king! But after not too many years – we do not know how many – his rule turned sour. The Lord decreed that the succession would be given to another man – one after God's own heart (13:14). Saul became, in effect, a 'lame duck' king, although he continued to hold the reins of power for a reign of some four decades. And the turning-point which precipitated God's rejecting him was, as we shall see, a moment of presumptuous impatience in which he determinedly disobeyed the will of God. He could not wait a few hours for God! And from that day forth, the early promise of Saul's reign was to dissolve into a pattern of spiritual declension which would continue to cast its louring shadows across the national life of God's people for many a long year. At length, with the accession of David, the heavenly light of spiritual revival would burst forth upon the people of God and give them the king of God's choice (Deuteronomy 17:14–20).

War with the Philistines [13:1–7]

The first verse is a statement of the accession formula for Saul. The extant Hebrew manuscripts have lost some of the original figures which would tell us both his age and the length of his reign. The Hebrew actually gives Saul's age at accession as one year old and his reign as two years long! Our Bible translations cannot resist attempting a reconstruction of the missing facts. Acts 13:21, however, gives a round figure of forty years for his reign, while his age at accession – thirty years old – appears in some Septuagint manuscripts (the third-century B.C. Greek Old Testament) and may even be borrowed from David's age at his accession! (2 Samuel 5:4).[1]

Early on in his reign, Saul decided to go to war with the Philistines.[2] Perhaps he was emboldened by his success over the Ammonites (11:11). More pointedly, he probably wanted to prove the value of his new army (13:2). Hitherto, Israel had tended to act defensively, for the simple reason that the army consisted of mass citizen levies from the tribes. Saul had, it seems, established a standing army and was in a position to take action without calling out the militia (and without having to give a good reason for a war of aggression against such a formidable enemy). He '**chose three thousand men from Israel**' and he sent his son Jonathan with '**a thousand**' against a Philistine garrison which then occupied the city of Geba in the territory of Benjamin (13:2).[3]

This has all the makings of a classic 'border incident' – a time-honoured method for manufacturing a war that will both unite the nation and, it is hoped, lead to territorial expansion. This is how Italy began her war with Ethiopia in 1935 (the Wal-Wal incident), Japan her war with China in 1937 (the Marco Polo Bridge incident) and Germany her war with Poland in 1939.

Saul's stratagem was at first successful. First-strike attacks against unsuspecting targets tend to be cheap victories – as witness Pearl Harbour, on 7 December 1941. Saul had the excuse that he needed to call out the men of Israel for an all-out war on their perennial enemies! With the sound of a trumpet throughout the land, the people were called to muster at Gilgal (13:3–4). War is so glorious! For the young especially, war always begins with intense excitement, a sense of elation and, indeed, over-weening optimism. For the experienced, there is only the anticipation of the inevitable cost.

Israel began paying the price immediately. The Philistines advanced to Saul's base at Michmash in overwhelming strength and Israel melted away. They '**hid in caves and thickets, among the rocks, and in pits and cisterns. Some Hebrews even crossed the Jordan to the land of Gad and Gilead**' (13:5–7). Their humiliation was, it would seem, complete. In embarking upon a war of aggression, Saul had made his first major mistake and brought the judgement of God upon his people.

Impatience with God [13:7–10]

Saul retreated on Gilgal with such of his army as had not, as an old soldier would put it, gone 'over the hill'. The inspired chronicler records, with solemn economy of expression, that they '**were quaking with fear**' (13:7). Saul was to wait there for '**seven days, the time set by Samuel**' (13:8). This takes us back to Samuel's instructions in 10:8, which could not have been fulfilled in the gathering at Gilgal recorded in 11:14–15, but must have been a prophetic reference to this occasion.[4] The days slipped by and Samuel did not appear. And as the days passed, Saul's soldiers deserted so that his once proud host was reduced to a single battalion of infantry (13:15).

It was at this point that Saul made the most important mistake of his reign. He directed that '**the burnt offering and the fellowship offerings**' be sacrificed to the Lord. '**And Saul offered up the burnt offering**' (13:9). This does not mean that he made the offering with his own hand, but that he did so with the co-operation of the priests – as, for example, David and Solomon did legitimately on a number of occasions (2 Samuel 24:25; 1 Kings 3:4; 8:63). Saul's sin was to *command* the offering of sacrifices when he had no proper authority for doing so. He was to wait for Samuel, but the pressures of the moment and the impetuosity of his spirit led him to 'jump the gun' and arrogate to himself the role of the prophet. This was to prove a most costly transgression. And the sad irony was that he had no sooner offered his sacrifice than Samuel strode into the camp (13:10).

Facing the consequences [13:11–22]

Just about everybody was angry with Saul. The Philistines were angry and the prophet Samuel was angry. No doubt a large number of Saul's subjects were angry as well. His plans were in ruins and his kingdom was being overrun by the enemy. As if this were not enough, two further consequences of his actions were added to his woes. One was personal, while the other was national.

1. Saul was deprived of a dynasty (13:11–15)

When Samuel arrived, so to speak, at the eleventh hour, he was confronted with the proof of Saul's desperate folly and he challenged his actions with characteristic forthrightness: '"**What have you done?**" asked Samuel' (13:11).

Saul's response is very understandable, however inadequate it may be as a justification for what he did. He was, he claimed, forced to do what he did by the rapidly deteriorating military situation and the non-appearance of the prophet. The constraints of piety confirmed him in this course, he suggested, for he felt it necessary to seek '**the Lord's favour**' (13:12). This sounds very plausible and we can certainly identify with the sense of crisis which must have crowded in on Saul's mind that afternoon.

Samuel, however, was not impressed by Saul's explanation. And he laid into Saul with one of the most trenchant rebukes in all of Scripture history. He characterized Saul's action as foolish and disobedient to the command of God, although no details are given to us of the instructions which had been violated. It is assumed that we can grasp the essence of the problem from what we know of the law of God and the recorded circumstances of this incident. If the crime was not exactly spelled out in precise detail, the punishment surely was – and with solemn severity. Saul would not be succeeded by his son. There would be no dynasty, no house of Saul, to sit upon the throne of Israel '**for all time**'. Indeed, the Lord had decided to seek out '**a man after his own heart**' who would be appointed '**the leader of his people**' (13:14). Saul therefore left Gilgal with his six hundred men in the knowledge that while he would continue to rule as king, he would never have the joy of knowing that his royal mantle would be passed to his son and the succeeding generations of his house.[5]

2. Israel became a demilitarized zone under Philistine occupation (13:16–22)

Raiding parties scoured the land and suppressed all manufacture of iron and iron implements. Military weapons were denied to Israel and the Israelites were obliged to go to their conquerors for agricultural equipment and even for the sharpening of ploughshares and cattle-goads. Saul's little war had cost the people of God very dearly.

Why?

Why did all this come to pass? What did it all mean? What can it possibly mean for modern man and modern society? These are some of the questions that leap at us from these, to us remote, events.

1. Perhaps the most obvious, and certainly the most vexed point for biblical interpreters, is the gravity of Saul's offence as reflected in the severity of his punishment. One commentator is uncomfortable with the 'harshness of Samuel's retort'.[6] Another sees Samuel's 'recorded harshness and refusal to compromise' as arising from 'unhappy experiences as a boy in Shiloh' – surely the triumph of popular psychology over the clear meaning of the Word of God![7] Gordon is surely correct in seeing the real issue as that of 'Saul's obedience to Yahweh'.[8] The interval of seven days was a test of Saul's faith and, as C. F. Keil and Franz Delitzsch point out, 'When Saul proceeded with the consecrating sacrifice ... without the presence of Samuel, he showed clearly enough that he thought he could make war upon the enemies of his kingdom without the counsel and assistance of God. This was an act of rebellion against the sovereignty of Jehovah, for which the punishment announced was by no means too severe.'[9]

The reason why some people have difficulty with the rigour of Samuel's condemnation of Saul's disobedience lies within their own hearts and not in any manifest injustice on the prophet's part. Matthew Poole, writing in the seventeenth century, put his finger on the problem exactly and stops the mouths of those who would gainsay the Lord's dealings with Saul: 'Men are very incompetent judges of God's judgements because they see but very little, either of the majesty of the offended God, or of the heinous nature and aggravations of the offence. . . men see nothing but Saul's outward act, which seems small, but God saw with how wicked a mind and heart he did this, with what rebellion against the light of his own conscience. . . with what gross. . . distrust of God's providence; with what contempt of God's authority and justice; and many other wicked principles and motions of the heart, unknown to men.'[10]

What searching words! And so full of reverence for God and his Word! And what a comment on modern scholarship that the most humbling and discerning comment on the text should come from a man who preached the gospel over three hundred years ago! How easily we can sit in judgement on the inspired, infallible and inerrant Word of God! But who are we to search the mind of God and challenge what we imagine to be his defective attitudes? We repeat the sin of Saul ourselves! We think we know better than the Holy One of Israel – we who do not even know the deceitfulness of our own hearts! (Cf. Jeremiah 17:9.) Who are we to decide which sins are little sins, when the Word tells us that to be guilty of *one* point of the law of God is to be guilty of all? What we ought to do is to plead for God so to enlighten our understanding and spiritual discernment that we can truly know ourselves as he knows us. Then, knowing how sinful sin is and how holy God is, we might gain the victory, in Christ our Saviour, over the subtle snares that wind their lilliputian threads around our souls and inhibit the movements of spiritual growth in our lives.

2. The obvious point of continuing application is that we are called to obey God and be satisfied in our hearts with straightforward faithfulness to his revealed Word. The word of Samuel to Saul was the command of God. And it was simply a contradiction of God for Saul to go his own way. It was also a retreat from the blessing of God, because the Lord's way is truly the way of happiness and fulfilment as a child of God.

It is never the Lord's intention merely to test – i.e., try to trip up – the believer. His purpose is entirely positive and wholly redemptive in thrust. It is possible for us to lose sight of this, especially if we are sensitive to our sins, or are prone to become morbid about them. If we look only at the thunderings of Sinai and the majesty of the law of God, we may well sink into a spiritual Slough of Despond as we think on our shortcomings. We may be tempted to fear that God plans to judge us over some decisive sin at some point in the future. We may therefore become racked by a lack of assurance that the Lord loves us, because we feel all our sins so keenly.

What we need to realize, however, is that sensitivity to sin is a work of grace and an evidence of the indwelling work of the Holy Spirit in our Christian life. It is not a cause of despair, nor is it designed to be an engine of discouragement. God has not given us a spirit of fear, but of power, of love and a sound mind (2 Tim. 1:7 AV).

3. When understood in relation to the whole purpose of God revealed in Scripture, even this sad account of Saul's failure contains a message of God's saving grace. Saul himself was not left without ongoing testimonies to the grace, presence and power of God in his life. That he was to end his life in the gall of bitterness and as a suicide can lay no charge of lovelessness or lack of patience at God's door. Saul went to hell with his eyes open, in spite of God's unmerited goodness to him over many years. But arching above the tragedy of Saul is the promise of a Saviour, for this is the distant goal of the declaration that God had appointed a king after his own heart (13:14). David points to the Son of David, the Lord Jesus Christ. And in Jesus we have the gospel in its fulness. He has died to conquer the sins of his people and bring them to eternal life, free from all that comes between us and our holy God. All the sins of believers are washed away by his perfect sacrifice for sin. Having come to Christ in saving faith, we are to be discouraged *no more* – not even by our own shortcomings. Rather we are to continue to live repentantly and believingly, looking to Jesus as the author and finisher of our faith. We can leave the things that are behind – leave them at the cross and the empty tomb – and press on towards the goal of our heavenward calling in our risen and victorious Saviour, the Lord Jesus Christ.

References

[1] See R.W. Klein, p. 122.
[2] J. C. Laney, p. 46, suggests that the reference in 13:1 to 'two years' (NIV's **'forty-two'** includes forty added, from Acts 13:21, by the translators) refers to the time he had been reigning. His rendering of 13:1–2 is, 'Saul was one and . . . [perhaps forty] years old when he began to reign, and when he had reigned two years over Israel then Saul chose for himself three thousand men of Israel. . .'

[3] See R. P. Gordon, pp. 93, 132.

[4] C. F. Keil and F. Delitzsch, pp. 101–103.

[5] In Genesis 49:10 it was prophesied that 'The sceptre will not depart from Judah.' How can this be squared with 1 Samuel 13:13? The answer is to be found in Jeremiah 18:5–10, where it is made clear that even the most absolute pronouncements are made with a reservation of divine response to the response of men and women to the words of God. Saul disobeyed; the potential for a dynasty was forfeited.

[6] Klein, p. 127.

[7] W. F. Albright, quoted by R. P. Gordon, p. 134.

[8] Gordon, p. 134.

[9] Keil and Delitzsch, p. 130.

[10] M. Poole, *Commentary on the Whole Bible*, (London: Banner of Truth Trust, 1969), Vol. 1, p. 544.

12.
By many or by few

Please read 1 Samuel 13:23–14:52

'Nothing can hinder the Lord from saving, whether by many or by few' (1 Samuel 14:6).

The idea of snatching victory from the jaws of defeat is not merely an appealing element of romanticism. It has frequently been a necessity for the retrieval of many an otherwise seemingly doomed cause. The garrison of Lucknow, in the Indian Mutiny of 1857, was at the end of its tether when the bagpipes of Sir Colin Campbell's Scottish Highlanders signalled that relief was at hand. The military psychology of the British race and their American cousins almost assumes a run of initial defeats before the expected turn of the tide and the culminating triumph of superior arms. If there is an Alamo, there will soon be a San Jacinto; if an Isandlwhana, an Ulundi; if a Dunkirk, then an El Alamein; and for a Pearl Harbour, the most dreadful end of all – Hiroshima and Nagasaki. If Vietnam dented confidence in the mythology of the great come-back, the Falklands and Grenada perhaps rekindled the older, comfortable assurance that 'we' would win out in the end.

Perhaps Saul hoped for such a reversal of Israel's fortunes as he sat under his pomegranate tree near Geba[1] and contemplated the ruination of his kingdom under the Philistine yoke. His situation was desperate indeed. Philistine raiding parties scoured the land (13:17), Israel had been all but demilitarized by the proscription of all iron-working (13:19–22) and Saul's 'army' consisted of no more than six

hundred men together with Ahijah the priest and the ark of
God (14:1–3). Only a couple of kilometres away from where
Saul brooded over his predicament, the Philistine camp at
Michmash kept a confident vigil, secure in the knowledge
that their enemy was too demoralized to be much of a threat.

There is a chilling rhythm to the sins of men. Genuine
achievement begets pride and pride goes before a fall. And so
there is a cycle of action and reaction that, in the good
providence of God, has the effect of restraining human evil.
As with Shakespeare's Macbeth, 'Vaulting ambition o'er-
leaps itself.' And this recurrent impulse towards self-
destruction offers relief for the hard-pressed.

But there is another factor at work. And that is the mighty
intervention of God in strengthening the hands of his people.
The eye of faith sees this in the normal course of the
individual Christian's life. It can be discerned, with less
precision perhaps, in the movements of history as a whole.
God is not merely letting things happen. He is working out
his purpose as year succeeds to year. He has a purpose of
grace for his people. He has a plan of salvation for lost people
who still have not been brought to faith in the Lord Jesus
Christ. He is actively proceeding to a goal which is his
victory over evil in all its manifestations. And every step
forward along that road is a deliverance and a victory for
God's people. Just such a deliverance was about to take place
for Saul and Israel. The Lord was about to raise up a nation
prostrated by the folly of her king. In the course of this
revival we are given some insight into the character of the
two main actors – Saul and his son, Jonathan. And we see,
particularly in the case of Saul, something of the nature of
human perversity even in the face of overwhelming evidences of the Lord's favour. The overarching theme is that of
salvation – by many or by few – and, as we shall see, the Lord
first saves the many by the few and then the few by the many.

Salvation by the few [13:23–14:23]

The occasion of Jonathan's testimony to the power of God to
save **'by many or by few'** (14:6) was a military adventure by
this accomplished and godly soldier-prince. The expedi-

tionary force was not large – two men – but the implications of that statement were, and remain, universal and cosmic in scope! For here is a glorious universal principle of divine revelation, uttered in the midst of the most amazing illustration of its truth. This is one of God's absolutes. It admits of no modification and no explaining away. It stands as a constant encouragement for all who trust in the Lord. He can save for us today whether by many or by few!

1. Jonathan's raid (13:23–14:15)

What was to become the Battle of Michmash began in a very quiet way. While Saul seemed paralysed with indecision, his son Jonathan decided to take the bull by the horns and get on with the war. So he and his armour-bearer slipped out of the camp with the intention of attacking the Philistine outpost across the valley (14:1).

The situation was that Saul, in Geba (probably not Gibeah), was in the hills to the south of Michmash, where the Philistine base was situated. Although no more than a few kilometres apart, they were separated by a deep valley with cliffs on either side (14:4–5). Jonathan's plan was to approach the Philistine outpost on the other side and test their mettle. It is clear that Jonathan was aware of the demoralization of the Israelite force, but he also realized two vital factors that could entirely transform the situation. One was the power of God and the other was the tonic of a decisive victory, however limited to begin with. As Oliver Cromwell would trust in God and keep his powder dry, so Jonathan proceeded with that happy blend of lively faith in the Lord and a skilled tactician's eye! He began with holy optimism: '**Perhaps the Lord will act on our behalf. Nothing can hinder the Lord from saving, whether by many or by few**' (14:6). And he continued with intelligent deliberation. Jonathan was not foolhardy. He therefore applied a test. They would only cross over and give battle if the Philistine pickets gave them an invitation to come up to their side! This Jonathan would regard as a '**sign that the Lord has given them into our hands**' (14:8–10).

It is unnecessary to see this 'sign' as a supernatural intervention of divine revelation like Gideon's fleece (Judges 6:34–40; 7:9–15). To a military mind, a Philistine invitation to go up to them might well have been an indication of their contempt and therefore over-confidence in the face of an Israelite challenge. Jonathan meant to 'have a go' if given half a chance and he was confident in the Lord that he could strike an effective blow for his country. That opportunity was afforded by the mocking response of the Philistines. **'The Hebrews are crawling out of the holes they were hiding in'** shouted the sentries. **'Come up to us and we'll teach you a lesson'** (14:11–12). This was enough for Jonathan. **'Climb up after me,'** he said to his companion, **'the Lord has given them into the hand of Israel'** (14:12). He was fully persuaded that this was God's moment for decisive action.

The two men went down across the wadi and scaled the height on the Michmash side. Once at the top hand-to-hand combat ensued and in the mêlée that followed, twenty men perished (14:13–14). The effect of this two-man blitzkrieg was to strike terror into the ranks of the main body of the Philistines, who were no doubt lolling about in their lines with easy confidence. Theirs was to be a rude awakening! It was, in fact, **'a panic sent by God'** (14:16). The ground shook 'with the noise and tumult of the frightened foe'.[2] The Philistines were in flight!

2. Saul's intervention (14:16–23)
Saul's lookouts in Geba (rather than Gibeah) saw what was happening to the Philistines. Accordingly he assembled his troops, thereby discovering that Jonathan and his armour-bearer were missing (14:16–17). He did not, however, spring into action against the enemy. Saul called for Ahijah, the priest, in order that sacrifices be made and the Lord's will be sought. The reference to the **'ark of God'** being **'with the Israelites'** has caused almost as much tumult among biblical commentators as Jonathan inflicted on the Philistines! At that time, the ark was in Kiriath Jearim and it is generally supposed that its presence there was unbroken for the whole period between its return from the Philistines until David took it to Jerusalem (7:1–2; 2 Samuel 6:2; 1 Chronicles 13:5–6). Noting that the Septuagint – the Greek version of the Old Testament – has Saul calling for the 'ephod' rather than the ark, many biblical scholars have

concluded that the Hebrew text is corrupted at this point, that the ark was not in the camp but at Kiriath Jearim.[3] What was really with the Israelite army was probably that priestly vestment, the ephod, with its mysterious stones, the Urim and the Thummim, by means of which guidance was sought of the Lord.[4] Whatever the case, it is certain that Saul intended to consult the Lord in a regular manner. But even as he instituted this solemn and holy procedure, he changed his mind and ordered Ahijah to withdraw his hand, so that the men of Israel could be flung into battle without delay (14:18–20). Israelites in the service of the Philistines rebelled against their erstwhile masters and as more Israelites emerged from hiding and joined the fight, the Philistines were utterly routed. '**So the Lord rescued Israel that day**' (14:23).

The Battle of Michmash was, on the human level, Jonathan's victory. Saul did not exactly shine, for all that he intervened decisively in the end. His ambivalence to the things of God emerged once again in his use – or, as it turns out, his abuse – of the priest Ahijah and the ordinances of the Lord. In his initial indecision over the dissolution of the Philistine army, he called for Ahijah, in order to seek the Lord's will. But then he made up his own mind and summarily dismissed him. Saul gives us the impression that he felt he was supposed to be 'religious' and observe certain conventions at the appropriate times, but really had no deep convictions of his own. He used religion, as opposed to living a personal faith in the Lord. Even when he was, by his way of things, trying to do the right thing, he shortly fell into some folly (13:9–10; 14:24–47; 15:19–23) or irreverence (14:18–19). There was a fundamental lack of spiritual discernment in his attitude to God's ordinances. His religion did not fit the real Saul.

Jonathan, on the other hand, showed some spiritual quality. His confidence in the Lord grew as the day progressed. And he and his armour-bearer not only became the heroes of the hour but stand as an emblem of the triumph of faith in the Lord. 'Faith,' said Bishop Joseph Hall (1574–1656), 'is never so glorious as when it has most opposition, and will not see it. Reason always looks to the means, faith to the end ... How perilous a passage, O Lord, hast thou

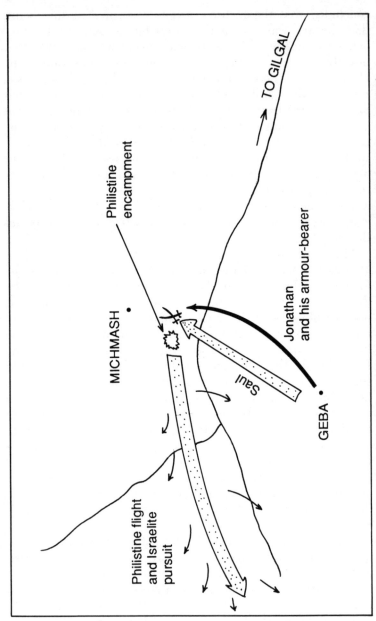

Map 6 The Battle of Michmash (1 Samuel 13:23 - 14:52)

appointed for thy labouring pilgrims! If difficulties discourage us, we shall but climb to fall. When lifting our feet to the last step, there are the Philistines of death, of temptations to grapple with, but give us faith, and we shall overcome the spite of earth and hell!'

Salvation by the many [14:24–45]

The battle was well on the way to being won when Saul did something that might well have snatched defeat out of the jaws of victory!

1. Saul's vainglorious vow (14:24–44)
Having demonstrated with unbecoming eloquence that he could do without the 'consolation of religion' (14:18–19), Saul immediately proceeded to take a solemn vow on behalf of all his soldiers: **'Cursed be any man who eats food before evening comes, before I have avenged myself on my enemies'** (14:24). Napoleon was unfortunately not around at the time to tell Saul that an army – even God's army – has to march on its stomach!

Underlying this culpable disregard for the welfare of his troops, not to mention its effect upon the scope of a victory that *others* had delivered to him on a platter, was Saul's utter self-centredness. Everything flows from an overwhelming egocentric urge for personal glory: it is a case of 'me . . . me . . . me' – **'before *I* have avenged *myself* upon *my* enemies'**. Let his men sweat, bleed and die! No, let them starve as well and drop dead of exhaustion, for *he*, Saul, must have *his* victory! Perhaps Saul regarded this as a fast and therefore an act of devotion pleasing to God, which would enhance the triumph of Israelite arms that day. If this was the case, it demonstrated once more Saul's peculiarly uncomprehending religiosity.[5] That kind of 'heavenly-mindedness' certainly is of 'no earthly use'!

Two general observations point us to some relevant lessons for us today. Firstly, by imposing such a vow, Saul was requiring more of God's people than God himself asked of them. This is a fundamental characteristic of what God's Word calls 'self-imposed worship' or, 'will-worship' [AV]

,ossians 2:23). The Pharisees of Jesus' time were past-
.isters at this kind of thing. They had constructed an
elaborate system of ritual righteousness above and beyond
what God had set forth in the Word. Jesus applied Leviticus
20:9 to them: 'But in vain do they worship me, teaching for
doctrines the commandments of men' (Matthew 15:9 AV).
And later, in passing judgement upon them, he said, 'They
tie up heavy loads and put them on men's shoulders, but
they themselves are not willing to lift a finger to move them'
(Matthew 23:4). This is called will-worship because it is the
enthronement of man's self-generated will in opposition to
the revealed will of God. Inevitably, this has calamitous
results, because it is precisely that from which we need to be
saved. It is the human problem already – by nature – and
therefore cannot be a solution to anything!

Secondly, unbiblical requirements lead to aggravated
evils. Saul's oath made a difficult enough situation considerably worse. Notice five harmful consequences of that
ill-considered oath.

a.   It led to Jonathan, his own son, unwittingly committing
a breach of the oath (14:25–27). Coming upon a honeycomb,
without any bees, Jonathan dipped into it and refreshed
himself with some honey.[6]

b.   Furthermore, it led Jonathan to an angry over-reaction,
when he was challenged by the other men, who had,
perforce, obeyed Saul's order of the day (14:28–30).
Jonathan was correct on all his three points. Yes, his father
had '**made trouble for the country**'. And yes! His '**eyes
brightened**' when he tasted a little of the honey. But to raise
his voice against the king was the ancient crime of *lèse-
majesté*, even if he was a prince of the blood! Yet what he said
was true! Had the men eaten of the plunder, the '**slaughter
of the Philistines**' would have been '**even greater**'.

c.   It also led the people into sin – that of eating blood
because of the over-hasty preparation of meat from the spoil
of the battle (14:31–35). The law was explicit on this point.
Meat was not to be eaten with the blood (Leviticus 19:26).
This was because of the provision, in Leviticus 17:10–12,

which reserved blood for the atoning sacrifices of the tabernacle. The reason given is that 'The life of a creature is in the blood' (Leviticus 17:11). In this way, the Lord maintained the integrity of the symbolic significance of the blood, in relation to atonement for sin, so that Israel might understand how necessary and how costly such atonement must be. In the death of Christ we have the once-for-all fulfilment of all that was signified by the bloodshed of the Old Covenant sanctuary (see Hebrews 9:11–10:18). Saul, to his credit, was quick to seek the remedy for this sin and made arrangements for the ritual purification of his men (14:33–35). The sad aspect of this was, however, that the first altar that Saul raised was not to give thanks for the victory, but to seek forgiveness for the sin that he, by his rashness, had precipitated.

d. It led, fourthly, to the diminution of Israel's victory (14:36–37). The Lord's will was sought about continuing the pursuit, but he did not answer and in this way permitted the Philistines to escape through the night.

e. Finally, it led to the exposure of Saul's ungodly despotism (14:38–46). It was shown to be an oath that could only be kept by committing more sin of the most grievous kind. To find why the Lord did not answer them, lots were cast and the lot eventually fell upon Jonathan. Jonathan confessed that he ate some honey and submitted, with evident chagrin, to the sentence of death: '**And now must I die?**' That Saul should then affirm in the strongest possible terms his intention to have his own son put to death is a chilling comment on the frightful state of his soul (14:44). He was, in fact, the guilty party. Jonathan had not consciously sinned. But because he had contravened Saul's oath and incurred the penalty that Saul had bound himself to carry out (14:24, 39), he became the focus of all the injustice of that oath. And, not least, he brought to the light of day the fact that God was angry with Israel because of Saul!

The warning this presents to Christians should be fairly obvious. There ought to be no heaping of extra-biblical rules and regulations upon anybody supposedly in the name of the Lord. God has spoken in his Word. Scripture *alone* is the the sufficient rule for faith and life. Adding to Scripture creates new, and actually fictitious, sins. But, sad to say, the

ffects upon the victims are far from fictitious. One need
look at the cults to see what that can mean in personal
.gedy. Nor are evangelical churches immune to the same
.emptation to add a little here and there to what God has
required of us. Let us be content with Scriptures and the
Christ of the Scriptures!

2. The many save the few! (14:45)
The people had a sense of justice, even if Saul did not. They
refused to permit the blameless hero of that day to go down
to needless death before the unhallowed ego of his
benighted father! Outrage drips from their every word: '**As
surely as the Lord lives, not a hair of his head shall fall to
the ground, for he did this today with God's help**.'
This was, in fact, God's verdict in the case. For once, the
voice of the people was the voice of God. Jonathan was
innocent. Rather, he was the victim of his father, who
'through his arbitrary and despotic command had brought
guilt upon Israel, on account of which God had given him no
reply'.⁷ God, in this roundabout way, humbled Saul before his
own people. From an individual and spiritual point of view, it
was a lesson about the pitfalls of pride, about the theology of
vows and about the sufficiency of God's revealed will as the
rule of faith and life. From a constitutional point of view, this
underscored the limits of kingly power. The 'divine right of
kings' (or presidents, chairmen, führers and caudillos) is a
human invention to justify absolutism and legalize state
terrorism against its own people. Nowadays, tyrants talk in
softer, euphemistic terms. They invoke 'the national interest'
and 'the will of the people'. But these are a 'front' for the
deification of a naked lust for power and a willingness to crush
all that stands in its way. Saul remembered what the people
did that day and he feared them (15:24). That is the dread
reality behind all the bravado of dictators. They fear the
people. But they ought to fear God even more.

God loves his people [14:46–52]

The final section of the chapter looks like an appendix or a
footnote and seems like a good candidate for no more than a

passing glance. There is, however, a wonderful principle hidden in this otherwise mundane passage.

Saul went on reigning as King of Israel. The Philistines **'withdrew to their own land'** (14:46). And year after year, Saul conducted successful campaigns against the nations who had been oppressing Israel for centuries (14:47–48). Saul and Israel were blessed with strength enough to forge a national integrity that could look the others in the face (14:49–52).

The point is that God loves his people, in spite of their faults. His love is constantly directed to the overcoming of their sins. His mercy sprinkles sinners with saving grace. And so, God's rebukes of sin and his message of salvation march side by side in the day-to-day experience of his people. He proves his love by coming over the mountains of our provocations. Even his discipline has a purpose of grace to those who have an ear to hear and an eye to see. His law was the way of true life, true liberty and the pursuit of true happiness for the Old Covenant people. That same law is, for ever, 'put in charge to lead us to Christ, that we might be justified by faith' (Galatians 3:24).

References

[1] Gordon, p. 132.

[2] Keil and Delitzsch, p. 140.

[3] Gordon, pp. 137–138; Keil and Delitzsch, pp. 140–1; Klein, p. 132 (note 18); Payne, p. 69.

[4] Keil and Delitzsch, p. 141.

[5] Gordon, p. 139.

[6] Klein, p. 138, gives a good explanation of the mechanics of Jonathan's action.

[7] Keil and Delitzsch, p. 147.

13.
Rejected by God

Please read 1 Samuel 15:1–35

'Because you have rejected the word of the Lord, he has rejected you as king' (1 Samuel 15:23).

Watching someone die is not at all like watching the endless carnage on prime-time television. The fantasy deaths on TV may, as has been alleged, engender a light view of death in the young. A cynic might counter that light views of almost everything are characteristic of young people anyway. It is hard experience that tends to concentrate minds and bring home the stark realities of life and death. Be that as it may, I can well remember, as a young man, my first face-to-face encounter with the death of a human being. It concentrated my mind in no uncertain way. While walking along Gorgie Road, a busy shopping street in Edinburgh, I saw an old man collapse on the pavement. I ran over to him, as did others, and was in time only to see him take his last breath. Life could be seen departing him. From red to blue to white, his colour betrayed the passage of his soul into eternity. It all happened so quickly; his body was whisked away in an ambulance and people went on shopping. As I went on my way what crowded in upon my mind was the great evil that death is and the terrible finality that it signals. And I thought about that most solemn of truths: 'It is appointed unto man once to die, but after this the judgement' (Hebrews 9:27 AV). That old man had crossed the great divide. One moment it was the sunshine of a Scottish spring; the next, a meeting with his Creator and his eternal destiny. How essential to be right with God before that moment of no return! But how wonderful, in such a context, is the gospel message of the very next verse in that ninth chapter of Hebrews: 'So Christ was once offered to bear the sins of many; and unto them that look for him shall he appear the second time without sin unto salvation' (Hebrews 9:28 AV).

The solemnity of death and divine judgement attends the events recorded in the fifteenth chapter of 1 Samuel. The account begins with God's command to Saul to destroy the Amalekites and it ends with God's rejection of Saul as king over Israel. Fearful though the fate of the Amalekites is, it is Saul who is centre stage and who is the truly tragic figure. As surely as Agag, the Amalekite king, was put to death by Samuel, Saul was executed by God. The tragedy had many acts to play before the curtain came down on Saul's life at Mount Gilboa (31:4). But from this moment on, as R. P. Gordon so aptly remarks, 'Saul is dead while he still lives.' And at the heart of his tragedy is the fact of his persistent refusal to obey the commands of God. Again, R. P. Gordon has a telling comment: 'In . . .13:7b–15a obedience was the stone on which Saul stumbled; here it is the rock that crushes him.'[1]

Saul and the Amalekites [15:1–9]

The narrative opens with Samuel coming to Saul with a command from God to wage war on Amalek and utterly exterminate them as a nation.

1. The ban on Amalek (15:1–3)
The Lord's command was unequivocal: the Amalekites were to be destroyed, '**men and women, children and infants, cattle and sheep, camels and donkeys**' (15:3). The term translated '**totally destroy**' is the Hebrew *herem*, which signifies a 'ban' or a 'devotion' to God for his exclusive disposition (e.g., Leviticus 27:28).[2] In this case, the Lord's disposition is one of judgement. The Lord had commanded the destruction of the Canaanite tribes as an essential part of Israel's possession of the promised land (Deuteronomy

20:16–18). The destruction of Amalek was not unconnected
with that process, for they had been the first people to war
against Israel on their way to Canaan. After that battle at
Rephidim – the one in which Israel prevailed as long as
Moses' hands were lifted up – God declared that he would
'blot out the memory of Amalek from under heaven' and
that 'The Lord will be at war with the Amalekites from
generation to generation' (Exodus 17:8–16; Deuteronomy
25:17–19).

This is the kind of Old Testament phenomenon that
makes many modern Christians somewhat uneasy. For God
to desire the extermination of a whole people seems exceedingly harsh. It appears, especially, to be so patently
indiscriminate – after all, it includes all the children and the
little babies. The inclusion of the livestock and the artefacts
of the culture so condemned only seems to add a strangely
barbaric air to this dark passage of the divine will. We
shrink from the violence and the blood and, most of all, from
the thought that it could be the will of the God who is love (1
John 4:16).

It is certainly natural that we recoil from death and
judgement. They are fearful things. We can take no
pleasure in the deaths of human beings, not even the death
of the wicked. And neither does God himself (Ezekiel
33:11). But we must understand the nature of God's perfect
justice. It must be served. And it is inevitable that it is only
served, in the end, with the irresistible force of the divine
sentence of death, physical and eternal. This enables us to
understand the meaning of the ban placed on the
Canaanites and the Amalekites.

Because these nations were indescribably wicked (and,
more especially, were the inveterate enemies of God and his
people and therefore the greatest threats to the establishment of the Old Covenant people in the land of
promise), God purposed to remove them from the face of
the earth. This, of course, was to involve the faithfulness of
Israel in carrying out the ban. Israel failed in this obligation,
with the result that for centuries they did not fully possess
the land and were, in the end, brought down by the false
religion of the nations they were supposed to have
expunged. The ban was a unique provision at that point in

the unfolding history of God's plan of redemption to preserve the spiritual and organic integrity of God's covenant people in the face of a very hostile and, indeed, satanic confederacy of evil. Precisely because this was a unique moment in the history of redemption, it is not the basis for an ongoing theology of 'holy war'[3] or the justification for a policy of extermination of 'infidels' and 'heretics'. Israel itself did not, as a rule, wage wars of that kind. Only in response to the command of God in particular instances and for the specific reasons given by God in these instances, did Israel engage in campaigns involving the ban.

What is of universal application is the truth that God destroys the wicked from the face of the earth – in every generation and, in the last great day, for ever! That destruction is death – first physical and second eternal death. It will reach into all ages, all generations and all nations, just as his salvation comes to people in all these categories. The destiny of the Amalekites is a picture for all time to follow of the destiny of the reprobate wicked, who will not bow the knee to God. And their judgement is no less severe than that of the Amalekites. Indeed, it is exactly identical. One by one, God's enemies will perish! Any sense of revulsion against God for his dealings with the Amalekites bespeaks a lack of willingness to face the fact of God's perfect holiness, the fact of the sinfulness of sin against a holy God, the fact that the wages of all sin is death, the fact that God is just in these judgements and, on a more personal level, the fact that I, the sinner, am fully deserving of the same condemnation for my own sins and that it is only of God's mercy that I have not been consumed (Lamentations 3:22). It must be said, with bated breath and solemn mien, that the ban on Amalek is being applied to the unconverted with every passing moment and its final and most awesome manifestation, when Christ returns to judge the world, will cause all that has gone before to pale into utter insignificance. That is why the gospel must be preached. We must reap a harvest for Christ, or the world will perish. Every generation is like a crop in a field. If it is not harvested, it rots and dies. The point is this: when we understand who God is, where history is going and how loving his purpose to save really is, when set against the background of the true nature of man's rebellion against God, we will be less squeamish about his dealings with the likes of Amalek and more urgently responsive to his call for repentance and faith, to the end that we might have eternal life in Jesus Christ his Son! Jesus asked the Jews if the Galileans executed by Pilate were more guilty than other Galileans and whether the 'eighteen who died when the tower in Siloam fell on them' were more guilty than 'all the others living in Jerusalem'. His answer was, simply and solemnly: 'I tell you, no! But unless you repent, you too will all perish' (Luke 13:1–5).[4]

2. Saul's execution of the ban (15:4–9)
Saul gathered his forces – the entire available manhood of Israel would have been required for an expedition of this nature – and marched on the Amalekites, who probably lived in the desert to the south of Gaza (15:4–5). Living among the Amalekites were the Kenites – the tribe of Moses' father-in-law, Jethro (Exodus 3:1; 18:1–12; Judges 1:16). They had enjoyed good relations with Israel all along and, therefore, did not fall under the ban (Numbers 10:29–31). They were given opportunity to withdraw and save themselves from the holocaust to follow (15:6).

Saul then fell upon the Amalekites and put them to the sword except for '**Agag and the best of the sheep and cattle, the fat calves and lambs – everything that was good**'. They were only willing to kill the people and the inferior livestock. The ban was applied very selectively. 'Agag' was the king of the Amalekites – the word probably is a title, rather than a personal name (see Numbers 24:7). Saul simply disobeyed the Lord's command to destroy all that fell into his hands. It should be noted that some must have escaped, for the Amalekites reappeared now and again until the last remnant was wiped out in the reign of King Hezekiah (27:8; 30:1; 2 Samuel 8:12; 1 Chronicles 4:43).

Samuel and Saul's disobedience [15:10–21]

'**Then the word of the Lord came to Samuel**.' And with it came Saul's epitaph: '**I am grieved that I have made Saul king, because he has turned away from me and has not**

carried out my instructions' (15:10 – 11). This is one of a number of instances in Scripture of God being said to 'repent' (Hebrew: *niham*) of an earlier action. (The NIV rendering, '**am grieved**', falls short of the mark.) God does not repent in a human sense: '**He is not a man, that he should change his mind**' (15:29; see also Malachi 3:6; James 1:17). From our changeable perspective, however, God deals with us in ways that interact with the changing circumstances of our lives. He orders our lives and does his sovereign, unchangeable will through the oscillations of human instability.

Samuel's response was to be '**troubled**' and to pray fervently through that night (15:11). He knew then what he had seen coming for some time: namely, that Saul was finished. Saul had disobeyed the Lord again and this had called forth the judgement of the Lord. Samuel was grieved about Saul's sad state. He wrestled in prayer, seeking forgiveness for him. He felt desperately sad for the fallen monarch. But God did not answer the prophet's prayer in the affirmative.

1. Self-deception (15:12–15)

When Samuel went next day to meet Saul, he found that the king had been busy. He had been to '**Carmel**' (not Mount Carmel, but a village near Hebron) and had set up a monument commemorating his victory. When Moses defeated the Amalekites, he had built an altar for the worship of God (Exodus 17:15–16). Saul's monument betrays his spirit of self-aggrandizement. Then he had gone down to Gilgal – 'a place of destiny for Saul,' says R. P. Gordon, 'whether in connection with the inauguration of his kingship (cf. 11:14f.) or – twice (cf. 13:7–15) – with its prophesied termination'.[5] There, Saul's reign would turn full circle as Samuel confronted the unsuspecting monarch.

Saul greeted Samuel's arrival with almost boyish excitement. He believed that he had obeyed God to the letter. '**The Lord bless you!**' he said, '**I have carried out the Lord's instructions**' (15:13). When someone is intent on sinning, he can do one of two things: he can sin boldly or he can redefine evil as good. The latter is psychologically and socially far more acceptable, because sinners prefer a pos-

itive image and like to convince themselves that they are
doing the right thing. Saul had gone this route. He was
self-deceived. He had persuaded himself that he had really
done the Lord's will, this time!

But his sheep were bleating an entirely different story!
Like the family parrot that tells the mother-in-law what her
daughter's husband really thinks of her, Saul's four-legged
Amalekites tell the true story of his self-praised devotion to
the Lord! (15:14).

And when he was challenged, Saul's ready tongue provided the most pious of explanations. With just a hint that it
was the soldiers that were really responsible rather than
himself, he suggested that they '**spared the best of the sheep
and cattle to sacrifice to the Lord**' (15:15). And anyway, '**We
totally destroyed the rest**.' How ready we are to cover our
sins with a pious excuse! Harmful gossip is redefined as
'sharing'. Oppressing the children is 'biblical parental
discipline'. Stealing your employer's time to use it for church
work is the Lord enabling you to serve him. The potential for
pseudo-pious self-deception is limitless. And so subtle is it
and so open is a mind bent on mischief to the siren call of
spurious innocence, that in no time at all we are convinced
that we are pure in heart! And grossly offended to be told that
quite the opposite is the case! The fact is that very little
human sin is overtly, blatantly, deliberately and confessedly
evil. Most of it is dressed up as a kind of goodness. It is often
splendidly attired in the garments of contrived justification.
And at the very least, the sinner does not take kindly to being
called what he is. We defend the citadel of self-deceit to the
very last syllable of protested innocence – the pretence of a
good name and an untarnished reputation.

2. Self-justification (15:16–21)

The Lord did not, however, spare Saul the full glare of the
light. The defence of piety was swept aside and the charge of
sheer disobedience and a desire for plunder was pressed with
unchallengeable authority: '**Why did you not obey the
Lord? Why did you pounce on the plunder and do evil in
the eyes of the Lord?**' (15:19).

Saul's response was to maintain his innocence and, more
explicitly than before, to blame the army (15:20–21). Armies,

especially victorious ones, are notoriously hard to control. But the truth is that Saul was guilty as charged. Even his protestation is an apparently uncomprehending admission of that guilt. He states, as if it were a badge of his faithfulness, that he had '**brought back Agag**'. Saul was not going to admit fault. His mind was made up!

Saul's response to rejection as king [15:22–31]

In the face of such intransigence, it fell to Samuel to pronounce sentence. The time was past for counselling sessions and attempts at reconciliation. And the time for excuses and evasions was gone for ever!

1. Rejected as king (15:22–23)

The heart of the matter was obedience to the Lord. '**Does the Lord delight in burnt offerings and sacrifices as much as in obeying the voice of the Lord?**' It was not that the making of sacrifices according to God's Word was unimportant. The point was that the external form without the inward obedience was rendered little better than an offence to God (Psalm 50:7–15; 51:10–19; Isaiah 1:11–17). The Lord was not – is never – interested in show and pretence. A fresh coat of paint can make crumbling walls look pretty for a little while, but will never prevent them from collapsing!

Hence the trenchant definition of Saul's sin against God. His rebellion is like '**the sin of divination**' and his '**arrogance like the evil of idolatry**'. He might as well have been worshipping other gods. Saul's will was his real god. In practice he had dethroned the Lord in his heart.

For this reason, the Lord rejected Saul as king: '**Because you have rejected the word of the Lord, he has rejected you as king**' (15:23). The sentence was final, even if it did not issue in his immediately being deposed. He would only reign on God's sufferance. It would only be a matter of time until God's king would replace the people's king.

2. False repentance and face-saving (15:24–31)

Saul's response is as pathetic as it is self-serving. His 'repentance' was worse than his sin. God's sentence had an

impact on him and he felt sorry. He knew he was in the wrong,
but he could not quite understand why. This comes out in the
way he persisted in his attempt to shift the blame onto his
army: '**I was afraid of the people and so I gave in to them**'
(15:24).

This was the repentance of a man who was afraid of losing
everything and, not least, of losing his standing with the
people. The bogus character of his contrition is further
confirmed by his concern that the prophet help him save face
with the people (15:25). At first Samuel refused, but as he
turned to leave, '**Saul caught hold of the hem of his robe,
and it tore**' (15:26). This provided a parable of what had
happened and the most solemn confirmation of the irrevo-
cable nature of that particular judgement of God: '**The Glory
of Israel does not lie or change his mind; for he is not a
man, that he should change his mind**' (15:29). Saul was
nothing if he was not stubborn. Even after that stern
restatement of God's displeasure, he desperately pleaded
with Samuel to '**honour**' him '**before the elders. . .and
before Israel**' (15:30). Samuel, who was a man (15:29),
changed his mind and went with Saul to engage in public
worship with the army of Israel (15:31).

The parting of the ways [15:32–35]

Samuel's deeper motive in going with Saul became clear
when, after Saul had worshipped God – with what kind of
conscience we can only surmise – he called for the Amalekite
king to be brought to him. He would do what Saul had failed
to do. He would execute God's sentence of death upon that
wicked monarch. Whatever confidence Agag entertained that
'**the bitterness of death**' was past was dashed by the prophet,
first with words and then with the sword. The sentence of
death was a strict statement of the law of retribution – the one
who had made many mothers childless would himself become
the dead child of a mother bereft of her offspring. That his
mother was probably dead does not detract from the notional
retribution enshrined in the sentence. Taking a sword,
Samuel executed Agag before the altar and to the glory of
God, in fulfilment of the terms of the ban on Amalek (15:33).

Samuel and Saul then went their separate ways and, according to the Hebrew text, Samuel **'did not see'** Saul again. This cannot easily be squared with 1 Samuel 19:24, where it is recorded that Saul **'prophesied in Samuel's presence'**. The solution in our translation is to interpret the text with ingenuous elasticity and say that Samuel **'did not go to see Saul again'**. Whatever the textual problems, the point is that Samuel was finished with Saul. Saul had crossed the reprobate's Rubicon. There would be no more warnings and appeals, no more entreaties and rebukes – only a fearful slide into the inevitable consequences of his true spiritual state. There is a way that seems right to man, but the end of that way is death.

Samuel mourned for Saul. No true messenger of God loves to bring a message of judgement. God's prophets weep for the sad state of the most wicked in this wicked world. The Lord Jesus Christ wept for a Jerusalem which, rejecting him, would be rejected by his Father God (Matthew 23:37–38). The delight of the Saviour and the saved alike is that people may come to love the Lord and enter into life in obedience to him. There is no pleasure in heaven over the condemnation of sinners: 'As surely as I live, declares the Sovereign Lord, I take no pleasure in the death of the wicked, but rather that they turn from their ways and live. Turn! Turn from your evil ways! Why will you die, O house of Israel?' (Ezekiel 33:11).

Saul did not like having his heart and conscience searched by the laser beams of God's Word. Neither do we. The Lord Jesus Christ calls us, against all natural inclination, to give our lives to him. He brings the Word to bear upon the darkest recesses of our thought and practice and – painful as it always is – he commands our repentance and our trust in him. And in this every believer has found true freedom and true happiness.

> Search me, O God, and know my heart;
>   test me and know my anxious thoughts.
> See if there is any offensive way in me,
>   and lead me in the way everlasting'
>   (Psalm 139:23–4).

References

[1] R. P. Gordon, p. 142.

[2] R. L. Harris (editor), *Theological Wordbook of the Old Testament* (Chicago: Moody Press, 1980) Vol. 1, pp. 324–5 (Article 744).

[3] It was convenient, for example, for Peter the Great, the Tsar of Russia, on 25 February 1711, to declare war on the Ottoman Empire as a holy war 'against the enemies of Christ'. [R. K. Massie, *Peter the Great* (New York: Ballantine Books, 1980) p. 548]. The misnamed 'Crusades' are the prime examples of this perversion of Scripture to imperialist expansionism.

[4] R. P. Gordon, pp. 147–8, perhaps represents the discomfort of many modern Christians with the idea of the ban, when he can only apply it to us today in an 'individualizing and interiorizing' of the concept. In his view the Amalekites for us today represent the spiritual warfare that each believer is involved in as per Ephesians 6:12. There is, in other words, a shrinking from the idea that God will destroy the nations that oppose him. The Christian faith, in keeping with the world-flight tendencies of modern Christians, is individualized and spiritualized. As suggested in this study, the fundamental line of application for all ages is that the wages of sin is death – both physical and eternal. The ban leaves us with a message of divine wrath, to be fled in terms of the gospel of saving grace in Christ. This is true for individuals and nations. To shrink from the ban (and, as C. S. Lewis has done, from the imprecatory psalms) as if it were unworthy of the God of the rest of the Bible, is to miss the point that God is perfectly just in all his ways. And, while he keeps mercy for thousands, he will by no means clear the guilty (Exodus 34:7).

[5] R. P. Gordon, p. 144.

PART III: David - The Lord's king

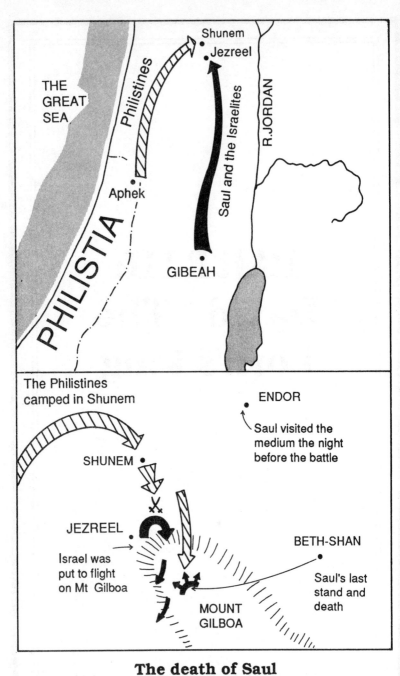

**The death of Saul
(1 Samuel 31)**

14.
The Lord's anointed

Please read 1 Samuel 16:1–13

'The Lord said to Samuel, "How long will you mourn for Saul, since I have rejected him as king over Israel? Fill your horn with oil and be on your way; I am sending you to Jesse of Bethlehem. I have chosen one of his sons to be king"' (1 Samuel 16:1).

The rejection of Saul paved the way for the rise of David and the flowering of the Israelite monarchy under that man after God's own heart (13:14). But there was no instantaneous transfer of the reins of power. It was not a case of, 'The king is dead. Long live the king!' The rejection of Saul did not herald his death or even his abdication. It only introduces us to the young man who would, after many trials, ascend Saul's throne and establish the dynasty that would bear his name for the centuries that followed. Saul's reign did not end when God rejected him. He continued to rule Israel for many years. And he was the means, in God's purposes, of crystallizing the transition of Israel from a loosely organized confederation of tribal families to a more tightly structured nation state. It is too easy to look at the life of Saul and lose sight of his practical qualities as a king and his positive contribution to the development of his nation. His personal failings tend to obscure his genuine achievements.

More pointedly, we can miss something of his role in the unfolding of God's plan of redemption, both for Israel and for the whole world. This is not too much to say, for, as Graeme Goldsworthy has observed, 'It is characteristic of the Old Testament persons and events that despite their

imperfections, they foreshadow the perfect which is to come
(1 Cor. 13:10). In fact it must be this, for if the fore-
shadowings were perfect they would no longer be mere
shadows and would become the solid reality. Saul, along
with the judges before him, is part of the historical foundation laid in the Old Testament for the revelation of the
perfect human king, Jesus of Nazareth, who mediates God's
rule.'[1] However aggravated the problems of Saul's reign
were, however wretched his spiritual state and his relationship with the Lord, it must be said that he was, in the
providence of God, the means of preparing Israel for a whole
new epoch in her experience of God's covenant favour. Saul
was a tragic figure. That is true. But that tragedy was
integral to the experience of Israel and both were to form
the arena in which God advanced the work of his kingdom
to the blessing of his people.

The anointing of David, son of Jesse, to be king of Israel,
heralded a decisive step forwards in God's plan for his
people. 'David's kingdom and reign in Israel,' wrote Patrick
Fairbairn, 'were from the first intended to foreshadow those
of Christ.'[2] What was in process of organization in Israel,
says Geerhardus Vos, was a 'theocratic kingdom under a
human ruler. In the days of Samuel, this movement began;
it found provisional embodiment in the rule of Saul, but was
not consolidated on a firm basis until the accession of
David. Henceforth the idea of this kingdom remains central
in the hopes of Israel. This human kingdom, however, is
only a representation of the kingdom of Jehovah Himself.'[3]
The Davidic kingdom was a flawed kingdom with a flawed
king and some successors that rivalled the Borgias for sheer
venality. David and his kingdom point to something better
that was yet to be revealed in Jesus Christ and it is often in
the contrast between the two that we see the connection and
the fulfilment.[4] We shall see more of this in future chapters
as we study the development of David's career.

Preparation [16:1–5]

We are always the children of our own time. Our personal
history integrates with the history of the period in which we

live. Even though we may not seem to affect the big picture very much, we know that it certainly influences our lives every day. And we believe, as Christians, that God is sovereign over both the larger movements of history and the smaller – but to us very large – events of our individual life-experience.

The same was true for David in relation to his preparation for the kingship in Israel. The providence of God in the broader canvas of the nation's life synchronized with the shepherd-boy's personal development, which was also under the providential care of God.

1. The nation's preparation can be summed up in the words of Hosea 13:11: 'So in my anger I gave you a king, and in my wrath I took him away.' The people's thirst for a king had been whetted by dissatisfaction with the theocratic republicanism of the period of the judges (8:20). Saul had been chosen – a man who was every inch a king. But he had rejected his appointed role as a theocratic monarch – God's deputy and vicegerent – and God had rejected him from being king (15:35).

On the face of it, this was not a promising situation. As Samuel grieved for Saul he no doubt also grieved for a nation plunged into the lamentable position of having a king who, in God's eyes, was no better than a usurper and a despot. But, as A.W. Pink commented, 'Man's extremity is always God's opportunity.'[5] So the Lord rebukes the prophet for his moping over the state of things and tells him to go to Jesse of Bethlehem, for he had '**chosen one of his sons to be king**' (16:1).

Three startling features of this turn of events suggest themselves as standing principles of the way in which God deals with men and nations in the course of his providence (i.e. history).

The first is that in the darkest moments of his people's experience, the Lord is preparing the brightest outpourings of his power and glory. This is the story of the Exodus, of the judges and of the advent of Samuel himself. It is also true of individual Christian experience (Psalm 107:6; Acts 16:29–34). It is a fact of Christian life that the Lord can bring us down very low, but it is to the end that we might be built up to be mature people in Christ (Psalm 119:67; 2 Corinthians 4:17).

A second principle is that God is slow to anger in the face of human provocation. He is longsuffering (Psalm 103:8). This may be for the purpose of bringing sinners to repentance; it is always for the manifestation of his glory (Romans 2:4; 9:22). We see this patient development in the transition between Saul and David. Saul's removal could wait. The Lord had plans for David. There would be a testing and refining process that would take years. And in that time it would be demonstrated that he, not Saul, was God's man for the throne of Israel.

A third principle evidenced in these events is that God chooses the weak, in the world's eyes, to confound the mighty (1 Corinthians 1:27–29). It is to Bethlehem that Samuel was sent to look for the man who would be king. This is the same Bethlehem Ephrathah of which the Scripture says, 'Though you are small among the clans of Judah, out of you will come for me one who will be ruler over Israel' (Micah 5:2; Matthew 2:6).

2. The providence of God is only the application of his absolute sovereignty to daily life. As he had prepared Israel for David, he had nurtured David for Israel. David and his family had no inkling of what was going to happen. When Samuel arrived at Bethlehem, the elders' reaction was one of considerable apprehension. They were completely unaware of any special providence involving David or, indeed, anyone else in Bethlehem. When they saw Samuel they apparently thought that something must be wrong. Are prophets always assumed to be prophets of doom, unless proven otherwise? At any rate, they felt constrained to ask him if he came '**in peace**' (16:4). As it turned out, he had come in peace, and he immediately arranged for a meeting at which the attendance of the elders and Jesse's family was required (16:5).

Behind this event, however, was a process of divine providential preparation of the lad who was to become the Lord's anointed later that day. Just as God had superintended the 'big picture' of national events, so he had prepared the personal experience of David for this moment.

And, as before, we see the evidences of the application of further basic principles of divine action in the course of human lives.

The fourth principle (in addition to the three above) is the simple truth that the whole course of our life is ordered according to the sovereign purpose of God. And that order is expressed in terms of covenant. God's dealings with men and women are covenantal. The Bible is the book of the covenant. We are either covenant-breakers (in Adam) or covenant-keepers (in the Lord Jesus Christ). We either belong to the covenant community or we are outside of it, in rebellion against the (covenant) claims of God.

David was a member of the covenant community of the Old Testament, Israel. He was a child of the family of God. And he was nurtured in a godly home and in a village where, from all appearances, the things of God were taken seriously. 1 Samuel 16:4–5 indicate the general spiritual concern in Bethlehem. And Jesse's family appears to have been sincerely devoted to the service of the Lord (20:29). Not least, David himself was taught from an early age about the covenant promises of God. Many years later, when he had vowed to build a permanent house for the ark of the covenant, he recalled that he had learned about the ark in his youth. 'We heard it in Ephrathah,' he said. Only later did he actually see it: 'We came upon it in the fields of Jaar [i.e., Kiriath Jearim]' (Psalm 132:6). Here was someone who was born into a covenant environment – both nation and family – and was, like Timothy in a later era, taught the Word of the Lord from infancy (2 Timothy 3:14–17). God had prepared him all through his life. And, before that, God had predestined each and every detail of that which came to pass in the fulness of the time (Ephesians 1:11).

A fifth principle is in evidence in the process by which David was selected. It is that whereas '**man looks at the outward appearance. . . the Lord looks at the heart**' (16:7). However great our wisdom, however fine our ability to judge character, we are always, at best, looking on the outside. We read the outward evidence of people's lives and reason our way into their motives. But the truth is that we cannot read the heart! God alone is the searcher of our inner being (1 Chronicles 28:9; Hebrews 4:12). We are limited to extrapolating from what we can see into what we can never see. Only God sees it all! Samuel, discerning a man as he was, could not tell whom God would choose to be king. And God humbled him by telling him the truth about the limitations of human finite discernment and by going on to choose Jesse's youngest son.

Anointing [16:6–13]

The contrast between the way in which Saul was chosen and the search leading to David's anointing is strikingly significant. Before there had been a public clamour for a king; here it was the special revelation of God that initiated the process. Before the man was chosen from the tribe of Benjamin; here the choice reverts to Judah, in accord with the promise of Genesis 49:10. It was God's choice 'from start to finish'.[6]

After the sacrifices had been made, and the general purpose of the visit explained to Jesse (presumably in connection with the '**consecration**' of Jesse and his sons (16:5)), the sons of Jesse were brought to Samuel. Eliab was the first. Like Saul, he was physically impressive and Samuel was disposed to believe that he would be the Lord's choice (16:6). This occasioned the revelation from the Lord that he was not the man – a re-emphasis, if you like, of the Lord's rejection of the criteria that had decided the appointment of Saul (16:7).

In quick succession the other sons of Jesse passed before Samuel. But it was not to be Abinadab. Neither was it to be Shammah. None of the seven sons of Jesse who were present that day was to be chosen (16:8–10). Inevitably, this puzzled Samuel. On enquiring of Jesse, he learned that there was another son '**tending the sheep**' (16:11). David, who was '**ruddy, with a fine appearance and handsome features**,' was brought from the pasture and the Lord told Samuel to '**Rise and anoint him**,' for he was the one (16:12). The prophet thereupon anointed him '**in the presence of his brothers**' and '**from that day on the Spirit of the Lord came upon David with power**' (16:13).

Two questions immediately come to mind in connection with this remarkable incident.

The first concerns the apparent secrecy of Samuel with respect to his true reason for being in Bethlehem and his examination of the sons of Jesse. The narrative breathes mystery on this point. Samuel's appearance was greeted with a sense of foreboding on the part of the elders of Bethlehem and the prophet told them no more than was necessary to allay their fears and provide an adequate explanation for his coming (16:5). But why the 'cover story'? The most satisfying answer would seem to be that the time was not yet ripe for God's choice of a new king to be revealed to the world. Hence the anointing was kept, as R. P. Gordon puts it, 'quasi-private'[7] and passed off as having some lesser unstated significance than the divine choice of a king. There can be no doubt that Jesse and his sons understood this process – and, specifically, the choice of David – as an act of consecration to the Lord.[8] It seems equally clear that the precise import of this consecration remained hidden to them. There is, perhaps, an analogy with the way in which Jesus progressively revealed himself to his disciples and to the Jews. He was for a time deliberately cautious in declaring his purposes and in exposing himself to the attention of his enemies. In this way, he avoided precipitating the crisis, which, when his time was 'at hand' (Matthew 26:18), would issue in his arrest, trial and death by crucifixion. Our Lord took his time to reveal himself in fulness. In a similar fashion, God did not fully reveal his purposes for David until the fulness of his time.

The other question that immediately arises is: what was the precise import of the anointing of David? What did it mean – for himself, for his family and for his future kingdom? The anointing itself was, as we have already indicated, shrouded in some mystery. We are not told how much Jesse and his family knew about what had transpired. We learn later that Eliab, the oldest brother, resented David and regarded him as conceited (17:28). At the very least, everyone would have understood the anointing to have been a mark of some distinction, however undefined at the time. Eliab probably resented being passed over in favour of his little brother. But it is doubtful that anyone anticipated that David would be the next king in Israel.

For the family, the immediate implication would simply have been one of blessing, in that a son of the household had been anointed with oil by the prophet, whatever they were given to understand it to mean. Some commentators believe that Jesse, though not his sons – excepting David – was told by Samuel that God had chosen David for the kingship. There is, however, no evidence to indicate that this was so and it is as well that we resist the temptation to speculate.[9]

For David, it meant that '**The Spirit of the Lord came upon**' him (16:13). Oil was the symbol of the Holy Spirit and anointing with oil symbolic of the endowment of the Spirit. In this way, Saul had been set apart to the service of God. The judges, though not anointed, were endowed with the Spirit of God (Judges 3:10; 6:34; 11:29; 13:25). The same can be said of *all* New Testament believers: every Christian is baptized by the Holy Spirit (i.e., receives and is indwelt by the Holy Spirit) upon coming to Christ in faith.[10] The point is that the outpouring of the Holy Spirit is a sign and a seal – and enabling power – for service to the Lord in terms of his everlasting covenant. There is no reason to believe that David was any less well-informed about the meaning of his anointing than was Saul at the same stage in the process which brought him to the throne. The internal witness of the Holy Spirit would have confirmed all that the words of the prophet and the theology of anointing with oil indicated as to his future role.

The kingship of Jesus Christ

God's ultimate purpose was to pave the way for the coming of the true and final King, the Lord Jesus Christ. David was to be the first king under the new order; Jesus was to be the last and once-for-all king of the house of David. In Christ, all the promises of the older covenant would be fully published and completely fulfilled as the new covenant in his blood, shed for sinners. David was to point God's covenant people more clearly than ever before to the coming of the Messiah, who would rule until his enemies became the very footstool of God (Psalm 110:1; Hebrews 1:13).

The practical thrust of all Scripture is to our faith; it is to show us where we stand with God and to direct us to the path of life in our risen Saviour. How do you know that you belong to the Lord? How can you know that the Lord is with you, as he was with David in his life? 'The best evidence of our being predestinated to the kingdom of glory,' wrote Matthew Henry, 'is our being sealed with the Spirit of promise, and our experience of a work of grace in our hearts.' And as David was tested over many years before the promise of his anointing was fulfilled in his accession to the throne, so the tests of faith are common to the experience of all believers and call forth the same trust that the sweet singer of Israel expressed so beautifully in many of his psalms (e.g., Psalm 62).

In charging his readers to be faithful to the Lord, the writer to the Hebrews said, 'We do not want you to become lazy, but to imitate those who through faith and patience inherit what has been promised' (Hebrews 6:12). Psalm 63 was written, we are told, in the wilderness of Judea, possibly when David was fleeing from the wrath of Saul. Here is the cry of a believing heart:

> 'O God, you are my God,
>   earnestly I seek you;
> my soul thirsts for you,
>   my body longs for you,
> in a dry and weary land
>   where there is no water.
> I have seen you in the sanctuary
>   and beheld your power and your glory.
> Because your love is better than life,
>   my lips will glorify you.
> I will praise you as long as I live,
>   and in your name I will lift up my hands.
> My soul will be satisfied as with the richest of foods;
>   with singing lips my mouth will praise you'
>
> (Psalm 63:1–4).

References

[1] G. Goldsworthy, *Gospel & Kingdom* (Exeter: Paternoster Press, 1981), p. 72.

[2] P. Fairbairn, *The Typology of Scripture* (Grand Rapids: Baker, [1900] 1975) Vol. I, p. 114.

[3] G. Vos, p. 203.

[4] R. P. Gordon, pp. 49f. Gordon's thesis is that in Christ 'The Davidic king has triumphed, but not in the Davidic way.'

[5] A. W. Pink, *The Life of David* (Swengel, PA: Reiner, 1974), p. 7.

[6] D. F. Payne, p. 82.

[7] R. P. Gordon, p. 151.

[8] See the article 'Anoint, Anointing', by Patrick Fairbairn in *The Imperial Standard Bible Encyclopedia* (Grand Rapids: Zondervan, 1957[1891]), Vol. 1, pp. 163–166.

[9] C. F. Keil and F. Delitzsch, p. 170.

[10] D. F. Payne, p. 83.

♥

15.
David and Goliath

Please read 1 Samuel 16:14–17:58

'David said to the Philistine, "You come against me with sword and spear and javelin, but I come against you in the name of the Lord Almighty, the God of the armies of Israel, whom you have defied"' (1 Samuel 17:45).

The whole point of any inauguration to some new sphere of employment is to mark the beginning in a special way. Most people, of course, just go to their work on the first day of their new job. For kings there is a coronation, for presidents an inauguration, for college professors an installation and for ministers of the gospel a service of ordination. These are designed to be a solemn, but happy, recognition of the privileges, the promises and the responsibilities of the work to which the individual has been called. They set a seal upon that person that is, for all the parties involved, a public witness of commitment to the work in view. This is, however, just the beginning. From this point, the real work must begin.

When David was anointed to be king over Israel, he was not even publicly or officially inaugurated in that office. Saul was still the king and would remain on the throne for a decade or more. David's anointing had been a semi-secret event and he had, no doubt, gone back to the sheep after the ceremonies were completed. He might well have wondered how real his anointing was. How would he ever begin to exercise this calling? By what conceivable route could he expect to ascend the throne? He may have been anointed by the Lord's prophet, but he was unheralded and untested. And there was already a king who showed no signs of poor health or a desire to abdicate in favour of a teen-age shepherd!

It is, as we saw, only through faith and patience that God's children inherit his promises (Hebrews 6:12). Such faith and patience are active graces of the Holy Spirit, not some stoical resignation that 'What will be, will be!' True faith prays and works towards the promises of God. Patience redeems the time spent waiting instead of wasting it in fears and frustrations. Faith and patience look for the Lord to open doors and bring about what to our eyes seems unlikely, if not impossible.

The Lord did not leave David with the sheep very long. Through a series of significant providences, David was to be called, first, to Saul's court (16:14–23) and, subsequently, to the battlefield in the valley of Elah, where he would face and vanquish the champion of the Philistine cause, the giant Goliath of Gath (17:1–58). In this way, David would burst upon the scene and, literally overnight, be transformed from relative obscurity to national hero.

The Spirit of the Lord had departed from Saul [16:14–23]

The great turning-point for both David and Saul was the anointing of David. Two verses capture this decisive moment: **'So Samuel took the horn of oil and anointed him in the presence of his brothers, and from that day on the Spirit of the Lord came upon David in power. Samuel then went to Ramah. Now the Spirit of the Lord had departed from Saul, and an evil spirit from the Lord tormented him'** (16:13–14). Both men underwent a signal spiritual change. Both men felt that change and knew it to be the Lord's doing. Both men also knew that at the heart of this change was not only their personal relationship with the Lord but their role in the national life of God's people.

1. 'Now the Spirit of the Lord had departed from Saul' (16:14)
Although the Holy Spirit had given Saul a 'spirit of prophecy' to fit him for his office as king (10:10), it is clear that his

heart was not renewed in the sense that he was born again and had come to love the Lord. Saul subsequently rejected God and persistently disregarded his revealed will. Consequently, God rejected Saul. When David was chosen, God withdrew even those gifts that he had given to Saul.

An important truth is taught here – one which is developed in the New Testament. It is that there are those who have 'shared in the Holy Spirit' and yet were never converted to the Lord and remain spiritually dead (Hebrews 6:4–6). They profess faith; they regard themselves as believers; they know a lot about the teaching of Scripture; but they are still dead in their sins. They have a lie in their right hand and will not see it (Isaiah 44:20).

Here is the difference between Saul and David. Saul 'shared' in the Holy Spirit but fell away from the Lord. In David's case, however, the Holy Spirit lived in him as a sanctifier – he was changed by the power of God. No doubt he was a believer before he was anointed and the Spirit came upon him with power. The point is that David truly loved the Lord and, for all his later sins and struggles, he persevered in the faith.

There is a question here for every Christian. Ask yourself, 'How can I, as I search my heart, tell whether I am like Saul or like David? How can I know that I am a true believer and not just a self-deceived, unconverted pseudo-believer?' The answer is that those who love the Lord keep his commandments (John 14:15). This is the first and most basic test. It was the test that Saul failed again and again. And it is in this connection – the willingness to follow the Lord's will and the enjoyment of practical godliness – that the sanctification of the Holy Spirit is experienced (1 Peter 1:2). There is a desire for ethical cleanliness. There is a hunger and thirst for righteousness (Matthew 5:6). There is a willingness to put off the old self with its practices and put on the new self, which is being renewed in knowledge in the image of its Creator (Colossians 3:9–10). There is an active clothing of oneself with the Lord Jesus Christ (Romans 13:14). You rejoice in victories over sin. You seek God's will with true sincerity of purpose. You love the law of the Lord. You delight in the Lord himself. And even though you fall into sin, you are sensitive to your failures. And the fact of that sensitivity and the fact of desire for the glory of God are evidence that the Holy Spirit is with you. Both Saul and David fell into sin. Both were sorry, but only David truly repented of sin and turned from it to serve the Lord afresh.

2. 'And an evil spirit from the Lord tormented him' (16:14)
This does not mean that God is the source of evil spirits. It simply emphasizes that when the Holy Spirit withdraws from someone, that person is easy prey for Satan and, indeed, for his own self-destructive sinfulness. In this case Saul was given over to the consequences of his sin and he fell into a severe depression of some kind. Satan had a free hand with Saul's heart. He became deeply troubled and his whole life plunged into misery.

His servants could see what was happening and they recommended a remedy. What did they advise? Did they suggest that Saul make his peace with God? Did they ask him to turn to the Lord in repentance and faith? Did they recommend that he seek the counsel of Samuel, the prophet of the Lord? No! Having diagnosed the need for heart surgery, they proceeded to prescribe a sedative! Find '**someone who can play the harp**'. Then his music would make the king feel better (16:16). And this was what happened, for later when the music was played, '**relief would come to Saul; he would feel better, and the evil spirit would leave him**' (16:23).

The power of music to 'soothe the savage breast' is well enough known. (It is also known to do the very opposite!) What is significant here is that Saul's depression became the means of bringing David to the royal court and to the service of Saul (16:18–22). It thrust David onto the national stage, albeit in a very modest way. It brought him face to face with Saul. The Holy Spirit left Saul and his house, but returned within the heart of David.

David, whose qualities were enumerated before Saul with all the fulsome praise so characteristic of the language of oriental courts, became not only Saul's musician but one of his armour-bearers. The Lord had taken David from the fields and placed him beside the throne!

The Spirit of the Lord came upon David [17:1–51]

The story of David's fight with Goliath is one of the best known and best loved of all literature. It has, needless to say, been romanticized to such an extent that the residual image in many minds is no more than that of a small, but clever and agile, boy triumphing over a very ungenial giant. The 'boy' was in fact a strapping young man probably in his late teens. But far more significant is the fact that he was endowed with the Spirit of God in power. The contrast is, of course, with Saul, from whom the Spirit of God had withdrawn. David rose from minor court functionary to national hero and potential king in the course of a few minutes in the Valley of Elah! This was not lost on Saul (18:8–15). Nor did it escape the attention of the people of Israel.

1. Goliath's challenge to Israel (17:1–11)
The Philistine army moved eastwards from their stronghold of Gath and crossed the Israelite frontier near Socoh in the Valley of Elah. There they were confronted by the assembled might of Israel. Battle-lines were drawn and the armies watched each other warily from their positions across the valley (17:1–3).

Then from the ranks of the Philistines a champion stepped forward and challenged the Israelites to send their champion and settle the matter in single representative combat. It was to be a case of 'winner take all' – and at stake was the very sovereignty of Israel! Although there was no precedent for such a procedure in the experience of God's people and therefore no absolute necessity for following such a course, there is no doubt that it was a humiliating moment for Israel. The reason was that Goliath simply struck terror into the hearts of the Israelites, from Saul right down to the lowest spearman! Goliath was **'over nine feet tall'** (3 metres) and he wore armour weighing about 125 pounds (57 kilos)! His spear was **'like a weaver's rod'** with a bronze point weighing some fifteen pounds (7 kilos) (17:4–7).[1]

No one would respond to the challenge of this man-mountain. Saul, who was a big man, was not willing.

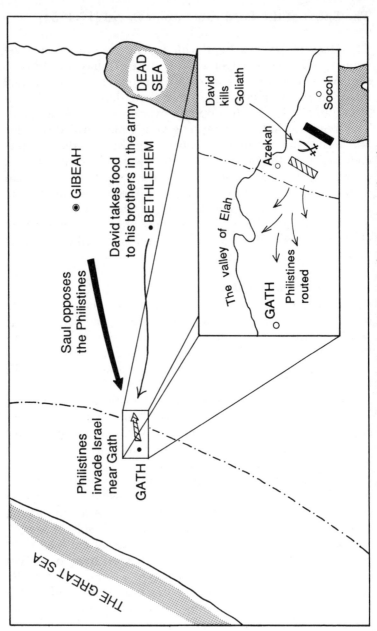

Map 7 - David and Goliath (1 Samuel 17)

Jonathan, who had bravely won the day at Michmash against overwhelming odds, did not step forward. Everyone was afraid. And a stalemate ensued (17:8–11).

2. David's acceptance of the challenge (17:12–40)
Every day for forty days, Goliath 'threw down the gauntlet' before Israel (17:16).

In the meantime, David had been commuting between Saul's court and his father's sheep at Bethlehem (17:15). It would appear that he was too young for military service, and that his status as an 'armour-bearer' to Saul was an honorary position (16:21).[2] This enabled Jesse to use David as a courier to take food to the three sons who were serving in the army (17:12–19). As David arrived, Goliath '**stepped out from his lines and shouted his usual defiance**'. As a result, '**David heard it**' (17:20–23). He also witnessed the terror of the Israelites and learned that Saul had promised wealth, his daughter in marriage and a tax-free future to the man who could kill Goliath (17:24–27).

David's interest in the problem of Goliath must have suggested strongly that the lad had some hopes of having a go at the giant. First, he was rebuked and ridiculed by his eldest brother. Then he was reported to Saul and summoned to appear before the king (17:28–31). The upshot of this was that David volunteered to take up Goliath's challenge: '**Let no one lose heart on account of this Philistine; your servant will go and fight him**' (17:32).

David had an old head on his young shoulders; this was a fruit of the indwelling of the Holy Spirit in his heart. He correctly diagnosed that Goliath was essentially a theological problem. When he said to the soldiers, '**Who is this uncircumcised Philistine that he should defy the armies of the living God?**', he was not indulging in youthful idealism, but expressing sober theological truth (17:26). He was speaking for God. The fact that Goliath was a walking fortress was beside the point. David realized that as the people of the God of the covenant, Israel had no right to cower before the enemies of the Lord. Rather, they should have claimed the promise of the presence and power of the Lord and taken the field in holy boldness in dependence upon the Lord. Israel's problem was faith – or rather the lack of it. Goliath was the symptom rather than the disease itself. The progression in David's thought was from the premise that Goliath and the Philistines were defying God when they defied Israel,[3] to the conclusion that no one ought to lose heart on account of the Philistine and finally to the conviction that he ought to be the one to fight Goliath. This suggests to us a very important fact of life that is so easily ignored: many of the most practical questions in life are essentially theological. For the Christian, sound theology is his practical day-to-day philosophy. Theological truth is father to God-honouring practicality. This is faith at work.

David was spiritually fortified by his experience of God's goodness in the past. When Saul quite reasonably pointed out that David was a boy set on doing a man's work, David told him how he had killed a lion and a bear while shepherding his father's flock: '**The Lord who delivered me from the paw of the lion and the paw of the bear will deliver me from the hand of this Philistine**' (17:33–37). He was confident in the Lord. His faith had been strengthened by his practical experience of God's goodness. First, the faith: 'I had fainted,' says the psalmist, 'unless I had believed to see the goodness of the Lord in the land of the living' (Psalm 27:13 AV). Then the strengthening experience of God's goodness: 'I love the Lord, for he heard my voice; he heard my cry for mercy' (Psalm 116:1). See also Psalms 71 and 73. And when David went out to fight Goliath, he went out as the shepherd whom the Lord had delivered from the lion and the bear. He refused Saul's armour and was content to use the weapons and the skills with which he was comfortable – his staff, his sling and five smooth stones from the stream (17:38–40). Israel was God's flock, Goliath no more than a predator and David stepped forward as the shepherd who would protect his sheep.[4] This is the symbolism of redemption itself. The psalmist sings: 'Hear us, O Shepherd of Israel, you who lead Joseph like a flock. . .' (Psalm 80:1). The God of the Covenant, Yahweh, 'is my shepherd, I shall not be in want' (Psalm 23:1). And the Lord Jesus Christ identified himself as 'the good shepherd' who 'lays down his life for the sheep' (John 10:11). Like Israel in the Valley of Elah, 'We all [i.e., lost humanity], like sheep, have gone astray, each of us has turned to his own way' (Isaiah 53:6). Like David the shepherd, Jesus the Good Shepherd came forward ready to give his life for the sheep. But David was merely a shadow of Christ. Christ took no weapons; Christ went not to fight, but to die, for as Isaiah prophesied,

'The Lord has laid on him
    the iniquity of us all.
He was oppressed and afflicted,
    yet he did not open his mouth. . .
For he bore the sin of many,
    and made intercession for the transgressors'
(Isaiah 53:6, 12).

3. David's victory over Goliath (17:41–51)
Seeing an Israelite champion crossing the brook, the Philistine paladin moved forward to close with him. Observing his opponent to be no more than a young lad armed with a staff – he could see neither sling nor stones – Goliath unleashed a torrent of contempt. **'Am I a dog,'** he sneered, **'that you come at me with sticks?'** (17:43). Then, cursing David **'by his gods'**, the giant declared that he would reduce him to carrion for the birds and the beasts (17:44).

David's response was both testimony and prophecy. The Philistine came with **'sword and spear and javelin'**. He had already invoked his false gods. But David came **'in the name of the Lord Almighty'** – Jehovah Sabaoth, the Lord of Hosts. Therefore Goliath would perish and the Philistine army would be scattered as carrion upon the land. The whole world would know that there was a God in Israel (17:45–47).

The fight itself lasted for no more than a moment. With one slingshot, Goliath was felled. David killed and decapitated the giant with his own sword (17:48–51). Goliath had gone the way of his god, Dagon, when he fell before the ark of the covenant – even to the loss of his head (5:4)![5] The Philistines' hero was as dead as their so-called god! And they knew there was a God in Israel!

The triumph of Israel [17:52–58]

Israel's victory was to be complete. They pursued the
fleeing Philistines to the gates of Gath and Ekron. The 'offal
of war' littered the highway as David's dire prediction was
fulfilled and the '**carcasses of the Philistine army**' were
given '**to the birds of the air and the beasts of the earth**'
(17:46, 52). Never had there been such a decisive victory for
the armies of Israel.

It was God's victory. All the circumstances make that
abundantly clear. One smooth stone in the hand of a
shepherd put all the conventional might of Saul's army in its
proper perspective. 'No king is saved by the size of his army;
no warrior escapes by his great strength' (Psalm 33:16). It is
surely significant that God had allowed Goliath to keep
Israel in fear and faithlessness for '**forty days**' (17:16),
before sending deliverance through the true anointed king!
Was Israel to remind herself of the forty years in the
wilderness of Sinai? Was she to remember that it was her sin
that kept her from the land of promise? Was she to be
persuaded afresh that there was still a God in Israel?

The instrument of victory was God's man. The contrast with
Saul's performance was not missed by the people of Israel.
Jonathan had delivered Israel at Michmash and Saul had then
marred the victory with a foolish order of the day (14:13–46).
David had now reversed Israel's fortunes completely and Saul
seemed only a spectator. David became the nation's hero. And
it was known that the Lord was with him. God had raised him
up to deliver his people and they knew it. From that moment,
Saul would decrease and David would increase. In the final
verses of the account of the victory, there is a record of Saul's
enquiring of Abner about David's background just as David
went out to meet Goliath. This is followed by the meeting of
David and Saul after the battle, where Saul asks David whose
son he is (17:55–58). Saul needed to know more about David,
most obviously, perhaps, because of the promises made to the
conqueror of Goliath (17:25).

It is, however, a turning-point for both men. Here is Saul,
the present king and there is David, the future king. And in
David's hand was the gory attestation that he was, indeed,
the Lord's anointed.

References

1 R. P. Gordon, pp. 155, notes that representative combat is rare in the Old Testament and that it 'is fitting. . . that a non-Israelite should be the instigator'.

[2] According to Keil & Delitzsch (footnote, p. 177), 'The appointment of armour-bearer was nothing more than conferring upon him the title of aide-de-camp.' David was probably not as well known to Saul as many assume from the account in 16:14–23. This would explain why he appears relatively unknown in 17:15, 31–40, 55–58.

[3] D. F. Payne, p. 90.

[4] D. F. Payne, p. 90.

[5] R. P. Gordon, p. 158.

16.
The price of popularity

Please read 1 Samuel 18:1–30

'Saul was very angry; this refrain galled him. "They have credited David with tens of thousands," he thought, "but me with only thousands. What more can he get but the kingdom?" And from that time on Saul kept a jealous eye on David' (1 Samuel 18:8–9).

One of the greatest ironies of human nature is surely that our strengths can often also be our weaknesses and our most notable successes can be our greatest snares. We so easily forget that we have nothing that we did not receive (1 Corinthians 4:7). Pride persuades us that we should get the glory. And the fact that 'Every good and perfect gift is from above, and coming down from the Father of the heavenly lights, who does not change like shifting shadows' (James 1:16) is quietly excised from our consciousness in favour of a spirit of self-congratulation. The excellent Thomas Brooks noted that there are always those 'that would hammer out their own happiness, like the spider climbing up by the thread of her own weaving'. But, he says, 'Of all the parts and abilities that be in you, you may well say as the young man did of his hatchet, "Alas master! it was but borrowed" (2 Kings 6:5). Alas, Lord! all I have is but borrowed from that fountain that fills all the vessels in heaven and on earth, and it overflows. My gifts are not so much mine as thine: "Of thine own have we offered unto thee," said that princely prophet (1 Chronicles 29:14).'[1]

If personal accomplishments only provided a temptation for the individual, the problem would at least be localized and containable. But pride is like a virus. When it invades success, it devours it to produce more of the virus and this serves to spread the disease and, inevitably, complicate the matter. There are at least three interactive aspects to the question. The first, as we have noted, is the temptation for the individual achiever to take the glory to himself. A second aspect is the public side of the same coin – the popularity snare or the personality cult. The mass of non-achievers vicariously enjoy the accomplishments of their hero, thereby indulging the same kind of pride that gives the glory to men rather than to God. Hero-worship is the way pride outflanks a lack of personal achievement and allows losers to glory in themselves! The third aspect is the response of jealousy in those who feel their own position or potential to be threatened by the success of others. One consequence of popularity is... unpopularity with some. And that has its own dangers.

We see something of this with David's rise to fame and fortune. After the victory at the battle of Elah and his spectacular victory over Goliath, David became the darling of Israelite public opinion. He was lionized as the deliverer of the nation! He rose to nationwide popularity – and justifiably so, since he had indeed been the instrument of national redemption! But here was the snare: popularity always has a price. Acclaim is the public aspect of individual achievement. In its train, it brings new challenges and unanticipated costs. David was soon to discover this and it was to dog his footsteps for the rest of his days. As we shall see, he responded to the challenges of his new-found fame with genuine piety and self-effacing humility. 'With all this concentration on David, however, the seeds of insecurity and jealousy are sown in Saul's heart, and they produce a tragic harvest.'[2]

Popularity [18:1–5]

After his summary despatch of Goliath, it was as inevitable as it was appropriate that David should be accorded the praise of a grateful nation. The text records three elements in David's rise from shepherd to celebrity.

1. The friendship of Jonathan (18:1–4)
The friendship of David and Jonathan was brotherhood by
adoption. They were likeable men who really liked each
other. At that battlefield audience, when David, still holding
Goliath's severed head, was brought before Saul, Jonathan
took an instant liking to him. He '**became one in spirit with
David, and he loved him as himself**'. After Jonathan was
killed at the Battle of Mount Gilboa, David would declare,

> 'I grieve for you, Jonathan my brother;
>   you were very dear to me.
> Your love for me was wonderful,
>   more wonderful than that of women'
>
> (2 Samuel 1:26).[3]

This friendship, sealed by a solemn covenant (18:3; cf.
20:41–42), is proverbial of the richness and closeness that
human friendship can attain. It is all the more remarkable,
however, for two reasons. One is the implication that
Jonathan was, in a sense, recognizing David as the next king
in Israel. Jonathan was the godly son of a wicked father and
there is some indication that he could see that the writing
was on the wall for Saul and his house. Did Jonathan discern
in David the Lord's choice for Israel's king? The gift of his
robe, tunic, sword, bow and belt may be an indication of
that awareness.[4] The other notable feature of this friendship
was to be Jonathan's role in preserving David's life against
the murderous efforts of his father.

2. Public approval (18:5)
Saul gave David military command – an indication, incidentally, that the shepherd 'boy' was not a child, but a
young man. David was evidently successful and this, in
turn, led to a promotion to '**a high rank in the army**'. He
had proved that his triumph over Goliath was no fluke.
David was confirmed as the national hero.

Jealousy [18:6–29]

The narrative again returns to the day after the victory over
Goliath and the Philistines. As they marched through the

towns of Israel, the women came out singing and dancing to greet the victorious soldiers (18:6–7). Their song included the lines:

> 'Saul has slain his thousands,
>   and David his tens of thousands.'

As R. P. Gordon has pointed out, the juxtaposition of 'thousand' and 'ten thousand' is used in Hebrew poetry to dramatize a cumulative effect.[5] For example, in Psalm 91:7 we read,

> 'A thousand may fall at your side,
>   ten thousand at your right hand. . .'

Unlike this and other similar usages (e.g. Psalm 144:13; Micah 6:7), in which the numbers are used cumulatively, the women's song used them by way of contrast and thereby suggested an unfavourable comparison between Saul and David. It looks more like the *faux pas* of an insensitive lyricist than an intentional slight to the king, but it cut too close to the bone for Saul and '**from that time on Saul kept a jealous eye on David**' (18:9). Saul had begun to suspect, if indeed he was not already convinced, that David was that one of his 'neighbours' whom Samuel had prophesied would supplant him (15:28). He was soon to act upon his fears.

1. Madness in his method? (18:10–11)

Like the wicked queen who could not stand being the second most beautiful woman in the land (you will recall that Snow White was the most beautiful), Saul seethed with resentment against David's increasing popularity. 'It is a sign that the Spirit of God is departed from men,' wrote Matthew Henry, 'if they are peevish in resenting affronts, envious and suspicious of all about them, and ill-natured in their conduct; for the "wisdom from above" makes us otherwise.' The man who hates his brother is a murderer (1 John 3:15). Saul's feelings for David now served to deepen his depression. Small wonder, then, that on one of these days when '**an evil spirit from God came forcefully upon Saul**' and '**while David was playing the harp, as he**

usually did,' Saul's composure snapped and in his rage he twice threw his spear at David. . . but missed. One can well imagine Saul apologizing later for doing such a thing. He was not himself. It was because he had been overwhelmed by an evil spirit. We are not told that he made any such apology. Whatever was or was not said, ambiguity would have shrouded Saul's motives. His mad impulse was, in truth, an indication of what was in his heart. But such actions are difficult to read at the time and men deemed irresponsible for their actions 'by reason of insanity' are given the benefit of the doubt, if not exactly excused. Only when Saul, with the perverse premeditation of a desperate man, began to devise thoroughly rational stratagems to eliminate David did he appear to be the murderer that he really was.

2. Method in his madness? (18:12–29)
In the cold light of day, Saul turned to more subtle methods of disposing of David. If there was madness in his earlier 'method' – throwing spears in a fit of anger – there was henceforth considerable method in his madness. The 'madness' is that perennial irrationalism of the sinner – the idea that he can actually overthrow the will of God and get away with it. Sin – all sin – is 'mad' in this sense. It flies in the face of inevitable destruction. The wages of sin is death and the history of human sin is a catalogue of ultimately doomed attempts to turn reality on its head. But the impossibility of lasting success never stopped a sinner yet. 'Long live death' is the battle-cry of sin – eat, drink and be merry, for tomorrow we die![6] Saul had embarked upon an impossible mission which could only end in self-destruction, whatever 'successes' he might achieve along the way. How unutterably tragic is Saul's plight, especially in view of the fact that he knew the truth about the situation: '**Saul was afraid of David, because the Lord was with David but had left Saul**'! (18:12).

Saul's first ploy was to remove David from court and give him a field command in the army (18:13–16). At one stroke this reduced his public 'visibility' and raised the possibility of death in battle. Unfortunately for Saul, David neither died nor disappeared! The Lord was with him (18:14) and success attended his every effort. Saul's scheme had proved to be counter-productive. The people loved David more than ever!

Saul's second stratagem was to use his older daughter Merab as a reward for a commitment from David to give himself more vigorously to '**the battles of the Lord**' (18:17–19).[7] This recalls the as yet unfulfilled promise to the man who could vanquish Goliath (17:25). Here it was cheapened to little more than a bribe. And underneath the bribe was the vilest hypocrisy of Saul, who could ask David to fight the Lord's battles, all the while looking forward to attending his funeral. David responded with genuine humility to the offer of a royal bride. In the interim, he preserved his life, no doubt by ensuring that the Philistines were the only ones to die for their country, and was rewarded by Saul, perhaps in a fit of pique, giving his daughter to another man.[8]

The third of Saul's machinations was a variation on the second. Saul's daughter Michal was '**in love with David**' (18:20–29). With no better motive than to make Michal a widow before she was married, Saul took occasion from this circum-stance to propose her marriage to David. To minimize any suspicion David might entertain as to the genuineness of the offer, Saul made the approach obliquely, through his officials. As before, David responded with characteristic humility, but signalled a positive attitude in indicating his interest in the bride-price: '**I'm only a poor man. . .** ' (18:23; cf. Genesis 34:12; Exodus 22:16–17). Saul jumped at this: all he would ask was for David to bring the evidence that he had killed 100 Philistines – the grisly proof to be their foreskins (18:25). Again, Saul's hope was that David would fall in battle. David agreed to the bargain, killed twice the number of Philistines, married Michal and plunged Saul into greater misery than ever before (18:26–29).

Saul's best-laid schemes had turned to dust. David was alive and was his son-in-law. And Saul was to be David's enemy for the rest of his days!

The Lord is your shade [18:30; Psalm 121:5]

David knew from his own experience what it meant to have the Lord as his shade, at his right hand (Psalm 121:5). The key to

David's success and safety was the fact that '**the Lord was with him**' (18:14). He knew the Lord personally. He knew the presence of the Spirit of God in his heart. And he therefore conducted himself in obedience to the Lord and with a lovely spirit of godly humility. '**David acted more wisely [NASB, 'behaved himself more wisely'] than all the servants of Saul**' (18:30, NIV footnote). And herein is a challenge to each and every one of us, for at the heart of the matter is a person's relationship to the Lord.

David exhibited an exemplary humility in his response to the praise of the people and his meteoric rise to national prominence and royal favour. Many a man has had his head turned by far more modest achievements. David did not behave like so many of our modern 'superstars' of sport and television, who seem to live for the 'lap of honour' and the plaudits of the multitude. The Lord asks us, as he asked Baruch so long ago, 'Should you then seek great things for yourself? Seek them not' (Jeremiah 45:5). It was sufficient for God's servant to know that the Lord would preserve his life and provide for him even as the self-aggrandizers and self-seekers around him were falling apart. Jesus warns his followers against the seductive lies of the praise of men: 'Woe to you when all men speak well of you, for that is how their fathers treated the false prophets' (Luke 6:26). Let us fix our eyes upon the Lord Jesus Christ and look for his approval. 'If we commit our souls, and bodies, and characters, and interests, our way and work into the hands of the Lord,' advises Matthew Henry, 'he will bring all to pass that is good for us, and carry us safely through all, to that blessed world where treachery, envy and malice finds no admission, but perfect love will prevail for evermore.'

References

[1] Thomas Brooks (1608–80), *Precious remedies against Satan's devices*, (London: Banner of Truth, 1968 [1652]), p. 195.

[2] R. P. Gordon, p. 159.

[3] D. F. Payne, p. 161, refutes the recent speculations of certain writers who see a homosexual relationship behind this florid encomium.

[4] R. W. Klein, p. 182.

[5] R. P. Gordon p. 160. D. F. Payne, pp. 95–96, says that 'All that was

meant was that Saul and David between them had accounted for very large numbers of the enemy.'

[6] The slogan 'Long live death' (*Viva la muerte!*) was coined during the Spanish Civil War by the Nationalist General Millan Astray. Astray, the founder of the Spanish Foreign Legion, was almost an advertisement for the madness of his slogan – he had one leg, one arm, one eye and only a few fingers on his one remaining hand. See Hugh Thomas, *The Spanish Civil War*, (New York: Harper & Row, 1963), pp. 271–272.

[7] For a discussion of the 'battles of the Lord' see W. C. Kaiser, *Toward Old Testament Ethics*, (Grand Rapids: Academie Books, 1983), pp. 172–180.

[8] The sons of this marriage were to be executed in retribution for Saul's massacre of the Gibeonites, an Amorite clan bound by treaty to Israel (2 Samuel 21:1–6, cf. Joshua 9).

17.
God is my strength

Please read 1 Samuel 19:1–24

'O my Strength, I sing praise to you; you, O God, are my fortress, my loving God' (Psalm 59:17).

'Oh, choice song!' wrote Charles Haddon Spurgeon of the fifty-ninth psalm, 'My soul would sing it now, in defiance of all the dogs of hell!'[1] For all who love the Lord Jesus Christ, these words are neither theory nor emotive rhetoric, but sober reality that lifts the soul from earth to heaven. It says to the believer in Christ that his life is 'hidden with Christ in God' (Colossians 3:3). This is true of our life now in this present world and of our life that is not yet – that of glory in the presence of our Father-God and his incarnate Son, the Lord Jesus Christ. This is to say that our history – the whole of history including our personal daily experience – is in the hand of the God who is the strength of his people. All the events that impinge upon our lives are in the sovereign control of God. And when these events appear threatening to us or actually harm us, we have the Lord's assurance that they are working together for good to those that love God (Romans 8:28). God has placed *all things* under the feet of the risen Christ and appointed him to be head *over everything* for the church (Ephesians 1:22).

It is to be emphasized that this is not a statement about the Christian's inward, subjective perception of what is going on in and around his life, as if his faith were merely a psychological help in coping with otherwise unintelligible and often hostile events. The Lord is the believer's strength both objectively, as the sovereign predestinator of the course of history, and in his experience as the one who indwells his people by the Holy Spirit. The obverse of this coin is, of course, that the godless and unbelieving are bound to feel somewhat alone in the universe, exposed to the random and brute reality that surrounds them and possessed of no more assurance about the meaning of their lives and the facts of their personal history than what they can subjectively create for themselves out of the nothing in which they believe. Human beings ache for certainty and meaning in life. They want to think there is some meaning to life, some purpose beyond mere existence and some future other than the grave. This is why modern secularized man has shrunk from the stark atheism implicit in secular humanism. 'An atheist,' as Franklin D. Roosevelt once quipped, 'is a man with no invisible means of support.' So modern man is into the neo-paganism of 'New Age' thought or the mysticism of Eastern religions, in his quest for meaning and the comfort of an 'invisible means of support' – anything except the only true source of meaning and purpose, the gospel of Jesus Christ.

The Word of God calls us to true meaning and purpose – to new life in fellowship with God, through faith in Jesus Christ as the Saviour of sinners. God reveals himself as the refuge and strength of his believing people – 'an ever present help in trouble'. And the witness of every true child of God is:

> 'Therefore we will not fear, though the earth give way
>   and the mountains fall into the heart of the sea,
> though its waters roar and foam
>   and the mountains quake with their surging'
>   (Psalm 46:1–3).

For the believer knows that all the apparent uncertainties and the hostilities of this world will ultimately serve God's purposes. Whatever anyone may do, like the king spoken of in the Proverbs, his 'heart is in the hand of the Lord; he directs it like a watercourse wherever he pleases' (Proverbs 21:1). He is in control and loves his people. Saul may fling javelins at David, but the loving purpose of God is furthered

rather than hindered. Believers – and they alone – have the
biblical warrant to walk confidently before God and men in
this world of uncertainty and wickedness. And the history of
David's multiple deliverances from the wrath of Saul beautifully illustrates this truth and seals it as a privilege to be laid
hold upon in dependence upon the Lord by all his people
everywhere.

Jonathan's faithfulness [19:1–7]

David was a marked man because he was God's man. And
because his enemy was the king, he was, on the face of it, in
a very vulnerable position indeed. But the Lord's arm is not
shortened that it cannot save. With solemn irony, the Lord
was to draw the very instruments of David's deliverance
from Saul's own family and even Saul himself.

Saul had determined to put David to death and ordered
his son and his servants to see that this was done (19:1).
Jonathan, however, out of his friendship for David, not only
warned him but interceded with Saul with a view to saving
his life. Jonathan arranged for David to hide near to the spot
where he would speak with his father – some think this was
to enable him to communicate the result of his conversation
to David without exciting any suspicion that they had been
in collusion,[2] while others believe it was to allow David to
eavesdrop and assess Saul's attitude for himself.[3] Jonathan
succeeded in presenting a solid case for David's innocence
of any wrongdoing. Saul was, for the moment, convinced
and, typically, over-reacted by binding himself, in the most
pious language, to the sparing of David's life (19:4–6). God
used Saul's own son to restrain the king's murderous intent
and, for a season, '**David was with Saul as before**' (19:7).

Had this been the end of the matter, we would have
rejoiced in the goodness of God as he brought Saul to a
change of heart and a reconciliation with David. We know
too much, however, to take this exchange at face value.
With the hindsight afforded by what we have already
learned about the character of Saul, the prophecy of Samuel
as to his future and, of course, our advance reading of the
first book of Samuel, we know it to be but another sad

indication of his sin-sick spiritual state. The reconciliation was to be ephemeral, the solemn vow a transient travesty.

And what are we to learn from this? Surely it points up the great complexity of human nature in general and human sin in particular. The child of Adam has another father, who is the father of lies. Jesus told the unbelieving Jews of his day that they could not and would not understand and accept him and his message because they belonged to their 'father, the devil' who is 'a liar and the father of lies' (John 8:44). Saul was living a lie. That is why he could so easily make pious vows and contradict them almost in the same breath. His repentance was worse than his sin. This kind of inconsistency is what makes it virtually impossible to know such a man. There is nothing with which to get to grips. The 'real' Saul was a will o' the wisp. No one ever quite knew which Saul was the real one, because good men, at least, wanted to believe the God-talk and the changes of mind for the better. The recurrent oscillations between recalcitrance and repentance only made it more difficult to declare the man an incorrigible hypocrite. The answer is, surely, that the 'real' Saul was not one or the other but *both*! He was the complex of contradictory words and actions that Scripture history records him to have been. It is because he had something of a sense of right and wrong, somewhat of a fear of other people's opinions, perhaps even a sneaking fear of God, and an intelligent enough awareness of the fact that politics is the art of the possible – in other words, he was not as given over to a reprobate mind as he could have been or as he was later to become – that he was such a welter of apparent inconsistencies. This is what we all are by nature as those who do not receive 'the things that come from the Spirit of God' (1 Corinthians 2:14) and it is what we will remain, growing worse and worse (Romans 1:18–32), unless born again by the Holy Spirit and converted to Christ in repentance and faith (John 3:3–7; Acts 3:19). Without a saving change, a sinner is a mess. He hardly knows himself. He thinks he is wise, when in fact he is a fool (Romans 1:22). And even though he knows that God will judge wickedness, he goes on doing it as if he had a death-wish and encourages others along the same fatal road (Romans 1:32). This is why we need so much to be saved by the free grace of God in Jesus Christ!

Michal's ruse [19:8–17]

David only had to gain another victory over the Philistines for Saul to relapse into his former ways. Again the king was afflicted by this mysterious '**evil spirit from the Lord**' and, in a repeat of earlier circumstances, threw his spear at David with intent to kill him. He missed, however, and David made good his escape. Perhaps thinking this would be another of Saul's passing fits of anger, he went home to his wife (19:8–10; cf. 18:11–12). So much for Saul's vow to spare David! Of such, the apostle Peter says, 'The proverbs are true: "A dog returns to its vomit," and, "A sow that is washed goes back to her wallowing in the mud"' (2 Peter 2:22). Saul wanted David dead! And this time, there would be no turning back!

It was as well that Saul's children had more of a sense of justice than their father. It was one of these inexpressible ironies of providence that two of them were bound in personal covenant with David: Jonathan, in a covenant of fraternal love, and Michal in a marriage covenant. The Lord had placed his 'fifth column' inside Saul's own household! This only added to Saul's bitterness against David, but it was God's provision for the young man's survival (20:30–31).

Saul still dithered, as he had before the Battle of Michmash. Had he been at all resolute, then, like the Gestapo or the KGB, he might have sent his men through the front door in the small hours of the night. But he waited, and by the morning the bird had flown! Michal had persuaded David to flee, let him down from a window and played for time by the clever ruse of filling his bed with '**an idol**'. Then by lying to Saul's men, she kept them guessing up to the very last moment (19:11–16). David was, by that time, well on his way. Grieved by his daughter's perfidy, Saul asked in a hurt tone, '**Why did you deceive me like this and send my enemy away so that he escaped?**' In response, she lied again and exculpated herself at her husband's expense by claiming that David had forced her to help him on pain of death (19:17).

The inspired historian offers no moral commentary on Michal's behaviour and leaves us to draw our own conclusions. Again, I believe, we are presented with all the pathos of the human condition in its confused complexity.

There is the suggestion, in the ready availability of a household idol (*teraphim*), that her personal religion involved elements of Canaanite idolatry. Her later inability to understand David's dancing before the ark of the covenant – and the Lord's judgement upon her attitude – also indicates a heart not right with God (2 Samuel 6:16–23). This helps us understand why, in an emergency in which she very bravely did the right thing and helped her husband escape, she turned, as A.W. Pink puts it, 'to fleshly schemings and devisings'. Pink goes on to observe that 'From a natural viewpoint Michal's fidelity to her husband was commendable, but from a spiritual standpoint her deceit and falsehood were reprehensible.'[4] To our modern ears, so finely tuned to the wavelength of situation ethics and sensitive to the existence everywhere of so-called 'grey areas' and to the over-riding force of 'pressure', this seems a harsh judgement. Would we not do the same? Very possibly! Perhaps, too, we would launder our consciences with the many excuses afforded by such flexible casuistries? The lies of desperation are invariably unnecessary anyway. Godly composure would, at the very least, have served no worse and, at the best, been a testimony to the grace of God. Michal's first lie was totally superfluous. Her second lie, however, was an addition of fuel to the flames and a betrayal of her absent husband. She loved her husband, but she did not love principle and, consequently, was unable to resist the temptation to malign David and feed her father's wrath against him – in order, one presumes, to waylay a potential reprisal against herself. Through her courage, the Lord saved David's life but she nowhere gives evidence of trusting the Lord for the safety of either her husband or herself. Even so, it cost Michal a great deal to go against her own father, especially one whom she knew to be capricious and tyrannical. But let us pray that if we are ever put to a test of this kind, we will be enabled to trust in the Lord fully and bear faithful testimony to his perfect righteousness.

Saul's trance [19:18–24]

David fled to Samuel at Ramah (a mere two miles from Saul's capital at Gibeah), told him all that had transpired

and, together, they went on to '**Naioth**', which may not be a
place name but a 'camp' or complex of buildings outside the
town, perhaps a seminary similar to Elisha's school of
prophets (2 Kings 6:1–7).[5]

David's flight to Samuel can only be seen as an appeal to
God for his help. He sought sanctuary with the great
prophet of Israel and, in effect, cast himself upon the mercy
of the Lord. This was to set the scene for one of the most
intriguing and, indeed, mysterious interventions of God's
Spirit ever recorded in the Word of God.

Three times, Saul sent men to seize David and three times
they were reduced to utter helplessness by a prophetic
ecstasy induced by God's Spirit. When Saul in his frustration took the road to Ramah in an attempt to do the job
properly, he too was overwhelmed by the same spirit of
prophecy, to the extent that he too lost all control over his
actions – but for far longer and with more dramatic and
humiliating effect. The king threw off his robes and lay on
the ground in his undergarments '**all that day and night**'
(19:19–24).

Saul was utterly humiliated by this experience: '**This is
why people say, "Is Saul also among the prophets?"**'
(19:24). D. F. Payne notes that 'No criticism whatever is
implied of Samuel and the company of the prophets which
he superintended; but it is plain that Saul's actions were the
object of scorn, as he lost all dignity.'[6] There was no
blessing for Saul in that experience of prophetic utterance.
It was an experience divorced from any positive prophetic
function and, needless to say, it is not an experience which
any believer would seek for himself. God sovereignly intervened and manifested his power in such a way as to express
his disapproval of Saul's intent towards David and to expose
him to the self-destructive folly of his ways.

And David, of course, was able to escape once more.

'The Lord my fortress'

The military metaphors that Scripture uses to illustrate the
Christian life can sometimes leave us with the feeling that
we are supposed to live our days as if besieged in a castle,

desperately fending off the assaults of a myriad of enemies, waiting for the relief expedition that will take us away to heaven. This is to misunderstand God's plan for his people and, indeed, to misread the metaphor itself. When I read a psalm that speaks of God as my refuge and strong tower, I think of the royal castle of the Scottish kings in Stirling. It stands on its rock, towering over the populous and fertile lowlands of the Forth valley. From its battlements there is an incomparable view of a pleasant land, its rich fields dissected by the sinuous windings of the river Forth and, in the distance, the purple mountains of the Highlands. The castle is a fortress. It has been besieged many times in its 800 years. On Midsummer's Day in 1314, it witnessed the carnage of Bannockburn where Scotland's independence was regained. But within its massive walls stands the palace of James V. There are gardens inside and outside the castle. One has a bowling green. The king and queen could walk in the sequestered safety of their garden and enjoy the vistas of their beautiful domain.

This is a parable of the way that the Lord is the refuge and strength of the Christian. He surrounds us with his favour as a shield. He keeps the feet of his saints. His unseen hand guards our heart and directs the very details of our daily life. He keeps us safe in the heat of the battle. But all is not strife and struggle. He also leads us by the still waters and restores our soul. He lays a bountiful table for us, even in the presence of our enemies. And he brings us home to live in the house of the Lord for ever. Our Shepherd is our strength and fortress (Psalm 23). And as David knew that the Lord was his strength, so all who love the Lord today have the assurance of his preserving love through all their days.

References

[1] C. H. Spurgeon, *The Treasury of David*, (Grand Rapids: Guardian Press, 1976 [1870–85]), vol. III, p. 81.
[2] C. F. Keil and F. Delitzsch, p. 194.
[3] R. P. Gordon, p. 163.
[4] A. W. Pink, p. 59.
[5] R. W. Klein, p. 198.
[6] D. F. Payne, p. 102.

18.
An uncertain future

Please read 1 Samuel 20:1 – 21:10

'Then David fled from Naioth at Ramah and went to Jonathan and asked, "What have I done? What is my crime? How have I wronged your father, that he is trying to take my life?"' (1 Samuel 20:1).

The darkest part of the night, we are told, is just before the dawn. Quite often, the same may be said of Christian experience. The darkest discouragements and the deepest failures have often been dramatically superseded by the richest spiritual blessings of God's grace. This is frequently the case when someone is converted to Christ. The tax collector in Jesus' parable could only bow his head, beat his breast and cry out in anguish of soul, 'God, have mercy on me, a sinner' – so great was his sense of spiritual dereliction. But he 'went home justified before God' (Luke 18:13–14) and we cannot doubt that this meant that his burden was lifted and his soul filled with the new song of those who know the Lord and what it means to be saved by grace. It is also true from time to time in the course of the Christian's life. There are waters to pass through and trials to be faced, but the Lord assures us that though weeping may endure for a night, joy will come in the morning (Psalm 30:5). God's goodness is all the sweeter because it contrasts so brilliantly with the shadows of hard times and the gloom of personal failings.

Sometimes, however, the Christian can go through the very opposite experience. We can be surrounded by the evidences of God's love towards us; we can be exhilarated in our hearts by a sense of his presence, his mercy, his forgiveness and his gracious promises for the future; and suddenly we falter, doubts arise, we are tempted to fear the future and we start to behave as if we had never known the Lord and had never been convinced of the reality of his grace towards us in the past. There can be many reasons for such 'rapid and great alternation of feeling'.[1] It may relate to personality type; it may be a very specific matter of unrepented sin, masked till that moment, perhaps, by a superficially emotional religious expression; or it may be something as prosaic as body chemistry or physical tiredness; or, as we believe was the case with David, it may be the pressures of distressing circumstances, crowding in upon the mind and, for the moment, obliterating the comforts and the joys of all the evidences of the Lord's favour. The nearness of the Lord and the steadfast exercise of faith in Christ are ever-present needs for a life of consistent holiness before God and men. It is something of this that we see in 1 Samuel 20–21, through the window of David's experience as he fled from Saul. David had been harried by Saul and his life threatened, but God had demonstrated – particularly by the direct intervention of his Spirit at Ramah (19:23–24) – that his favour surrounded David like a shield and that, as the Lord's anointed, he was invulnerable to the evil designs of Saul. As we shall see, however, this did not keep David from what we might call 'spiritual edginess'. As he fled from Saul, he also retreated somewhat from the Lord and lost that quiet confidence which had been so much a part of him from his anointing by Samuel to his rise as the national hero of Israel.

The narrative begins with David in '**Naioth at Ramah**' and ends with his voluntary exile in Gath, with the Philistines. There are also two distinct phases in his flight: first, his four-day visit to his friend Jonathan (20:1–42) and second, his visit to Ahimelech, the priest, who ministered at the tabernacle, by then relocated to Nob from Shiloh (21:1–10).

A friend in need is a friend indeed [20:1–42]

1. The first day – David and Jonathan covenant together (20:1–23)
David left Samuel and sought out Jonathan, evidently anxious to enlist his aid in sorting out things with Saul, if at all possible.

Plaintively, he asked his friend, '**What have I done? What is my crime? How have I wronged your father, that he is trying to take my life?**' (20:1). This is the heart cry of all victims of injustice in every age. Even to have the semblance of a rational explanation would fortify the persecuted. But this only comes with time and spiritual discernment. The initial response reflects the shock and fear at the onslaught of unprovoked hostility. David had not yet become settled in heart and mind as to the meaning of what was happening to him. He was casting about desperately for an escape from the situation, of course, and was so consumed with doubts and fears that it is quite clear that he was not exercising that quiet trust in the Lord which, as an old man fleeing Absalom, would enable him to write with evident composure,

> 'I lie down and sleep;
>   I wake again, because the Lord sustains me
>   I will not fear the tens of thousands
>   drawn up against me on every side'
>
> (Psalm 3:5–6).

Jonathan's answer suggests that he was unaware of the recent turn in his father's attitude to David. He was sure that Saul would do nothing without his knowing about it and expostulated, more in frustration than in disbelief of David's testimony, '**Why would he hide this from me? It's not so!**' But David assured him with a solemn oath that what he said was absolutely true: '**Yet as surely as the Lord lives and as you live, there is only a step between me and death**.' Jonathan was convinced and committed himself to giving David whatever help he might need (20:2–4).

a. *David's request* (20:5–11) was that Jonathan ascertain Saul's intentions. The following day was to be the '**New Moon festival**' – a religious and civil festival celebrated on the first Sabbath of the month (Numbers 10:10; 28:11–15; 2 Kings 4:23; Isaiah 1:13; Amos 8:5) – and David was expected at Saul's table on that and the succeeding days. So he asked Jonathan to give an excuse for his absence, should Saul notice it and enquire about him. The excuse to be offered was that he had asked to go to Bethlehem for '**an annual sacrifice. . . for his whole clan**' (20:6). This was, of course, a lie. David would remain nearby to hear how Saul reacted to his absence.

b. *Jonathan's response* (20:12–23) was threefold.

Firstly, he promised to provide David with an honest report of Saul's disposition and to ensure that he could escape in the event that Saul intended to kill him (20:12–13).

Secondly, he acknowledged that God would destroy David's enemies (20:13–17). 'The implication was that one day Saul would be judged by God, and David would be Israel's new king.'[2] The way in which Jonathan blessed David indicates that the root of his conviction, and therefore the reason why he had a deeper loyalty to David than to his father, was that David was truly the Lord's anointed and the chosen successor of Saul. He said, '**May the Lord be with you as he has been with my father**' (20:13). In view of this, Jonathan asked David for an undertaking to spare him and his family at such time as the Lord would '**cut off every one of David's enemies from the face of the earth**' (20:15). David agreed and they bound each other in a solemn covenant. This covenant was kept by both men and is a wonderful testimony to what true friendship ought always to mean. Either man could easily have reneged on it. David was in Jonathan's power at that moment; later, Jonathan's son, Mephibosheth, would be in David's power (2 Samuel 9:1). But at no time did their commitment to one another falter.

Thirdly, Jonathan also made practical arrangements to communicate his findings about Saul's intentions to David by means of a secret sign involving the use of arrows (20:18–23).

2. The second day – nothing said (20:24–26)
When David did not appear on the Sabbath of the New Moon, Saul noticed his absence but said nothing. He assumed that there was some cause of ceremonial uncleanness keeping him away.[3]

3. The third day – Saul's anger (20:27–34)
On the second day of the feast, Saul noted David's absence and enquired of his son as to his whereabouts. When

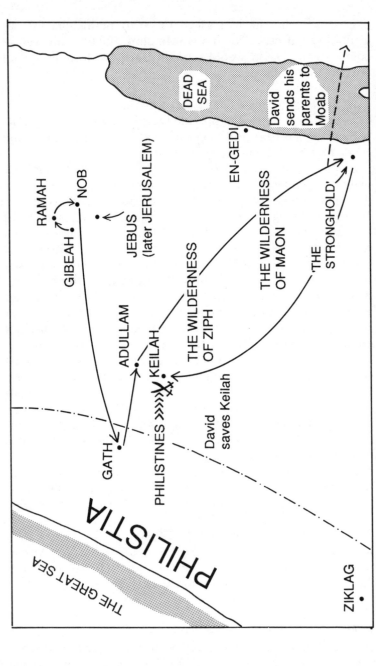

Map 8 : David's wanderings. Part 1 (1 Samuel 19:18 - 23:4)

Jonathan passed on David's cover story and implied that he had given David permission to go to Bethlehem, Saul became abusive towards Jonathan and commanded him to bring David to him, so that he could be put to death. Faithful to his friendship with David, the king's son objected and was himself obliged to dodge Saul's spear. Saul's intentions were clear to him. Jonathan left the table in anger and in grief, to fast for the remainder of the day in sorrow at his father's sin.

4. The fourth day – David's escape (20:35–42)
Next morning, Jonathan followed through with the agreed procedure for telling David that he should flee immediately. But in the end, it seems, David could not go without a personal farewell. They renewed their covenant and parted in tears, both aware that better days could not come until Saul was dead and aware also that this implied a permanent separation for them.[4] From that day until the death of Saul and Jonathan on Mount Gilboa, David was to be a fugitive from Saul's wrath. And so the two men went their sad and separate ways; Jonathan back to the town and David to an uncertain future, behind which stood the invisible guarantee of the loving purpose of the Lord.

The bread of the Presence [21:1–9]

David's next stop was the tabernacle, now relocated from Shiloh to Nob[5] and, of course, bereft of the ark of God, which was then in Kiriath Jearim. The chief priest at Nob was Ahimelech, grandson of Phinehas, the son of Eli who had perished at the Second Battle of Aphek.[6]

Ahimelech was perturbed by David's appearance on his doorstep. His guarded enquiry as to why David came alone indicated that he knew something was wrong. Such an important personage would not normally travel without a retinue. Whatever his suspicions, they were sufficiently allayed by David's 'confidence trick' about a top-secret mission for the king. His men, he said, were to meet him later at a certain place (21:2). He had just two favours to ask of the priest.

The first was for '**five loaves of bread, or whatever you can find**' (21:3–6). As it turned out, the only available bread was the consecrated bread from the Table of the Presence which was only to be eaten by the priests (Exodus 25:30; Leviticus 24:5–9). This the priest was willing to give to David providing he and his men[7] were not ceremonially unclean (see Exodus 19:15; Leviticus 15:18; Revelation 14:4). The consecrated bread – also known as the showbread or 'the bread of the Presence' – consisted of twelve loaves put out on the table in the Holy Place, symbolically in the presence of the Lord (Leviticus 24:5–9). After removal from the table, they could be eaten by the priests – thereby symbolizing God's provision for the needs of his people.[8] Ahimelech's willingness to give this bread to David indicates that he recognized that the claims of compassion as well as the symbolism of God's provision would be well served in giving what was a ceremonial privilege of the priests to a man who was in genuine need. It is not, as one writer suggests, that the moral obligation to sustain David's life superseded the ceremonial obligation to restrict the bread to the priests, as if the two were in opposition.[9] Rather, as our Lord made clear in Mark 2:25–28, the true meaning of the ceremonial law of the showbread was expressed in its being given to David as an act of compassion and mercy providing for real need; the law was fulfilled, rather than superseded. 'Believers,' said Matthew Henry, 'are spiritual priests and the offerings of the Lord shall be their inheritance; they shall eat the bread of their God.'

The second request was for a weapon and, as it happened, the sword of Goliath was the only one available (21:8–9). That the sword was there for David to retrieve it reflects the ancient practice of laying up the symbols of national redemption in places of worship. The modern manifestations of this tradition – retired regimental colours, covered with the battle honours of centuries of warfare – are to be seen in parish churches all over the British Isles.

Ahimelech's largesse towards David, whether or not it was extracted by deception, was bound to be regarded as treasonable by Saul, should he ever hear of it. Tragically for the priests of Nob, as it turned out, the informant was present to observe David's transactions with Ahimelech. Why Doeg the Edomite was present – '**detained before the Lord**' – we are not told. But he was later to be the executioner of Ahimelech and the priests of the tabernacle (22:9–10, 18–19).

Into exile [21:10]

This section properly ends with 21:10: '**That day David fled from Saul and went to Achish king of Gath**.' Nothing demonstrates David's fearful confusion more than his flight to Gath. David had been given every assurance from the Lord that he would be kept from the murderous hand of Saul and had seen with his own eyes how the Lord had neutralized the king's most decisive efforts to arrest him. The events of his escape called him to stand his ground rather than run away. But oppression makes many a wise man mad (Ecclesiastes 7:7). And David ran to Jonathan and then to Ahimelech, spraying his path with lies and deceptions that were later to stain his conscience with blood (22:22). And finally he fled the country and went to the Philistines, the enemies of the Lord's people! Even to us, across these intervening millennia, this was obviously an act of desperation. What business could he have with the Philistines? Would he be any safer with them? How would the people of Gath react to the man who had killed Goliath of Gath walking into town sporting the giant's own sword? In Philistia he would be surrounded by enemies; in Israel he had a bedrock of sympathy among the people and many friends who would help him. Above all, the Lord was unchangingly resolved to see him through his troubles and bring him to the throne. For all the problems, staying in Israel was likely to be the surer – and safer – course.

David's flight to Philistia – which, as we shall see, was short-lived for the reasons stated above – was a failure of faith. To leave the land of promise carried the implication of practical disbelief in the promises of God to his people. In the history of Ruth, for example, the migration of Elimelech and Naomi from Bethlehem in a time of famine is seen as just such an instance of faltering faith in the Lord. After a sad life in Moab, Naomi returned to Bethlehem on hearing that 'The Lord had come to the aid of his people by providing food for them' (Ruth 1:6). The very name of Bethlehem – literally, 'house of bread' – clothes the whole transaction with symbolic covenant significance. Exile was regarded as a curse. 'How can we sing the songs of the Lord while in a foreign land?' sang the exiles in Babylon (Psalm 137:4). The possession of the land and residence in the land were matters both of covenant blessing and practical godliness. Why? Because it was God's land or, as one writer has put it, 'God's throne area'.[10] It could never be an act of faith in the Lord to turn away from the land. When David crossed that frontier he was backsliding from the will and the promises of God.

Is your future uncertain?

Not one of us knows what a day will bring forth (Proverbs 27:1). God has not revealed his secret will for our lives. And even though we have the general framework of the promises of God's Word upon which to hang our prayerful aspirations, the fact remains that we can only look to the future in terms of faith as opposed to sight. We do not see the future. David had unusually specific promises about his future. He had been anointed by the prophet Samuel to be Israel's next king. He had been endowed in a special way by the Spirit of God. But this did not mean that everything thereafter was plain sailing. Saul was still king, although a man of reprobate mind willing to keep his throne by murderous means. David was torn by the contradiction that these circumstances offered to his faith. God had made promises but Saul was still there and seemed to be in the saddle, for all that he had failed to kill David so far. David had the spiritual jitters. He was rattled. We surely know this feeling very well. We simply start to doubt the Lord and we begin to tremble about the future. We fear. . . and fear. . . and fear. And every revolution of these fears in our minds seems to accelerate the panic and cause us to cast about despairingly for reasons and solutions, although our thoughts never stop long enough to formulate anything of any substance or sense. This is the stuff of which harsh words and rash decisions are made – and even complete nervous breakdowns. Just as a dew-pond can dry up under a hot sun to a shallow saucer of cracked earth, the human heart, if the certainties of faith evaporate, dries out, shrivels and cracks up under the strain of hopeless fears. This was what was happening to David. Just as surely it has happened to many of us from time to time.

Did David need to leave Samuel and Israel? Did David need to lie to Ahimelech and thereby bring down the wrath of Saul on the priests of Nob? Did he think that God could not preserve him? Was the future as uncertain to God's eyes as it was to David's? 'We blame not David for using with all diligence the means of safety,' wrote Charles Simeon, 'but it became him to believe the Word of God, and to be satisfied that Saul should not prevail against him. Faith is not to supersede, but to encourage our efforts, and to assure us of a successful end.'[11] Yet even David's visits to Samuel and the tabernacle have little of the flavour of faith seeking the will of God. There is no record of Samuel's or Ahimelech's counsel to David. It seems inconceivable that the prophet or the priest would have sent him off without a word of guidance. We know that David asked Ahimelech to enquire of the Lord for him (22:10). But when it comes to deeds it is the prosaic level of the need of food and a sword that dominates the transaction. The Word of God just does not figure, in practice. Indeed, David's contacts with the priests has something of the air of the way many people today will attend church in a crisis, presumably out of a desire to allay their fears, but with no evident interest in personal discipleship to the Lord or any long-standing commitment even to the outward observances of their new-found 'religion'. David was a believer, but believers can sometimes be very inconsistent with their own, genuine faith. Personal disaster is the test of personal faith.

The best of men are weak, and remain so, on this side of heaven. But the Lord Jesus Christ is greater than our hearts and his mercy is new every morning. He declares in his Word to every believer, 'Sin shall not have dominion over you' (Romans 6:14 AV). He has promised never to leave us or forsake us. He is the guarantor of all our tomorrows until he takes us to glory. And we need to learn with the apostle Paul that as our life here is Christ, even our death will be gain (Philippians 1:21). That is a statement about the confidence with which the Christian may face the future. Because the Christian's life, every day, is Christ, then the worst that the enemy can do – that is, attempt to put us in hell through death (for that is the essential meaning of death) – is turned into gain, in Christ. We do not know what may happen tomorrow, but the Lord does. And that is the practical as well as the theological-theoretical answer to the uncertainties that flood so easily into our minds and tempt us to turn from his promises to the arm of the flesh.

> 'I lie down and sleep;
>   I wake again, because the Lord sustains me.
> I will not fear the tens of thousands
>   drawn up against me on every side.
> Arise O Lord!
>   Deliver me, O my God!
> Strike all my enemies on the jaw;
>   break the teeth of the wicked.
> From the Lord comes deliverance.
>   May your blessing be on your people'
>
> (Psalm 3:6–8).

References

[1] Archibald Alexander, *Thoughts on Religious Experience*, (London: Banner of Truth, [1844] 1967), p. 34.

[2] J. Carl Laney, *First and Second Samuel*, (*Everyman's Bible Commentary*, Chicago: Moody Press, 1982), p. 64.

[3] See Leviticus 11–15 and comment in R. P. Gordon, p. 168.

[4] They were, in fact, to meet once more (see 23:16–18).

[5] Nob is thought to be the modern Mount Scopus, outside Jerusalem (see Isaiah 10:32; Nehemiah 11:32), J. Carl Laney, p. 65.

[6] The line of priests from Eli included his son Phinehas, grandson Ahitub, and great-grandsons, Ahimelech and Ahijah (see 1 Samuel 14:3; 22:9; 1 Chronicles 24:3).

[7] There is no indication, prior to David's lie about the secret mission, that he had any companions. The Lord Jesus Christ, as recorded in Mark 2:25–6, speaks of men who were with David and who ate of that bread. He mentions Abiathar rather than Ahimelech (his father). David's lie was about the fictitious mission, not about having men with him.

[8] R. P. Gordon, p. 170.

[9] J. C. Laney, p. 65.

[10] R. J. Rushdoony, *The Institutes of Biblical Law*, (Nutley, N.J: Craig Press, 1973), p. 491.

[11] Charles Simeon, *Expository Outlines on the whole Bible*, (Grand Rapids: Zondervan, 1956), p. 215.

19.
A new beginning

Please read 1 Samuel 21:11 – 22:5

'David left Gath and escaped to the cave of Adullam. When his brothers and his father's household heard about it, they went down to him there. All those who were in distress or in debt or discontented gathered round him, and he became their leader' (1 Samuel 22:1–2).

If there were no winter, we should never see the beauties of the spring. The annual return of life, leaf and colour derives a unique appeal from its dramatic contrast with the grey prospect of the preceding months. Winter, by being so dead, ensures that spring is an exciting revelation of new life.

The winter of Saul's discontent had cast its gloomy net for David. By the grace of God, it had come up empty. David had, however, continued to run from Saul. He had plunged into a winter of his own making, a time in which his fears triumphed over his faith, a dark interlude in which, though clearly a believer, he began to live as if God had abandoned him – as if all God's past blessings and future promises were to no effect.

Christians have no difficulty in identifying with David's experience. We are bone of his bone and flesh of his flesh. We know what it is to struggle with sin – and we know what it is to fail. We feel for David, not only in his predicament but also in the confused wavering of his beleaguered soul. Whenever God's providences seem to run counter to his promises, faith is challenged. It is so much easier to walk by sight than to walk by faith (2 Corinthians 5:7). But walking by faith is of the essence of discipleship to the Lord and it is inevitable that that faith will be tested. It is, however, precisely the trial of our faith that works patience and results in 'praise and honour and glory at the appearing of Jesus Christ' (James 1:3; 1 Peter 1:7 AV).

Time out: David in Gath [21:11 – 22:1]

It took a lot of gall, or else it was blind desperation, for David to walk into Gath looking for political asylum. By now, David was a legendary exterminator of Philistines. He was even armed with the sword of one of Gath's favourite sons, the late great Goliath, whom David had felled with a stone in the valley of Elah. Perhaps David entertained fond notions of a quiet respite among the Philistines. We are not told what plans he had for his stay in Gath, but whatever they were, it soon became clear that he had jumped from the frying pan into the fire.

At first, it seems that Achish, the King of Gath, received David with a degree of hospitality. He might well have clapped him in irons or even lopped off his head, but he did neither. His advisors, however, were somewhat less sanguine about the advent of the conqueror of Goliath: **'Isn't this David, the king of the land? Isn't he the one they sing about in their dances: "Saul has slain his thousands, and David his tens of thousands"?'** (21:11). Like Saul, they interpreted the girls' plauditory ditty rather negatively – and with more reason, for the slaughtered 'tens of thousands' were their own kith and kin! David was a marked man and in the greatest of danger! He was discovering that a celebrity has no hiding place and, more pointedly, that the Lord's anointed king was not going to be allowed to escape his calling! Like Jonah in a later generation, David was to find his flight arrested by an unseen hand and his steps redirected to the path of God's purpose. David soon heard about this counsel of Achish's advisors and he knew that the writing was on the wall. He **'took these words to heart and was very much afraid of Achish king of Gath'** (21:12). He decided to escape as soon as he could. But how? That was the question.

David determined to feign insanity. He **'acted like a madman'** scribbling graffiti on doors and drooling down his beard (12:13). This had the desired effect. Achish had nothing more to do with him. '**Am I so short of mad-men. . . ?**' he asked '**Must this man come into my house?**' Thus freed from the attentions of his host, David made good his escape from Philistia and returned to Israel (21:14 – 22:1).

David had completely fooled the Philistines. And it certainly was a *tour de force*. It was the kind of ingenuity – perhaps we might call it, with sneaking admiration, devilment – that adds lustre to the exploits of heroes and villains alike. Our inclination is to enjoy his discomfiture of the unwitting Achish! And it is just not in our nature to see this incident in a negative light; still less as the low-water mark of David's spiritual development. Before we shrug it off, however, we need to see that there is a deeper, less laudable, perspective on David's behaviour.

In the first place, effectiveness is not proof of the rectitude of any action. David's ploy was effective but cannot be said to reflect very well on him. It was a carnal stratagem. The spirit that took him to Gath in the first place was operative in his desperate grab for self-preservation. He was still leaning on his own understanding rather than waiting upon God in an honest and dignified spirit of dependence upon his grace. Compare the Lord Jesus Christ and the apostle Paul before their captors: no lies, no faking madness. . . just simple, open-faced and infinitely courageous trust in the promises of God! We are so used to the idea of using deception to gain good ends that we tend to write off transparent honesty and dignified submission to whatever God's hand provides as some kind of starry-eyed idealism. The Lord delivered David from Achish of Gath, but he has not promised to honour lies and trickery, even in a good cause. How can the perfect righteousness of God be served by chicanery? What sort of a witness is it to behave exactly like the world? Could David's behaviour conceivably commend David's God to the Philistines? Not in a hundred years! No more can any subterfuge, whether in a good cause or not. If our behaviour is indistinguishable from that of the world that does not know the Lord, then we cannot be doing the Lord's work. We are called to be holy, as God is holy.

In the second place, we must understand that a real struggle was taking place in David's soul. He wrote Psalm 56 in Gath and it expresses his anxiety and his fears in vivid terms. Later, in the relative safety of the cave of Adullam, he wrote Psalm 34 and it, in contrast, is full of renewed spiritual composure. Good men do strange things under pressure. The godly Thomas Cranmer, Archbishop of Canterbury in the reign of Mary Tudor, first saved his life by recanting his Protestant convictions, having been forced to watch the burning of the martyrs Latimer and Ridley. But he repented of his weakness, revoked his recantations and died a martyr's death on 21 March 1556. The life of faith cannot be lived without doing battle with the enemy of our souls, but in Christ our Saviour we shall be more than conquerors!

In the third place, it is an unbreakable principle of God's Word that we should not 'go on sinning, so that grace may increase' (Romans 6:1). God permitted David to play the fool, just as he had permitted him to do many other less than faithful things. The Lord used this to save his life. God saved David in his folly.[1] No sinner was ever saved any other way! But God saves from sin. To plan to go against God's express will – and supposedly to achieve that very will – is not only irrational but extremely dangerous. Paul warns us solemnly against the delusion that continuing in sin will actually increase grace!

David understood the positive import of this truth for his own life when he came to pen Psalm 34:

> 'A righteous man may have many troubles,
>   but the Lord delivers him from them all;
> he protects all his bones,
>   not one of them will be broken'
>
> (Psalm 34:19–22)

David knew the meaning of grace for the backslider and restoration to reconciled fellowship with the Lord. If you have had your Gaths, then may the Lord bring you to the cave of Adullam and the tenderness of spirit of that inspired song of David. God's perfect love casts out all fear (1 John 4:18).

Back on the right track: the cave of Adullam [22:1–5]

If David's 'time out' in Gath was the low point of his flight from Saul, then the cave of Adullam was where he got back

on the right track with the Lord. There he became truly one
of those men of whom 'the world was not worthy. . . They
wandered in deserts and mountains, and in caves and holes
in the ground' (Hebrews 11:38). The cave in question was
near the town of Adullam, some sixteen miles south-west of
Jerusalem (Joshua 15:35; 2 Chronicles 11:7). His family
joined him, as did about 400 men. He then arranged asylum
for his parents in Moab – the native land of his great-
grandmother, Ruth – and betook himself to '**the
stronghold**' and waited to see what would happen.[2] The
Lord had other plans for David, however, and sent the
prophet Gad to him to bring an end to this interlude in his
wanderings, roust him from his desert fastness and set him
back on the road to the throne. '**So David left and went to
the forest of Hereth**' (22:5).

What is the significance of this phase of David's life? I
would suggest that it was a time of vital importance for both
his personal development and his future effectiveness.
Three aspects come to the fore.

1. A time of spiritual reflection and restoration

We have already seen that David's experience in Gath
occasioned the composition of Psalm 34. It was also about
this time that David wrote Psalms 57 and 142. Both psalms
are models of how to pray in the most oppressive circumstances. They both powerfully illustrate the truth that 'It is
through the channel of our helplessness that God commu-
nicates his strength to us. In our spiritual warfare the
smallest degree of self-sufficiency may stand as a barrier
between us and His help. And it is by the door of self-
confidence that Satan often brings us low.' But David calls
'in all his conscious weakness' and 'through faith and prayer
help came to him from above'.[3]

> 'Have mercy on me, O God, have mercy on me,
>   for in you my soul takes refuge.
> I will take refuge in the shadow of your wings
>   until the disaster has passed.
> I cry out to God Most High,
>   to God, who fulfils his purpose for me'
>   (Psalm 57:1–2).

And his prayer and praise rise to the recognition of specific blessing in his current fugitive state:

> 'Set me free from my prison,
>> that I may praise your name.
> Then the righteous will gather about me
>> because of your goodness to me'
>
> (Psalm 142:7).

The man who fled in terror from Saul, who lied to Ahimelech and played the fool in Gath had been brought to 'a renewed sense of God's favour, and fresh experience of his mercy towards his children'.[4] So whereas he had been constantly on the move, both physically and in the turmoil of his troubled heart and wavering faith, now he can declare with rising joy, 'My heart is fixed, O God, my heart is fixed: I will sing and give praise. Awake up, my glory; awake, psaltery and harp: I myself will awake early. I will praise thee, O Lord, among the people: I will sing unto thee among the nations' (Psalm 57:7–9 AV). Worship flows from the Holy Spirit's gracious workings within our heart. David knew he was saved and that assurance of personal faith could only lead to the praise of his Father God.

2. A time of preparation for the future

Some 400 men '**gathered round**' David at the cave of Adullam. Perhaps because the word 'discontented' is used in describing some of them – '**All those who were in distress or in debt or discontented gathered around him**' (22:2) – we might be tempted to think that this was an assemblage of malcontents and even brigands.[5] However motley a crew it may have been – and no doubt there were all sorts of people in it – the general tone was high rather than low, as subsequent events make clear. The '**discontented**' were 'those who have creditors' and the implication would appear to be that these and others were seeking David's leadership because of the oppressive and basically unjust treatment they had been receiving under Saul's regime. However many rascals and hangers-on there were, there is no doubt that the discipline and integrity of David's band were exemplary.

This was a faithful remnant of men who were to become committed to David and to the Lord. For this reason, incidentally, the cave of Adullam has even been honoured in the name of a number of Christian congregations. This is quaint to modern ears, perhaps, but it represents a spiritually discerning grasp of the nature and significance of the cave of Adullam. There was the Lord's king with the Lord's remnant – a picture of the church in the wilderness.

3. A time for obedience to the Lord's commands
David was not permitted to dally either in the cave of Adullam or 'the stronghold'. The prophet Gad, who became one of David's 'court prophets' in later years (see 2 Samuel 24), brought God's orders that he go up to Judah forthwith. David obeyed this command immediately. He acted upon God's Word. He was on the move – for God! There is an undeniable sense of a transfer of initiative and momentum from Saul to David, David was, perceptibly, going over to the offensive after a period of defeatist defensiveness. The Lord had brought him to a new beginning!

A picture of Christ's church

The Old Testament people of God were the church of their time. The events of that era, and especially the mighty acts of God in redeeming his people for himself, afford us many a pointer to the later unfolding of saving love in the person and work of Jesus Christ.

The temptation to spiritualize Old Testament events and treat their every detail as parables for New Testament Christians is to be restricted. David and the so-called 'malcontents' of Adullam are surely not a 'type' (i.e., a prophetic foreshadowing) of 'the first coming to Christ of his people' or 'their subsequently *going forth* "unto Him without the camp" (Heb. 13:13)' (original emphasis).[6] At the same time, there are lessons to be learned. In the experience of the saints of former generations, there is a picture of the challenges facing the church today. Faithful Christians have often experienced the kind of rejection that David and the men of Adullam went through. Sometimes the church has been, and is, from time to time and place to place, an outcast remnant. As such she rallies to Christ and cries out for deliverance. When persecuted in one place, she flees to another. And in the midst of danger from hostile forces, she seeks and does the will of her Lord!

Christ is our Captain. Unlike David, he is a sinless leader, and a perfect King, the Saviour of the world. He says to us, 'Don't be afraid, little flock,' 'Take heart! I have overcome the world.' Even in trying circumstances, there are caves of Adullam, where, as it were, we may sit awhile in quietness of heart and, having cast our burdens upon the Lord, begin again with him in a revived assurance of his love and a renewed commitment to the righteousness of his kingdom.

References

[1] D. F. Payne, p. 113.

[2] 'Stronghold', (Hebrew, *mesuda*), has been identified with Masada, the place of the suicidal 'last stand' of the Jewish revolt in A.D.73 (Y. Aharoni and Michael Avi-Yonah, *The Macmillan Bible Atlas*, New York: Macmillan, 1973, 92). Others, more cautiously, regard it as of uncertain location, possibly an unspecified place in Moab (R.W. Klein, p. 223).

[3] M. Campbell, *From Grace to Glory – meditations on the Book of Psalms*, (London: Banner of Truth, 1970), p. 57.

[4] D. Dickson, *A Commentary on the Psalms*, (London: Banner of Truth, 1959 [1653–5]), vol. 1. p. 343.

[5] R. P. Gordon, p. 172, sees them as 'an assortment of social malcontents and derelicts' without recognizing the possibility of their having valid grievances under the tyrannical reign of Saul. Keil and Delitzsch, p. 223, more judiciously note that these 'discontented' men 'ripened into heroic men under the command of David' and the bravest of them are listed in 1 Chronicles 12 (compare 2 Samuel 23:13; 1 Chronicles 11:15–19).

[6] A.W. Pink, p. 84.

20.
Enquiring of the Lord

Please read 1 Samuel 22:6–23:6

'When David was told, "Look, the Philistines are fighting against Keilah and are looting the threshing-floors," he enquired of the Lord, saying, "Shall I go and attack these Philistines?" The Lord answered him, "Go, attack the Philistines and save Keilah"' (1 Samuel 23:1–2).

The cave of Adullam was a watershed in David's life. Until the flight that led to Adullam, he had always entertained the hope of a reconciliation with Saul and a return to the normal life of the court and the service of king and country. It was devastating to David to realize that Saul saw him as an ever-present threat to his throne and was determined to kill him. He saw clearly that the hatred of Saul towards him was implacable. And this terrible realization – that there was no hope of a return to the warm relationship of earlier days – laid waste David's assurance of the Lord's blessing and brought him to desperate self-reliance and utter confusion of face. He fled from Saul but he did not exactly flee to the Lord! His faith wavered. He despaired. He ran. He lied. He even sought asylum with the Lord's enemies, the Philistines. And throughout this dark passage, David, though a true believer in the Lord, behaved like a man who had lost his spiritual moorings. He had, in truth, lost his way!

The Lord was still with him, to watch over him. And no doubt there were times when David cried out to the Lord in his desperation and confusion. Backsliders often pray, but their prayers are like their actions at such times – a welter of confusing, sometimes hysterical, thoughts. Indecision,

panic, consternation, trepidation and hopelessness all con-
spire to produce a sense of floundering weightlessness.
Actions become guesses looking for a miracle; prayers mere
words that thrash the heavens and are dissipated in the
tumults of the soul. The prayer of faith rests on more solid
ground. But the Lord does not desert his people, however
far away he may seem to them. David was passing through
the waters, but the Lord was with him (Isaiah 43:2).

As the Lord brought David out of this spiritual maelstrom,
the fruit of revival in his soul began to flow from his pen.
Psalms 34, 57 and 142 came, as we have already seen, from
this period. More were to follow. Towards the end of his life,
David reflected on earlier days and recalled an incident from
the Adullam period that beautifully illustrates the new
direction in his life. The Philistines were in Bethlehem and
David conceived a longing for a drink of water from the well
near the gate of that town. The 'three mighty men' –
Josheb-Basshebeth, Eleazar and Shammah – heard this and
took up the challenge. They infiltrated the Philistine lines
and brought back some water for David. It is, of course, of
such acts of romantic heroism that 'mighty men' are made!
David's response was to clothe that heroism in a corona of
self-sacrificial holiness. David refused to drink the water, but
poured it out before the Lord, declaring it to be 'the blood of
men who went at the risk of their lives' (2 Samuel 23:13–17).
The loyalty of 'the Three' was answered by their leader's
godly recognition of the value of their love and their lives.

David was not 'out of the wood' yet. He would continue to be
a fugitive from Saul and have many narrow escapes. From this
point on, however, he was imbued with a spirit of confidence
in the Lord and began to act as a true king should. His support
grew and the hapless Saul became increasingly isolated and
embittered. Saul had taken the road that was to end in death
on Mount Gilboa, while David, through many perils, would
come to Mount Zion as the Lord's anointed king!

Preparation [22:1–5]

God prepared David for his next trial in that transitional
period between Adullam and 'the stronghold'. We have seen

in the previous study how he made provision for the safety
of his parents in Moab and how the prophet Gad came to
tell him, in the name of the Lord, to go to '**the land of
Judah**', where, after all, the issue between Saul and himself
would have to be settled.

What was absolutely vital to any progress was David's
willingness, without question and without delay, to obey the
Lord's will as it had been revealed to him by the prophet
Gad. There is no greater or more effective preparation of
any person for a fruitful and happy life than the implant-
ation of a readiness to receive with meekness the engrafted
Word which is able to save (James 1:21 AV). This is the
proof that someone loves the Lord (John 14:15). Without
such a readiness, David would have remained spiritually
paralysed. But the Lord took him 'out of the mud and mire'
and set his 'feet on a rock,' giving him 'a firm place to stand'
(Psalm 40:2).

Predicament [22:6 – 23:1]

In the meantime, events were taking place which put
David's predicament in sharp relief.

1. The massacre of the priests (22:6–23)
One day, a priest named Abiathar arrived at David's camp
with a most horrific story. He told how Saul had completely
destroyed the Levite community at Nob, including his
father Ahimelech, and that he alone had succeeded in
escaping! (22:20–21).

It transpired that when Saul heard about the movements
of David and his men, he had begun to berate his officials
for conspiring against him. Would David give them lands or
position? Why did no one tell him that Jonathan had made a
covenant with David? He even told them, '**My son has
incited my servant** [David] **to lie in wait for me, as he
does today**' (22:8). Saul was so full of hatred and fear that
he trusted no one and so he treated them all as if they were
his enemies. This is often the way with dictators. Their
advisors are too scared to tell them the truth. It was said of
Mussolini, for example, that by the time he took Italy into

World War II, it had been nearly twenty years since he had heard the truth about the state of the Italian armed forces! It is not easy to bring bad news to a tyrant. In such circumstances a climate of fear and distrust builds up on both sides. Only the 'yes-men' and the sycophants speak up and it is axiomatic that their contributions will be self-serving.

On this occasion, Doeg the Edomite was able to inform Saul of the fact that David had visited Ahimelech, the high priest, at the tabernacle in Nob. Whatever Doeg saw and heard at Nob, it is clear that he was a false witness, in that he was quite content for Saul to believe that Ahimelech had a treasonable intention in giving assistance to David. An honest witness would have reported David's deception and exonerated the priest. But Doeg was the kind of man with an instinct for what his master wanted to hear. It is interesting, too, that Doeg mentions that Ahimelech '**enquired of the Lord**' for David (22:9–10). Was this true? There is no mention of this in the inspired historian's account of the meeting itself (see 21:1–9), although Ahimelech's defence may imply that such an enquiry was made (22:15). This is, however, not conclusive. Doeg might well have lied on this point, so as to persuade Saul to think the worse of Ahimelech, even to believing that the priest had sought the blessing of God for actions on David's part which he must have known to be treasonable.

Saul was certainly willing to condemn the high priest on Doeg's testimony. Even Ahimelech's spirited and transparently honest defence did nothing to shift the irate king. Just as Henry II of England, two millennia later, wished to be done with Archbishop Thomas Becket, Saul intended to be rid of his meddlesome priest! Ahimelech and his family were summarily condemned to death!

But none of Saul's officials moved to carry out his sentence. They were '**not willing to raise a hand to strike the priests of the Lord**' (22:11–17). Saul then ordered Doeg, the foreigner from Edom, to execute his sentence. With grim efficiency, Doeg murdered eighty-five priests, including Ahimelech. Nob, the town of the priests, was razed to the ground and all its inhabitants put to the sword. Saul had his Lidice[1] to inspire the loyalty of his subjects! Saul had acquired that hallmark of all true tyrants – he had declared war on his own people and had added mass murder to the instruments of his government.

Such horrific crimes are easily understood, if we look no further than the evil machinations of Saul's mind. This is what unrestrained sin can do and 'There, but for the grace of God, go we!' There is, however, a deeper level to be considered, namely the interplay of human evil and the will of God. God's purposes are never thwarted by human sin. Even though monstrous evils may be perpetrated against the Lord's people, the Lord has promised that the very gates of hell shall not prevail against his church. The 'wrath of man' will praise the Lord (Psalm 76:10 AV). This is not always clear at first, but in the case of Saul's massacre of the priests, at least three strands of the divine purpose are immediately evident.

The first is the fulfilment of the warning to Israel about the excesses of a monarchy that goes wrong. 'When that day comes,' said the Lord through Samuel, 'you will cry out for relief from the king you have chosen, and the Lord will not answer you in that day' (8:18). Saul was turning sour. And the Lord had told them so.

The second is a further stage in the fulfilment of the prophecy against the house of Eli (2:31–36; 3:13–14). The massacre of the eighty-five priests took the line of Eli that much nearer to extinction. 'It was,' says Matthew Henry, 'the accomplishment of threatenings long since pro- nounced against the house of Eli. . . though Saul was unrighteous in doing this, yet God was righteous in per- mitting it. Now God performed against Eli, at which the ears of them that heard it must tingle. No word of God shall fall to the ground.'

The third is that this sealed, for David, his calling before God. He recognized his responsibility for bringing down Saul's wrath on Ahimelech and his family (22:22). And in assuring Abiathar that he would be safe if he stayed with him, David was affirming that there was no road back: '**The man who is seeking your life is seeking mine also**' (22:23). In a mixture of sorrow, outrage and solemn resolve, David wrote a song that, under the inspir- ation of the Spirit of God, pronounced God's judgement upon Saul and Doeg:

'Why do you boast of evil, you mighty man?
Why do you boast all day long,
you who are a disgrace in the eyes of God?'

'Surely God will bring you down to everlasting ruin:
He will snatch you up and tear you from your tent;
He will uproot you from the land of the living.'

'But I am like an olive tree
flourishing in the house of God;
I trust in God's unfailing love
for ever and ever'

(Psalm 52:1, 5, 8).

David knew, with the deepest assurance of faith, that he must be about the business to which the Lord had called him.

2. The seige of Keilah (23:1)

Curiously – but significantly – the next challenge to David came from the Philistines and not from Saul. They crossed the border from Gath and besieged the town of Keilah, which was a mere three miles from Adullam.[2] It was harvest-time, the traditional season for such raids.[3] The significance of this development was, of course, that it posed the question for David, whether he would serve his people as a true king should, or simply preserve himself against the day when Saul had been overcome and he would be undisputed monarch in Israel. Did David believe he was already the Lord's anointed king? Or did he believe it was only a future possibility? Keilah challenged his faith and required that he act upon it immediately. The kingship was no longer a theory. David's predicament called for action!

Performance [23:2–6]

There can be little doubt that David was possessed of a holy confidence in his God-given call to be the king of Israel. Furthermore, since Abiathar succeeded his father as Israel's high priest, every vestige of the mantle of legitimacy had

been irrevocably removed from Saul. Saul had been rejected
by God as king; now the oracles of God – the high priest and
the ephod (see 23:6) – had been removed from him. He was
little more than a chapter waiting to be closed.

The coming of Abiathar to David's camp therefore held a
constitutional significance. He was the priest of the tabernacle. Gad, whom God had sent to David to counsel him,
was a true prophet of the Lord. And David, of course, was
the anointed king who, according to God's purpose, was to
replace the rejected, but still ruling, Saul. This triad of
prophet, priest and king constituted God's stamp of
authority upon David's enterprise. Although David always
respected Saul as the Lord's anointed king and adopted a
defensive rather than an offensive posture towards him,
there is a sense in which he now represented a kind of
'government in exile' of the people of God.

Firstly, David acted as the true, godly king and took the
field in defence of the realm (23:1–5). He sought the Lord's
will respecting the Philistine siege of Keilah. The Lord
directed him to attack the Philistines. When his men
expressed their honest fears – after all, they were constantly
under the threat of attack from Saul – David again enquired
of the Lord and the Lord assured him of victory (23:1–4).

While Saul sulked, David fought. The Philistines were
defeated and Keilah was relieved (23:5).

Secondly, David committed himself to seeking the Lord's
will by the appointed means (23:6). Abiathar accompanied
David to Keilah. He had with him the vestments of the high
priest – the garment called the ephod. This had a
breastplate with the mysterious stones, the Urim and
Thummim, which were used in determining the Lord's
will.[4]

David exemplifies the simple, yet momentous, faithfulness that ought to characterize every true child of God. He
sought the Lord's will according to God's commands (23:2);
he was not deflected from his spiritual responsibilities by
the fears of others (23:3); he persevered before God's throne
until he was assured of God's will (23:4) and he obeyed the
Lord's will with despatch (23:5). David might have enquired
all day and put off his obedience until a more convenient
time. When the Lord Jesus Christ calls, the time is now! He

has called us to a new direction for our lives. A direction is a way. Jesus is that way, the truth and the life.

References

[1] The town in Czechoslovakia destroyed by Hitler's SS as a reprisal for the assassination of Reinhard Heydrich, the brutal 'Reichsprotektor' of Bohemia.

[2] A glance at a map of Israel reveals how small an area was involved in the various wars and wanderings of David. The country was, and is, rugged and communications in those days favoured the mountain goats more than the humans.

[3] R. P. Gordon, p. 176.

[4] R. P. Gordon, p. 85, gives an extensive description of this oracular device.

21.
Gracious victory

Please read 1 Samuel 23:7–24:22

'I know that you will surely be king and that the kingdom of Israel will be established in your hands' (1 Samuel 24:20).

Few men have had as many narrow escapes in a short time as did David in his flight from Saul. During this time of intense trial, David experienced an astonishing series of gracious providences. If anyone was a trophy of grace, it was the 'sweet singer of Israel'. And if his life hitherto had been a testimony of God's goodness towards 'the man after his own heart', then the events which followed were to be a testimony to God's grace in the heart and actions of his servant. We surely discover how much mercy is in a man's heart when we fall into his hands. David was given an opportunity to kill Saul and, arguably, could have solved his problem at one stroke. But David spared Saul's life. Far from being vindictive and vengeful, he showed humility and even tenderness towards the king. And in so doing he won a greater victory by far – a victory over the powers of darkness – a victory which moved Saul to tears and to the recognition that David was a righteous man, God's man – the man who would be king in Israel!

David practised what the apostle Paul was later to preach to the New Testament church: 'Do not be overcome by evil, but overcome evil with good' (Romans 12:21). This very searching truth is, sad to say, too easily shrugged off as the relatively unattainable mark of exemplary saintliness. In fact, it is the bottom line in the relationship between our faith and other people! Nothing reveals more the reality of the love of Christ in your heart and mine – or more starkly indicates its absence – than the way we treat those whom we believe to have done us some wrong. A vindictive spirit argues a lack of grace in the heart, evidences an unforgiving spirit and, most of all, demonstrates a sad incomprehension of both the nature of Christ's substitutionary atonement for sin and a lack of practical experience of the claims of Christ's death upon our thought, words and actions. David, in this respect, points us to Christ and to the redemptive transformation that we need in order to be holy as he is holy.

On the move again [23:7–29]

The scene is set for us by an account of David's further wanderings and yet another very narrow escape from Saul. You will recall that David had sallied forth from the forest of Hereth (22:5) to raise the Philistine siege of Keilah (23:1–6). He acted as a king should, in defence of the realm. In the process, he completely upstaged Saul, who had, of course, let the people of Keilah shift for themselves. But he had also exposed his position so as to invite a search-and-destroy mission from the irate king.

1. Keilah – discovering God's will (23:7–13)
Saul wasted no time in going to Keilah when he heard that his rival was there. The prospect of bottling up David and his guerrillas in a walled city appealed to Saul far more than having to save his fellow-countrymen from the Philistine yoke. He even had the nerve to attribute his opportunity to the good providence of God! So he '**called up all his forces for battle, to go down to Keilah to besiege David and his men**' (23:7–8).

On hearing of this development, David promptly sought the Lord's will through the ministrations of Abiathar the priest, who was in possession of the high priestly ephod, which was employed in discerning God's will.[1] David had already heard that Saul intended to destroy Keilah just because he was there. The king had started at Nob in the manner he meant to continue! Any hint of assisting David would issue in the execution of a ban against any town or village. David also asked whether the inhabitants of Keilah would give him up to Saul. He fully understood the bleak prospects for these people if they did not dissociate themselves from him. The Lord's answer on both counts was in the affirmative (23:9–12).[2]

David and his men – now six hundred strong – withdrew from Keilah and '**kept moving from place to place**'. Saul, meanwhile, did not go down to Keilah (23:13). David had done nothing but good in both going to and departing from Keilah. He had been their deliverer – even in leaving them! It was with a sense of accomplishment and, more importantly, with an awareness of the favour of God towards them, that David and his men marched away from the scene of their first victory. 'He who fights and runs away, lives to fight another day.'

2. Ziph – encouragement and treachery (23:14–24)

No body of men as large as David's band could have sustained itself without the happy concurrence of the local population. The converse was true, as soon became apparent, for when the inhabitants were unsympathetic there was no alternative except to flee to a safer place. At first, however, the wilderness of Ziph seemed safe enough. David played 'hide and seek' with Saul in these hills for quite some time and Saul never touched him (23:14).

Jonathan, Saul's son, evidently did know how to find David, because one day he turned up in David's camp in the forest of Horesh (23:15–18). Jonathan came '**and helped him** [David] **to find strength in God**'. He encouraged David by reaffirming his conviction that the latter would be king. He knew that he himself would, at most, be '**second**' and he added that his father Saul was well aware that this was going to come to pass. They made a covenant together, no doubt in the terms of their earlier pact (18:3; 20:12–17), and then they parted, never to see one another again this side of eternity.

The quality of a man may be gauged by the quality of his friends and the depth of his friendships with them. David and Jonathan were men of the highest quality. Jonathan was the friend that stuck closer than a brother (Proverbs 18:24). The 'glue' was a shared fellowship in the love of God. 'Fellowship' is a much devalued word these days, even in Christian circles. It has come to be equated with a merely social camaraderie. We have 'fellowship meals' and 'times of fellowship' in modern church life, in which, it must be said, much of the 'fellowship' consists in light-hearted conversation on general subjects, with or without a definite spiritual and biblical content. Such times are helpful in getting to know people and in the fostering of a sense of oneness in the body of Christ. And it is certainly appropriate – and inevitable – that in such general social events involving a wide range of people and ages there should be happy Christian socializing. At that limited level, it is an expression of fellowship. But fellowship must be experienced at a much deeper and more personal level. True fellowship is the sharing, in terms of 'like precious faith' in the Lord Jesus Christ, of the interrelated experiences of tragedy and triumph as they arise in the course of the Christian life. David and Jonathan would have enjoyed the table-talk at many a feast and many a camp-fire, but their fellowship was forged in the serious things of life and in the interplay of testing times and the powerful influence of the Holy Spirit. Jonathan first covenanted to be David's friend as the latter came before Saul with the severed head of Goliath in his hand. Successive covenants between them arose in life-threatening situations and in a context where it truly cost Jonathan to be a friend to David. True fellowship is the sharing of our lives in Christ – believing the same truth, striving for the same holiness, bearing one another's burdens, rejoicing with those who rejoice and weeping with those who weep. David and Jonathan exemplify the depth of such spiritual bonds and offer a corrective to any tendency to reduce fellowship to a species of *bonhomie*.

'The treachery of the Ziphites forms a striking contrast to Jonathan's treatment of David.'[3] We are not given the reasons for their antipathy to David. Perhaps they simply saw no advantages in having a large band of men in the neighbourhood, especially since they would probably be called upon to provide them with the necessities of life! A person needs to be animated by solid convictions before being willing to sacrifice part of an already fairly modest standard of living – especially in favour of an outlaw! The Ziphites were clearly not persuaded that David was the man for them. So they undertook to deliver him into the hands of Saul (23:19–20). Saul was duly appreciative and sent them off to scout about for David's hiding-places (23:22–24).

3. Maon – providential deliverance (23:25–29)

When David heard that Saul was on the move against him, he retreated to the Desert of Maon, some eight miles south of Hebron (see map). The Ziphites did their work well, for Saul was closing in on David and seemed certain to capture him, when word came of a Philistine invasion and he '**broke off his pursuit of David and went to meet the Philistines**' (23:28). David had been saved by the providential hand of God! This was commemorated in the name given to that place of deliverance: Sela Hammahlekoth, the 'rock of smoothness,' i.e., of slipping away or escaping.[4] The wider events of history are also God's providences for individuals. He manipulates the activities of the wicked to honour his promises to believing people. How often we think fearfully about the future and its potential troubles! But the Lord is on the throne! And, in his infinite wisdom and power, he will effect the salvation of his people even through the kinds of events that might otherwise be seen as threatening.

David had every reason to be confident in the Lord. In Psalm 54 he expressed his reliance upon God in the face of the Ziphites' alliance with Saul:

> Surely God is my help;
>   the Lord is the one who sustains me.
> Let evil recoil on those who slander me;
>   in your faithfulness destroy them.
> I will sacrifice a freewill offering to you;
>   I will praise your name, O Lord,
>   for it is good.
> For he has delivered me from all my troubles,
>   and my eyes have looked in triumph on my foes'
> (Psalm 54:4–7).

David knew, says C. H. Spurgeon, 'that yet he should look on his haughty foes, gazing down on them in triumph as now they looked on him in contempt. He desired this as a matter of justice and not of personal pique. . . Could we keep out of our hearts all personal enmity as fully as the psalmist did in this Psalm, we might yet feel equally with him a sacred aquiescence and delight in that divine justice which will save the righteous and overthrow the ma-licious. . . let us trust that if we are as friendless as this man of God, we may resort to prayer as he did, exercise the like faith, and find ourselves ere long singing the same joyous hymn of praise.'[5] Even though obliged to flee to En Gedi near the Dead Sea shore (23:29), David was imbued with a steadfast assurance of his ultimate victory in the strength of the Lord.

The constraints of grace [24:1–15]

Almost immediately a situation arose which, on the face of it, presented David with a golden opportunity to take a short-cut to that anticipated triumph of the Lord. Saul, having disposed of the Philistine threat (23:27), took up the pursuit of David once again and moved with a force of 3,000 men to a place called the Crags of the Wild Goats (24:1–2). This is a limestone area and is riddled with caves wonder-fully suited to the concealment of bodies of men. In the providence of God, Saul turned aside into one of these caves in order to **'relieve himself'** (24:3; literally, 'to cover his feet' – a Hebrew euphemism equivalent to our 'spending a penny') and, lo and behold, David was hiding in that very cave!

1. David spares Saul's life (24:3–7)
There is an understandable tendency for us to leap at the opportunities – 'open doors' we call them – of God's providence, as if the opening up of a more or less obvious course of action implies that it must be the Lord's will. Favourable circumstances would seem to suggest the Lord's leading in that particular direction. And here was Saul, the mortal enemy, delivered 'on a platter', all alone in the cave

and totally unaware of his danger. Had not the Lord delivered him into David's hands? Had God not given David the opportunity to solve his problem with Saul? David's men thought so and suggested that it was the fulfilment of a particular promise from the Lord (24:4).[6]

David nevertheless resisted this advice. He did, however, sneak up on Saul and cut off a piece of his robe, which, presumably, had been thrown across a boulder on the cave floor. Even this action, which may seem little more than cheekiness to us, gave David pangs of conscience, for he realized that he had demeaned the royal dignity. Saul was still 'the Lord's anointed' (24:5–6). David therefore dissuaded his men from killing Saul and Saul picked up his robe and left (24:7).

The meaning of this incident, surely, is that God was testing David. In a sense it was the ultimate test of trust. And it turned out to be the triumph of right principle over clear – and providential – opportunity. The 'open door' was there. Many a modern Christian would point to these circumstances, say that 'Everything is working out' and that 'It seems to be the Lord's leading' that I take the indicated steps to secure the necessary solution to my problem. But an 'open door' is not, in itself, proof of God's will. Circumstances, in God's provi-dence, are not a substitute for the principles he has revealed in his Word, the Bible. The 'open door' is susceptible of serious misinterpretation. At most it is a trying of your faith – a means of making you think about the path of obedience to the Lord's will! How then can a course of action be decided upon? A.W. Pink wisely points us to the answer: 'An accurate knowledge of God's Word, a holy state of heart. . . a broken will, are absolutely essential in order to clearly discern the path of duty in important cases and crises. The safest plan is to deny all suggestions of revenge, covetousness, ambition and im-patience. A heart that is established in true godliness will rather interpret the dispensations of Providence as trials of faith and patience, as occasions to practise self-denial, than as opportunities for self-indulgence' (cf. Psalm 37:5–7; Isaiah 28:16).[7]

2. David proves his innocence (24:8–15)
The essayist Francis Bacon said that 'Revenge is a kind of wild

justice.' Getting our own back is in the blood of the human race. Retaliation is the reflex action of injured pride. And that is why it is such a shock when someone we have wronged responds with a serene and humble spirit. 'A gentle answer turns away wrath' (Proverbs 15:1). Why? Because it disarms the opposition. It removes any pretext for further wrangling. It embarrasses with kindness and creates a situation in which the other person's conscience cannot but be melted with a degree of shame unless, sadly, it has become so hardened as to brush off the conciliatory approach with contempt and unrepentant antagonism. Doing genuine good to an enemy 'will heap burning coals on his head,' says the writer of the proverb (Proverbs 25:22). These 'coals' hasten the refining of the raw ore. The goal is to overcome evil with good (Romans 12:21).

David provided for all time a beautiful model of the way in which the Lord's people ought to handle their vindication against injustice and injury. David heaped 'burning coals' upon the hapless Saul. No sooner had Saul emerged from the cave than he was hailed by David in the most respectful of terms. The recognition of that voice and the instant realization of how near he had come to eternity must have pierced Saul's heart like an arrow. But then to hear what David said! He pressed seven points upon his persecutor.

He declared his innocence of the charges falsely brought against him by those to whom Saul had listened (24:9).

He declared his commitment to principle, in that he had not raised his hand against the Lord's anointed (24:10).

He presented practical proof of the truth of his words by producing the portion of robe he had cut off in the cave (24:11).

He solemnly declared that judgement belonged to the Lord and indicated that he had no intention of exacting justice by his own hand in the future (24:12).

He appealed to his known personal history as a proof of his harmlessness to Saul and a confirmation of the veracity of his words (24:13).

He expressed true humility (24:14).

He cast himself upon the mercy of God (24:15).

David was constrained by the grace of God. And he won a gracious victory, beside which Saul's death in the cave

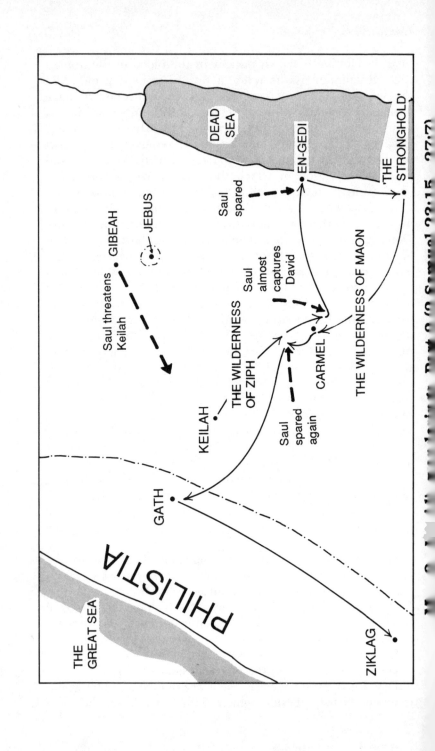

THE GREAT SEA

PHILISTIA

GATH

ZIKLAG

KEILAH

THE WILDERNESS OF ZIPH

Saul threatens Keilah

GIBEAH

JEBUS

Saul spared again

CARMEL

Saul almost captures David

THE WILDERNESS OF MAON

Saul spared

EN-GEDI

DEAD SEA

'THE STRONGHOLD'

would have been cheap indeed. 'He that is slow to anger is better than the mighty; and he that ruleth his spirit than he that taketh a city' (Proverbs 16:32 AV). The challenge this offers to the way we deal with friends and enemies alike is as searching as it is obvious. Consider David and imitate his faith! (Hebrews 13:7).

The reluctant realism of the reprobate [24:16–22]

As surely as David had heaped 'burning coals' upon Saul's head, so that unhappy sovereign melted with emotion and delivered the most sorrowful confession of his life. He greeted David as a son and **'wept aloud'**. He confessed that David was **'more righteous'** than he. He reflected on David's generosity in sparing him in such circumstances. He wished the blessing of God upon David for sparing his life. And, most significantly of all, he gave voice to the very thing that he had dreaded all along, that David would be king. Consequently, he requested that David undertake to spare his descendants and preserve his family name. David agreed and they went their separate ways. David had won a victory. . . for the moment.

Saul's confession was deeply emotional and it was profoundly revealing of what he knew in his heart of hearts to be true about both himself and David. Sorrow dripped from every word. The tears were real, the words sincere. It was Saul at his most candid, for the protective shell of lies and hatred had been largely stripped away by David's godly witness. None of it would last (26:1–6). And when this confession was repeated later, David certainly did not believe it trustworthy (see 26:21 – 27:1).

The point is that there is a difference between godly sorrow that 'brings repentance that leads to salvation and leaves no regrets' and worldly sorrow that 'brings death' (2 Corinthians 7:10). Saul's sorrow was of the worldly, unrepentant variety. It was the honesty of hell that made his tears flow. There is a reluctant realism in the reprobate lost, here and in hell. Lost sinners in hell know what lostness means. Their agony is only compounded by their undying hatred for the way of salvation in Jesus Christ. Their sorrow is real, but they have made a covenant with the very cause of that sorrow and are in agreement with Sheol (Isaiah 28:15). Saul could not bring himself to true repentance. He had set his face against the Lord. His confession, said Matthew Henry, 'was sufficient to prove David innocent, even his enemy himself being the judge; but not enough to prove Saul himself a true penitent. He should have said, "Thou art righteous, and I am wicked," but the most he will say is this, "Thou art more righteous than I."' David's grace-filled witness brought Saul as near to repentance and saving faith as a sinner can come without actually being converted. But for all the weeping and the recognition of the consequences of his spiritual state and manner of life, Saul was still committed to his own way. He was never evangelized more winsomely than by David on that day, but he held to his eternally suicidal course anyway.

The victory was won in David's heart and life and extended to the vanquishing of the evil planned by Saul. May the Lord work such gracious victories in our hearts and glorify his great name in the redemption of sinners and the vindication of his everlasting righteousness.

References

[1] W. H. Gispen, *Exodus*, (Grand Rapids: Zondervan, 1982), pp. 267–270, has an extensive and helpful discussion of Exodus 28:15–30, which describes the construction of 'the breastpiece for making decisions' used by the high priest in discerning the Lord's will. See also J. G. Murphy, *Commentary on the Book of Exodus*, (Minneapolis: James Publications, 1976 [1868]), pp. 315–319.

[2] Edersheim, p. 295, notes that the Lord answers the questions one at a time, even though David asked both together at first (23:11). Edersheim says this is significant, without saying what the significance was. Keil and Delitzsch, pp. 229–230, see this as related to the way the Urim and the Thummim worked – that this means of arriving at a decision could only give one answer at a time. W. H. Gispen, p. 267, notes speculation that the Urim and Thummim were stones that gave either a 'yes' or a 'no' answer. J. G. Murphy, p. 317, sees the Urim and Thummim as all twelve precious stones mounted on the breast-piece and views their use as no more than a symbolic wearing of the breast-piece in the act of praying for guidance before the Lord and rejects any idea that stones moved or lit up to give answers to these enquiries (p. 318). Murphy, correctly I believe, keeps the focus on the symbolic sacramental significance of the breast-piece and says that the Lord conveyed his will by means of audible and

other means – but not magic and the movement of stones.

[3] C. F. Keil and F. Delitzsch, p. 231.

[4] *Ibid.*, p. 233.

[5] C. H. Spurgeon, *The Treasury of David*, Vol. III, p. 10.

[6] No such promise is recorded in Scripture. It could either have been an otherwise unrecorded oracle from the prophet Gad (Klein, p. 239), a complete fabrication to impel David to action (Gordon, p. 179), or an interpretation of known assurances from God that David would triumph over his enemies (Keil and Delitzsch, p. 235). The only sure thing is that they wanted Saul dead!

[7] A.W. Pink, p. 116.

22.

A rose between two thorns

Please read 1 Samuel 25:1–44

'David said to Abigail, "Praise be to the Lord, the God of Israel, who has sent you today to meet me. May you be blest for your good judgement and for keeping me from bloodshed this day and from avenging myself with my own hands"' (1 Samuel 25:32–33).

In the closing days of British rule in India, the leader of India's Moslems, later to be the founder of Pakistan, Mohammed Ali Jinnah, was invited to meet the viceroy, Lord Louis Mountbatten. Jinnah was, by all accounts, a stiff and formal individual. He knew that he would be involved in a photo session with Lord and Lady Mountbatten. He expected that Lady Mountbatten would be in the centre with the viceroy and himself on either side. So he prepared a little speech to mark this moment – a remark that he thought would be appropriate. When the time came for the photo, however, Lady Mountbatten did not stand in the centre – she slipped round to Jinnah's left, so that he was in the middle, a Mountbatten on each flank. But poor Jinnah had decided on his speech and out it came anyway, one of the greatest 'howlers' of international politics: "Ah," he said beaming, "a rose between two thorns!"[1]

As the incident involving David, Nabal – a wealthy farmer – and Abigail – Nabal's wife – indicates, David would not have perpetrated such a *faux pas*. He knew that the men were the thorns and the intelligent and beautiful Abigail was truly a rose! The gist of the story is that David sent ten young men to Nabal on what was evidently the Hebrew equivalent of a fund-raising drive! Nabal insulted them and sent them away empty-handed. When David heard of this, he reacted angrily and set off with 400 of his men to exact retribution. Abigail, meanwhile, had been informed of her husband's rude rebuff of David's men and, at the pleading of her servant, set off to intercept David and, she hoped, head off the disaster that was looming for Nabal and his household. She succeeded in her quest and even drew from David an acknowledgement of her good judgement and an implicit recognition that he would have been wrong to kill Nabal. Later, when Nabal found out how his wife had saved him from catastrophe, he was terrified, went into a coma and in ten days was dead. Abigail subsequently became David's wife and forsook the comforts of home for a fugitive's life with her new husband.

This incident, as we shall see, is related to the accounts of both episodes in which David forbore to take the life of King Saul when he had clear opportunity to do so (24:1–22; 26:1–25). The central theme throughout all three events is that God is the avenger and vindicator of injustices perpetrated against his people. 'David learns that, if he withholds the avenging sword, God will act on his behalf.'[2]

We should note that the inspired historian records the death and burial of Samuel (25:1). This quiet insertion marked a point of no return for David, Saul and Israel. Although Samuel had long before 'abdicated' his judgeship in favour of the rule of Saul as king (12:1–25), he had continued to exercise a crucial role in Israel as the premier prophet of God. The afterglow of the old Hebrew republic lingered on in Samuel's person and ministry and with it, perhaps, the notional possibility of some remarkable resolution of the problems emerging with the monarchy under Saul and the rift between David and Saul. Samuel's death was the end of an era.

Two wrongs don't make a right [25:2–13]

It was essential to David and his men that they have the support of a sympathetic population. No body of 600 men and many more camp-followers (see 27:2–3) could hope to sustain itself without the practical assistance of the local farmers. It would have been fatal to David's cause had he acted like a brigand chief and lived off the fat of the land by coercion and pillage. If good relations were to be maintained there had to be a *quid pro quo* for such succour as he received. What David offered in return for their material support was protection (25:15–16). He did not offer a 'protection racket', in which he undertook not to inflict loss upon those who paid him a suitable bribe. He acted as a true king for his people, in that he, as Nabal's servant testified, was '**a wall**' around the shepherds and their flocks '**night and day**'. His supporters would, however, have to weigh the risks of aiding a man who could offer no defence should Saul decide to vent his spleen on them as he had on the priests at Nob!

1. Nabal's insult (25:2–11)

Nabal lived up to his name, which means literally, 'a fool'. He was not a fool in the conventional sense of the term, for he had everything that this world had to offer – wealth, influence and a beautiful wife. But in terms of God's definition of a fool, he certainly was one. It may be true that 'A fool and his money are easily parted.' But Nabal was not an idiot to be gulled into making himself a pauper. He was a 'rich fool' like the fellow in Jesus' parable – he stored up things for himself but was not rich towards God (Luke 12:13–21).

His foolishness – like all true foolishness – concerns his relationship to the Lord. All sin is sheer foolishness, for it is the contradiction of God. The way he dealt with David was foolish at the obvious level that it is not prudent to insult a man who has the power to do you great harm. But he was foolish at the deeper level of offending God through rejecting his servant in a contemptuous and uncaring manner. David had been kind to Nabal, for all that it was unsolicited. At the very least, he could expect common courtesy. As the Lord's anointed, and a well-known national figure with an unimpeachable personal history, he was entitled to some respect, if not indeed the assistance of his brethren, the Lord's people!

Nabal may have been a descendant of godly Caleb (25:3), but he shared none of his spirit. He dismissed David's embassy with utter contempt. He characterized David as a runaway servant and betrayed not the slightest perception of his exalted calling and destiny (25:10–11).

2. David's over-reaction (25:12–13)

David's men were humble and restrained. Not so their leader! David was incensed by Nabal's insulting rebuff and decided to exact an entirely disproportionate revenge by descending upon Nabal with 400 armed men with the purpose of killing him and all the males in the household. He aimed, in other words, to remove Nabal's name from the face of the earth! (25:33). For one insult, rivers of blood were to flow! This was the complete triumph of unsanctified temper over the claims of God's grace. Why did David succumb to such unbridled anger? Bear in mind that this was the same man who, shortly before, had refused a golden opportunity to kill Saul – a man who had made repeated attempts on his life in the past and was set to try again in the future! Why be so kind to Saul and so ferocious towards Nabal? How could he overcome Saul's evil with good, but be completely overcome by evil in the face of Nabal's insult? Had he forgotten that two wrongs don't make a right?

The answer may be related to David's differing expectations of these men. From Saul, he expected hostility and was, in a sense, inured to it. He had come to terms with Saul's attitude and saw clearly how God wanted him to respond to it. By the grace of God, and not without many struggles, he had been enabled to respond to the threat from Saul in a God-honouring manner. But from Nabal he expected a friendly response. After all, he had done nothing to provoke him or give him any cause to be abusive. So when that unprovoked insult came from Nabal it came as a nasty surprise. And it is nasty surprises that always tend to raise the hackles and give occasion for the temptation to over-react. We are vulnerable at such moments, not only to the flushes of our own sinfulness but to the influences of demonic suggestion. Hence the prayer that our Lord taught us: 'Lead us not into temptation, but deliver us from evil.'

This teaches us that without the upholding power of the Holy Spirit and the deliberate and diligent exercise of a faith that looks to the Lord before leaping into action, we

shall soon fall into sin and begin to reap its evil consequences. David would be reminded by this failure that he
still needed the saving hand of God to keep him from
falling. Salvation from sin is an ongoing experience of the
grace of God in Christ, as he applies the benefits of Jesus'
once-for-all sacrifice for sin in the lives of his believing
people.

We are also taught that past successes do not prevent
future failures. 'Ups' in life are often followed very quickly
by 'downs'. The football team that convincingly beat good
opposition last week can itself be humbled this week by the
team at the bottom of the league. Our worst sins sometimes
follow on the heels of our greatest spiritual victories! Why?
'Because,' as A.W. Pink suggests, 'we are less conscious of
our need of God's delivering grace. Peter was bold before
the soldiers in the Garden, but became fearful in the
presence of a maid.'[3]

This also sheds light on why we are sometimes 'softer' on
our enemies than we are on our friends. We expect more of
our friends than we do of our enemies. Disagreement
between friends is a test of friendship and it is one that is
frequently failed. That is why divisions in otherwise doc-
trinally and practically close fellowships can be so intense,
even when very small points of difference are involved.
What a need we have for consistent holiness before the
Lord! Let us learn from David's mistake with Nabal and
grow up in Christ to the full stature of mature Christian
discipleship!

A woman who fears the Lord [25:14–31]

'Charm is deceptive, and beauty is fleeting; but a woman
who fears the Lord is to be praised' (Proverbs 31:30). The
myth that women were regarded as little better than goods
and chattels in the Old Testament period is thoroughly
exploded by the history of Abigail, the worthy wife of
worthless Nabal. Here was the kind of woman that the
writer of Proverbs 31:10–31 had in mind, when he penned
that most memorable passage. Abigail, like the wife of
Proverbs 31, feared the Lord and was also charming and

beautiful. And she put all her gifts to good use to turn back the tide of David's wrath before it broke upon the house of her obnoxious husband. She was indeed the rose between two thorns.

1. Informed by a servant (25:14–17)
The servant who informed Abigail of Nabal's snub of David spoke with a frankness born of both desperation and long acquaintance with his master's boorishness. Clearly, he had a high regard for Abigail and, equally clearly, she had long recognized that her husband was, as the servant said so openly, '**such a wicked man that no one can talk to him**' (25:17). Abigail looks like the competent wife who had been called upon before to rectify some of her husband's pig-headedness. Men like that rarely know how much they owe to the faithfulness of their wives.

2. Sending a gift (25:18–19)
Abigail needed no convincing and she wasted no time. She assembled a generous gift of food and drink and sent it on ahead with her servants, thus emulating the procedure adopted by Jacob when Esau and his 400 men were approaching, also with a reckoning in view (Genesis 32:6–21; 33:11–12). Then she set out to meet David. Needless to say, she did not discuss the matter with her husband. Wifely submissiveness does not extend to initiating fruitless arguments, still less to potentially suicidal delay.

3. Meeting with David (25:20–31)
The meeting between David and Abigail is clothed with divine irony. Just before they met in '**a mountain ravine**', David had been complaining about Nabal and had solemnly foresworn himself to kill every *male* in Nabal's household (25:20–22). Then, lo and behold, he was confronted by a *female* from that selfsame quarter! So the Lord arranged that his initial contact would be with someone he would have to listen to (a woman) rather than someone he had sworn to put to the sword (any male connected with Nabal)! The Lord had employed Abigail to waylay David's vindictive vow in that lonely ravine and bring him to a change of heart!

Abigail's address to David was a brilliant spiritual *tour de force*. It was 'a masterpiece reflecting feminine charm, wisdom and grace'.[4] There is an unmistakable sense of the presence of the Spirit of God in everything she said and did in this remarkable interview. She was a lady of high spiritual quality – a fact that was not lost on David, as subsequent events were to prove (see 25:39). Note the three components of her appeal for David's clemency towards her husband.

Firstly, she humbly took the blame and appealed for a hearing (25:23–25). She frankly admitted the folly of Nabal – '**His name is fool, and folly goes with him**' – and indicated that things would have been different had she been there when David's emissaries met with her husband. This form of blame-taking is regarded by some scholars as a 'conventional way of initiating a conversation with a superior' with the guilt referring to 'anything. . . blameworthy in the ensuing interview'.[5] This turns the flow of the text on its head, however, for there is no reason to believe that Abigail was not reflecting a genuine influence she might have had upon her husband had she been present to nip his surliness in the bud. If she said she felt she was to blame, then let her be taken at her word.

Secondly, she made restitution in kind to David, by presenting the kind of gift which the young men had requested in the first place – perhaps even more ample than their open-ended but modest request (see 25:8). And she sought forgiveness for Nabal's insult (25:27–28). The linking of restitution and forgiveness is highly significant. Today, it is commonly assumed that forgiveness is a purely mental adjustment in the mind of God. This is an all too common and very serious error. People think saying 'Sorry' almost bestows a right to be forgiven! In the Bible, however, forgiveness and restitution are always inextricably and inseparably linked (see Exodus 22:1–17).[6] Restitution, with the goal of accomplishing salvation for sinners, was the reason for the death of Christ as the substitutionary atoning sacrifice for sin. God did not just 'forget it' – he exacted the full and absolutely necessary penalty for sin required by his perfect law. In seeking forgiveness, the element of restitution must be present, because only in this way is it possible to make good the actual loss brought about by the sin in question. If you steal a car, it is not enough to say sorry and return it as if nothing happened. Damages appropriate to the loss are to be paid. The victim is entitled to more than the return of his property plus some warm thoughts about forgiveness. He must be compensated for losses incurred. The criminal, on the other hand, must realize the practical consequences of his victimization of the other party and be required to make proper restitution.

Thirdly, she acknowledged David as the rightful king of Israel (25:28–31). He would have '**a lasting dynasty**' for he '**fights the Lord's battles**'. However great the efforts of his persecutors, his life would be '**bound securely in the bundle of the living by the Lord**'. And when he was king, she suggested, he would not want to have on his conscience '**the staggering burden of needless bloodshed or of having avenged himself**'. Finally, she asked that when the Lord brought him success, he would remember her.

What made this appeal so powerful was the connection Abigail made between the Lord's purposes and David's personal interests. God's way is the happiest way for his people. What is in the Lord's interest is in our interest, simply because he loves us with an everlasting love. Abigail raised David's eyes from his hurt pride and set them on the glorious panorama of God's loving purposes for his life.

Two practical points are to the fore in Abigail's presentation.

The first is that God is the avenger of injustice. This was the lesson David had learned when he could have killed Saul in the cave, but did not (24:12). This was the lesson he had so quickly forgotten in his reaction to Nabal's insult.

The second is that to destroy Nabal's household would have destroyed his peace of mind and his personal integrity. His standing as the Lord's king would not have been enhanced by such an action. Indeed, he would have shown himself to be little different from Saul. He would only have been sacrificing his subjects on the altar of unhallowed pride.

Praise be to the Lord! [25:32–44]

The sweetest victories are always snatched from the jaws of defeat. But no one in his right mind would ever deliberately

choose such a course. In the Christian life, we would be
blessed indeed to go from day to day in the full enjoyment of
a quiet and truly God-honouring life, without trials and
tribulations disturbing our progress. We have every warrant
to pray for and aspire to just such a life – one of victory in
Jesus Christ our Lord. Jesus did not, however, promise his
followers a rose garden. In the world we shall have tribulations. We have to battle with the remaining power of sin in
our own lives and are involved in the cosmic conflict of the
powers of darkness and the power of God. But the Lord has
promised that he will perfect his strength in our weakness
and that we shall gain the crown of life through overcoming,
in the one who has overcome the world. We cannot be 'more
than conquerors' without engaging in the kind of costly
spiritual conflict that prevails against the most ferocious
opposition. Such victories are sweet because of the manner
of their accomplishment: that is to say, because of the
overwhelming sense of the presence of the saving grace and
power of the Lord for our redemption – full, free, unmerited,
sovereignly gracious salvation through the once-for-all sacrificial death of Christ for the sins of the world. Such a faith
exultantly shouts, 'Praise be to the Lord!' and glories in the
marvellous goodness of God. Such was David's praise! And
such is the praise of all the Lord's faithful people!

1. Praise the Lord for wise counsel! (25:32–35)
David praised God for Abigail's wise counsel. If we are to
consider it a 'woe', when all men speak well of us (Luke
6:26), we should count it a blessing when someone loves us
enough to tell us the truth. David was not slow to recognize
the hand of God in his encounter with Abigail.

Firstly, he saw that it was the work of God (25:32). If
when we confess sin, we are to see it primarily as sin against
God, whatever its effects on those people against whom we
have sinned (Psalm 51:4), it is equally the case that all
kindness, irrespective of its immediate source, is to be seen
as the blessing of God, and he is to be thanked accordingly
(James 1:17). God had something to say to David – and
Abigail was his ambassador. And David realized that it was
God who was dealing with him, albeit through the witness of
Abigail.

Secondly, he deeply appreciated her and, therefore, invoked God's blessing upon her (25:33). It is always '**good judgement**' to minister faithfully to anyone. The truth spoken in love is not always appreciated for the privilege and blessing that it is. But David knew how much courage and discernment it took for Abigail to act as she did. And he commended her and prayed for her blessing in the future.

Thirdly, he acknowledged that she had been the means of his deliverance from committing a terrible deed (25:33–34). She had both saved lives and kept him from a tragic sin, that of avenging himself with his own hand. God's redeeming purpose had touched his soul in a fresh and living way.

2. Praise the Lord for upholding his people! (25:36–39)
Nabal had been oblivious to both the threat of disaster and the successful efforts of his wife to avert it – in more ways than one, as it happened. He, who was willing to let the real king starve, had been feasting like a king and became '**very drunk**'. Next day, after he had sobered up, Abigail told him the whole story. The shock was too much for Nabal: '**His heart failed him and he became like a stone**' and ten days later '**The Lord struck him**' and he died.

The fact that it was evidently the judgement of God upon Nabal was a confirmation that vengeance does, indeed, belong to the Lord. The justice of God, rather than the injustice of David's displeasure, settled with the sins of that wicked man. David therefore gave thanks to God for upholding his cause of offence against Nabal and also for keeping him from the wrong of taking the law into his own hands. It is significant that the Lord is said to have '**brought Nabal's wrongdoing down on his own head**'. God's acts of judgement seal the self-destructive effects of sin. Death is but the wages of sin for which the sinner is wholly responsible.

3. Praise the Lord for godly wives! (25:39–44)
Abigail had become an eligible widow. David wasted no time in proposing marriage and she accepted with suitable dignity and decorum. He also took another wife, Ahinoam of Jezreel, in keeping with the polygamous custom of the time, although not in accord with a proper understanding of the

Word of God. Saul had, meanwhile, married off Michal, David's wife and his own daughter, to another man – an indication both of his obsessive hatred for David and his total disregard for the law of God.

David surely praised the Lord for the day he met Abigail and for the fact that she later became his wife. She had proved her godliness in her earlier counsel to him. She confirmed that in the self-sacrificial way in which she followed him from her comfortable life at Carmel to life on the run in the wilderness of Judea!

These events – David's marriage and the 'divorce' of Michal – sealed the separation between Saul and David. But David had received further confirmations of the blessing of the Lord.

The Lord has given us all a million reasons for praising him! Even the difficult experiences of our life give cause to thank him. And all the obvious blessings can only multiply that refrain. The unconverted turn their backs on the Lord. They reject him as the source of their blessings and will often blame him for their set-backs. But the Christian knows that his life is hidden with Christ in God (Colossians 3:3). The Christian praises God for his whole life, for it is the unfolding of God's redeeming love towards him.

References

[1] L. Collins and D. Lapierre, *Freedom at Midnight*, (New York: Avon Books, 1976), p. 119.
[2] R. P. Gordon, p. 181.
[3] A. W. Pink, pp. 135–136.
[4] J. C. Laney, p. 74.
[5] R. P. Gordon, p. 184.
[6] For an excellent exposition of this theme see R. J. Rushdoony, *The Institutes of Biblical Law*, pp. 458–463.

23.
Playing the fool

Please read 1 Samuel 26:1–27:12

'Then Saul said, "I have sinned. Come back, David my son. Because you considered my life precious today, I will not try to harm you again. Surely I have acted like a fool and erred greatly"' (1 Samuel 26:21).

Only a real fool will claim he has never done foolish things in the course of his life. We have all felt like kicking ourselves over things we have done in the past. And the older – and ostensibly wiser – we become, the greater will be our sensitivity to human folly – our own and that of others. This, at any rate, is the theory.

In practice, foolishness – or, to use Saul's expression, 'acting like a fool' or 'playing the fool' (AV) – has been viewed with a degree of ambivalence. A fool is sometimes merely an object of fun, even of endearing fun. Hence the courts of kings used to have 'court jesters' or 'fools,' whose often self-deprecating inanities were a source of merriment to their masters. Such professional tomfoolery has always been a sub-division of the entertainment industry. At the same time, the word 'fool' has been reserved for the most bitter ridicule of the real or imagined inadequacies of those who have had the misfortune to fall under the contempt of intemperate critics. Occasionally these two categories of usage come together in the one person. Today, for example, people in the street will laugh at the antics of a drunk and, outwardly at least, treat his inebriation as a fount of mirth and even entertainment. But, at one and the same time, these bystanders can also be feeling that the drunk is a real fool for getting himself into such a wretched state. There is a tragi-comic air about the whole thing – but when the comedy is over the tragedy is always left. And in our heart of hearts, we know very well that there is nothing essentially humorous about a man who is only 'funny' because, through alcohol abuse, he is killing his brain and shattering his life (and perhaps the lives of many others). Tragedy and comedy are, indeed, separated by a fine line in our perception. 'Black humour' erases that line in rendering the tragic as an object of fun, but it does not alleviate the tragedy one whit. Foolishness, however, inevitably has a deeper layer of sad calamity, marching inexorably to a final crash. To respond to it with nothing better than a laugh is, at least, thoughtless insensitivity and, at worst, the cruel cynicism of hell itself.

In the Word of God, there is no ambiguity about the character of fools. The Lord's definition of the fool is a world away from conventional ideas of bumbling oafishness or amiable stupidity. The heart of biblical foolishness is the rejection of God and his Word. The fool says in his heart, 'There is no God' (Psalm 14:1). Fools despise wisdom and instruction (Proverbs 1:7). Those who turn to the worship of idols are fools (Romans 1:22). Calling someone a fool (Greek, *moros*, hence English, 'moron') is therefore viewed as a very serious business, not to be engaged in lightly (Matthew 5:22). Yet Paul could call himself a *moros* for the sake of Christ and so indicate the antithesis between the world and the gospel. To be regarded as a 'fool' in the world's eyes because of devotion to the Lord shows us two things: firstly, how far the world has turned God's definitions of wisdom and foolishness on their heads and, secondly, how inevitably radical true Christian witness must be in a world that is opposed to God.

Sin is foolishness. Spiritual blindness is the currency of fools. And wherever we are touched by personal sin or influenced by spiritual darkness, this foolishness casts its shadows across the soul. In 1 Samuel 26 and 27, we see how this can happen in the lives of both believer and unbeliever. Saul gives voice to the words which form a theme for these two chapters: '**Behold, I have played the fool and have erred exceedingly**' (26:21 AV). Saul was indeed a fool. He did not, however, believe that enough to change his ways. David, full of grace in his encounter with Saul, then lost his spiritual composure and played the fool by fleeing once more to Achish, the Philistine King of Gath! Foolishness, like crime, knows no frontiers! It is the native air of the lost sinner – in the biblical sense, he is a fool by nature. But it clings to the choicest of believers – as a clammy morning mist envelops and holds back the beauty of a summer day – until the sun of righteousness rises with healing in its wings (Malachi 4:2) and burns off these foggy tentacles of sin.

The unbelieving fool – Saul [26:1–25]

History almost repeated itself on this second occasion in which Saul's life was spared by the man he had been seeking to kill. For a second time, the Ziphites had informed Saul of David's whereabouts. The king set out with his army of 3,000 men and began to search that general area. David, however, was always one jump ahead of him: '**He sent out scouts and learned that Saul had definitely arrived**' (26:1–4). What followed showed David to be full of grace and Saul to be an unbelieving fool.

1. Sparing Saul's life (26:5–12)
Having seen for himself where Saul had camped, David decided to take a closer look. He asked two of his men – Ahimelech the Hittite and his nephew Abishai – for someone to accompany him on a night patrol into Saul's lines.[1] Abishai volunteered and David and he went off to Saul's camp. They were able to penetrate the very heart of the camp, where Saul lay asleep surrounded by his soldiers, because the Lord had put everyone, the sentries included. '**into a deep sleep**' (26:12).[2]

Abishai, quite understandably in the circumstances, saw this as a God-given opportunity to dispose of Saul once and for all: '**Today God has delivered your enemy into your hands. Now let me pin him to the ground with one thrust of my spear: I won't strike him twice**' (26:8). One commentator remarks that Abishai 'offers to do David's dirty work for him'.[3] There is no need to impugn his motives in this way, although one may question his discernment. Once again, we have a clear example of the essential ambiguity of the 'open door' of providential circumstances. If opportunity is automatically a mandate to act, then what need have we of principles? If the 'open door', *per se*, is equivalent to the will of God, then opportunism is holiness, irrespective of the nature or consequences of the act itself. Even a committed anarchist would blanch at such a philosophy. Even he sees the need of applying intelligence to the twists and turns of circumstance! The Christian should be the last person in the world to bow to any kind of opportunism – the last person to deal with providential occurrences in abstraction from the Word of God and the leading of the Holy Spirit into that truth.

David, however, had thought through this matter before and, under the leading of the Spirit of God, was persuaded that he could not touch the anointed King of Israel. And so he restrained Abishai and assured him that the Lord would deal with Saul: '**Either his time will come and he will die, or he will go into battle and perish. But the Lord forbid that I should lay a hand on the Lord's anointed**' (26:10, 11). Instead, they took Saul's spear and water jug and returned to their own lines in the hills above the camp. The principle that motivated David finds its echoes elsewhere in the Scriptures in the respect which is to be shown to civil government. We are to fear God and honour the king. We are to pray for princes and those in authority. We are to recognize that God has instituted civil government and it is to be obeyed. There is no divine sanction for assassination or regicide; or even for the removal, by violent revolution, of an unjust and oppressive tyranny.[4]

2. Challenging Abner (26:13–16)
From the safety of an adjacent crag, David called to Abner, the general commanding Saul's army. His words suggest that repeated calls had failed to rouse Abner from his slumbers: '**Aren't you going to answer me, Abner?**' (26:14). It seems unlikely that Abner did not suspect that it was David who called to him. His reply, '**Who are you who calls to the king?**' drips with anger and contempt against David, who had, after all, made light of Saul's power before

this (26:14). David, certainly, did not let him off the hook. He taunted him with the charge that, for all his accomplishments, he could not protect his master. '**Look around you**,' he asked, '**Where are the king's spear and water jug that were near his head?**' (26:16). This was no mere impudence. It was proof positive of two profound realities: the first, that God had cast his protective power around David to preserve him from Saul and, in addition, had rendered Saul helpless to defend himself; and the second, that David was innocent of all the charges laid against him by that unhappy monarch. David had spared Saul again and God had vindicated his cause.

3. Remonstrating with Saul (26:17–20)
Saul had, meanwhile, recognized David's voice (cf. 24:16) and took over the conversation from Abner. As on the earlier occasion, David offered a humble remonstrance to the king. He made three main points.

Firstly, he *pleaded his innocence* of any wrongdoing towards him, in terms which recognized the king's authority (26:17–18).

Secondly, he *threw himself upon the mercy of the Lord* [26:19). He proposed two theoretical alternatives to Saul.

Suppose, on the one hand, he (David) really was guilty of an offence against Saul and '**the Lord [had] incited**' Saul against him. In that case, the Lord might '**accept an offering**' (26:19). Should not the king, by implication, encourage him to make such an offering for sin and accept that as a resolution of the matter?

On the other hand, if he were innocent, and '**men**' had '**done it**', then they should be punished, for they were driving David away from his '**share in the Lord's inheritance**' and saying to him, in effect, '**Go, serve other gods.**'

Surely, he was saying to Saul, the answer is to lay the matter before the Lord? This David was willing to do. David was therefore saying, in effect, 'How do you respond to this, Saul?'

Thirdly, David *appealed to the king's conscience* (26:20). Surely the king would not wish to let him die in exile? '**Now do not let my blood fall to the ground far from the presence of the Lord.**' And he wondered if he – a mere 'flea' or a **'partridge in the mountains'** – were not beneath the king's dignity and unworthy of his attentions. Allowing for the flowery language of oriental formal address, there is here a genuine expression of David's humility before Saul. He was not a personal threat to Saul. It was the Lord, as Saul well knew, who was going to take the kingdom from him. It was rebellion against heaven which led Saul to scour the hills of Judea to do the impossible – thwart the will of the Lord!

4. Saul's confession (26:21–25)

Saul was totally disarmed by David's self-effacing generosity in sparing him once more and, not least, by his palpable righteousness. The world is more sensitive to genuine holiness than it cares to admit. And hostility gives way to wistful admiration, in the face of humble believing kindness. Saul felt suddenly dirty before David's gracious witness. He could see that David was a man of principle, whereas he knew that he was not. So, as he had on the earlier occasion in the cave (24:17), he confessed himself to be a sinner and admitted, 'I have acted like a fool, and have erred greatly.' He asked David to come back to his court and promised not to try to harm him in the future.

David was not taken in by this sudden *volte-face*. He had been at this place before. And however sincere Saul was today, he could not be trusted for tomorrow. David's response was simple, symbolic and spiritually submissive. David simply **'went on his way'**. He did this last in chronological order, but logically it was his fundamental response to Saul's confessed desire for reconciliation. He just did not believe he could trust Saul's word.

He parted, however, with a symbolic action – the return of Saul's spear, perhaps the very weapon which the king had thrown at him in the palace so long ago. It was as if David said to him, 'Here is the symbol of my faithfulness and your perfidy. Let us now see what you will do with it, once it is back in your hand. Will you keep your word, or will you again raise it against me?'

Finally, David expressed spiritual submission to the Lord as his guarantor and security: '**As surely as I valued your life today, so may the Lord value my life and deliver me**

from all trouble.' He put his trust neither in princes nor in the arm of the flesh – he waited for the Lord (Psalm 146:3; 40:1).

Saul was left to utter a rueful acknowledgement of David's future blessing and go on his way to his home (26:25). The two men would never meet again. David would flee the country and, in a little more than a year, Saul would be dead by his own hand on the battlefield of Mount Gilboa. His awareness of the truth of God did not change him. He was committed to his own way. Another moment of potential repentance and reformation had gone by and, in spite of his fine words, he had hardened his heart again. He was not only an unbelieving fool, he was a reprobate unbelieving fool. He was on a roller-coaster to hell. Like the boy who thought he could fly like Superman and jumped out of a third-storey window only to realize the truth that he was falling like a stone, Saul could do nothing to retrieve his situation. His face was set against the Lord. He gritted his teeth and held his course towards its bitter end. He loved his sins more than his soul, more than the truth, more than the Lord. This is the invariable path of the biblical 'fool'. Ignorance is the least of his problems. He knows more of the truth than he can bear to think about. He just hates it! That is the tragedy of the unbelieving fool. From the depth of his being he denies the obvious and clings to his lie: he will be **'like God, knowing good and evil'** (Genesis 3:5). He goes on in rebellion. . . but he also knows that he is doomed.

There are some important lessons here for Christians today.

First of all, notice that David kept the focus upon the claims of God's truth. In appealing to Saul he was in fact appealing to the justice of God! It was a God-centred testimony. He spoke of righteous principle, guilt before God, offerings for sin, and thus of forgiveness, of divine justice, the inheritance of God's people in the land and the curse of serving false gods. David took the problem to the foot of God's throne and laid it out in terms of obeying the Lord's will. And because of that spiritual emphasis, David backed Saul's conscience into a corner and obliged him to face the issues. Saul had either to agree with David or publicly reject God. Had David merely protested his innocence in a grieved and defensive tone and moaned about how nasty Saul had been to him, he would have given Saul a wonderful opportunity to snipe back at him. Why? Because in that case, the argument would be seen as no more than an exchange of contrary opinions arising from selfish motives. But as soon as he appealed to the Lord and his revealed will for dealing with sin, David moved the discussion to a higher plane altogether. The Lord, and not a mere matter of clash of personalities or individual disagreement, became the touchstone of all that he was saying. David left 'personalities' out of it; he did not pour out a litany of self-pitying woes and he did not try to put Saul in the poorest possible light by heaping up all sorts of arguments to prove his bad motives and unholy actions. He went straight to the claims of God. He was ready to submit to the scrutiny of the Lord – and he set that challenge before Saul.

Secondly, notice that David maintained a gentle and loving attitude towards his enemy. Too often, Christians under criticism – whether just or unjust, it does not matter – attack their critics like tigers. Disagreements in the church can be every bit as fierce and vicious in tone and tactics as anything in the non-Christian world. Why? Because the exercise of true faith is the radical contradiction of every natural impulse. It takes personal holiness – lively faith in earnest exercise – to believe that a soft answer turns away wrath. It takes faith overcoming the impulse of nature to do good to those who insult and persecute us and to exercise love towards our enemies (Matthew 5:11–12, 43–48). This does not rule out firmness in stating the truth – but it does mean a genuinely positive attitude. The crowning example of this was, of course, that of the Lord Jesus Christ, who wept for his enemies and was quietly submissive to his Father in the face of his tormentors and murderers.

Thirdly, notice that David prayed expectantly for the blessing of God in submitting to his will: '**As surely as I valued your life today, so may the Lord value my life and deliver me from all trouble**' (26:24). You will never distance yourself from sin until and unless you draw close to the Lord. Looking to him is looking to his nearness and blessing as we order our lives before him in loving obedience to his will. 'By faith,' Moses left Egypt and 'regarded disgrace for the sake of Christ as of greater value than the treasures of Egypt, because he was looking ahead to his reward' (Hebrews 11:26).

The foolish believer – David [27:1–12]

David had no confidence that Saul would leave him alone. However great his moral victories over Saul had been – and he did not discount the fact that the Lord had been with him through these incidents – they were tarnished by the realization that they were not likely to have any lasting effect. Saul would soon be on the hunt for him again.

Still, the Lord had preserved him up to that point and the evidence had piled up over the months and years that the promises of God were being powerfully fulfilled in his life. His confidence would be in the Lord, let Saul rage and the heavens fall!

But something cracked in David's mind and from the heights of moral victory over Saul he plunged into doubts that were to set him for a second time upon the road to Gath and refuge with his enemies, the Philistines. This transformation – between 26:25 and 27:1 – would shock us, were it not so much a recurrent feature of our own Christian experience. David practically gave up the struggle at a point where all the hard evidence indicated impending victory. . . at a point which, we know with the hindsight of Scripture, was very close to the final deliverance for which he fervently longed. How could he repeat his earlier error of leaving Israel for an illegitimate and illusory sanctuary with the Philistines? Why did he abandon what he knew to be the will of God – that as yet unrevoked word through the prophet Gad some time before, 'Go into the land of Judah' (22:5) – and try again the failed solution of earlier backslidings? Why is David the one who now 'plays the fool'?

1. The decision (27:1)
'But David thought to himself, "One of these days I shall be destroyed by the hand of Saul. The best thing I can do is to escape to the land of the Philistines. Then Saul will give up searching for me anywhere in Israel, and I will

slip out of his hand."' This succinct account of David's
thinking points us to the reasons for his sudden turn-about.

Firstly, David was a man. He was subject to human
frailty, physical and spiritual. Sin is always at the door.
With his eyes, he could see Saul's army march off. He could
easily imagine it marching back in a week or two. It took the
constant exercise of unwavering faith to see the promises of
God and the protective cover of his angels. It also took
vigilance and physical endurance to sustain body and soul
for himself and his followers in these rugged Judean hills.
David was probably very weary and just gasping for some
respite. When men are tired, temptation seems like a cool
drink and sin like a good night's sleep.

Secondly, David was worrying. He was worrying because
he was indulging in speculative thinking. The mythical 'law
of averages' was preying on his mind. Yes, he had been
delivered so far. . . but one day Saul would catch up with
him. David wanted to quit while he was ahead. He suddenly
doubted God's promises. He could not see taking any more
risks with Saul.

Thirdly, there is that strange phenomenon we call 'reaction' – the let-down after the big event. How often have we
seen, for example, that scintillating French national rugby
team dominate the run of play in an international game,
score some points so as to seem inevitable winners and then
virtually fall apart, to lose to a less talented side? So, in
spiritual things, good men in the aftermath of victories have
fallen back to old ways, almost without a struggle. There are
vulnerable moments in life and Satan is ready to exploit
them to his advantage.

Fourthly, David apparently did not enquire of the Lord as
to the proper course of action. On this occasion, he did not
season his thoughts with prayer. C. H. Spurgeon commented, 'In every other action of David you find some hint that
he asked counsel of the Lord. . . But this time what did he
talk with? Why, with the most deceitful thing that he could
have found – with his own heart.'⁵

In saying these things, we must not think the worse of
David. The Lord understands our weaknesses. David had
already endured far more than a lesser man could have
tolerated. But God calls us to faithfulness and promises to

perfect his strength in our weakness. Let us therefore learn
from David so that we may stand our ground in the day of
evil (Ephesians 6:13).

2. The bogus mercenary of Ziklag (27:2–12)

David, his men and their families sought asylum in Gath,
with the same Achish from whom David had perforce fled so
precipitously on an earlier occasion (21:10 – 22:1). Achish
received him, installed him in his own fief in Ziklag and
employed him as a foreign auxiliary, in much the same
fashion as the Romans used Germanic *foederati* to protect the
marches of their far-flung empire.

For his part, David achieved a twofold success in this
move. He succeeded in escaping from Saul's clutches (27:4)
and he also succeeded in ingratiating himself with his new
master, the Philistine King of Gath (27:12).

You will recall that on his first outing to Gath, David
secured his escape by pretending to be mad and thereby
fooling Achish into letting him go. This time, David succeeded in winning the trust of the King of Gath and he did it
by pulling off one of the most spectacular examples of
sleight of hand in the annals of biblical history. For sixteen
months, David pretended to be a mercenary in the service of
the Philistines. But he was a fake mercenary! He raided the
Geshurites, the Girzites and the Amalekites on the southern
border of Israel – the tribes hostile to Israel – while he told
Achish he was striking at Israel and her allies, the Jerah-
meelites and the Kenites.[6] Behind this farrago of lies, he
was destroying Israel's enemies root and branch, expanding
the borders of his future kingdom and winning popular
support among her people (27:8–11, cf. 30:26–31)! And
since 'dead men tell no tales', he carefully covered his tracks
by a rigorous policy of genocide – men, women, children all
perished. No one lived to enlighten Achish about the
activities of his tenant in Ziklag.

Brilliance and success are no proper measure of the
rightness of a course of action. These are certainly the
normal criteria of pragmatism. They are the common yard-
stick of achievement in our amoral humanistic society
today. David was brilliant and successful, but he
slaughtered whole communities and lied through his teeth

to Achish in the process. He had left his principles in the mountains of Judah and boxed himself into a corner where deceit and ruthlessness were the staples that kept him alive. He was trapped and, as we shall see in our next chapter, only the grace of God could save him from his unholy entanglement with the Philistines.

A final word

'Oh, what a tangled web we weave, when first we practise to deceive!' David was a believer, but he had gone to playing the fool anyway. The Lord was, however, not going to let him go on doing that indefinitely. There would be a reckoning, but there would be a deliverance as well!

David may have had pangs of conscience. Perhaps he prayed frequently to be delivered. We are not told. There is certainly no indication in Scripture that he felt himself to be playing the fool during that time in Ziklag. But the Lord never sent him to Gath. The Lord never sends anyone out to serve sin. The Lord's word is simple and full of his grace and power: 'Trust in the Lord with all your heart and lean not on your own understanding' (Proverbs 3:5). Paul, writing to the Colossian Christians, tells us to set our 'hearts on things above, where Christ is seated at the right hand of God' (Colossians 3:1). He goes on to urge us to put sin to death and clothe ourselves with love (3:14), the peace of Christ and gratitude to God (3:15). To be so changed by the power of God, we are to 'let the word of Christ dwell in [us] richly as [we] teach and admonish one another with all wisdom. . .' (3:16). Our Lord must instruct us. His Word must be in our hearts. We must love him with the deepest gratitude in our hearts for his saving grace and let his peace rule in our hearts. This is the only antidote to human foolishness. Commenting on the broken relationship between Saul and David, Matthew Henry reminds us, 'Men's transgressions against God are the cause of their enmities against each other, and no reconciliation among men is firm, which is not founded in and cemented by, peace with God through Jesus Christ. In sinning against God, men "play the fool and err exceedingly". This the believer perceives, repents of it, obtains pardon, and acts more wisely.'

References

[1] These were two of David's 'mighty men' – his elite force – and Abishai was one of the most accomplished of them (2 Samuel 23:18; 1 Chronicles 2:16).

[2] The same expression is used of Adam, when God anaesthetized him to remove the rib from which he formed Eve (Genesis 2:21).

[3] R. P. Gordon, p. 188.

[4] D. F. Payne, p. 137. Elsewhere, I have shown how the Bible's principles of civil government were expounded by John Calvin (G. J. Keddie, 'Calvin and Civil Government,' *Scottish Bulletin of Evangelical Theology*, **3**, 1 (Spring 1985), pp 23–33.)

[5] C. H. Spurgeon as quoted by A.W. Pink, p. 176.

[6] The exact opposite was the case. His campaigns were relieving pressure on the people of Judah and their Jerahmeelite and Kenite confederates. (These two tribes were closely associated with Israel, Judges 1:16; 1 Chronicles 2:5, 9, 25.) See R. P. Gordon, p. 192.

24.
Dilemma, deliverance and devotion

Please read 1 Samuel 28:1–2; 29:1–30:31

'David was greatly distressed because the men were talking of stoning him; each one was bitter in spirit because of his sons and daughters. But David found strength in the Lord his God' (1 Samuel 30:6).

Towards the end of World War II, London was subjected to incessant attack from German 'flying bombs'. This weapon chugged along rather loudly in flight and people soon recognized its distinctive sound. They waited with bated breath for the engine to cut out, for then, and only then, did the bomb fall through a brief but terrible silence to wreak its havoc on the city below. That silence before the explosion could seem endless and the bomb's concussion came no less as a surprise because it was so anxiously anticipated. Sometimes our life-experience can be like that fearful wait for the bomb to go off. Waiting for an important and expected event can seem like watching the pot that never boils. The most poignant example of this is, perhaps, the sad anticipation of the death of a terminally ill loved one. Almost to the last minute the waiting seems interminable, even cruel. We want it to end and we don't. But end it does and, paradoxically, the end is no less traumatic for being anticipated.

David probably wondered if his exile would ever end. He was a young man, perhaps around thirty years of age. For a good deal of his adult life a certain ambiguity had attended his progress, culminating in the open break with Saul and the years of fugitive flight at home and abroad. Would it ever end? When would the promises of God come to fruition? He must have wondered at times.

In God's timetable, the cataclysmic end of Saul's reign was at hand and the events that would both deliver David from his Philistine entanglement and catapult him to the throne of Israel were to unfold with unanticipated swiftness. The inspired historian's account of this period extends from 1 Samuel 28:1 to 2 Samuel 1:27 (the division of the one book of Samuel is an artificial imposition on the Hebrew text) and interweaves the actions of David and Saul in roughly chronological order, although, of course, their paths never crossed.[1] For the sake of simplicity, we will continue to focus in this chapter on an examination of David's movements prior to the Battle of Gilboa. In the next chapter we will look at Saul's last days, from his visit to the witch at Endor to his suicide on Mount Gilboa.

Dilemma [28:1–2]

The success with which David had hoodwinked Achish into believing he was a loyal mercenary with no future in Israel served David's purpose beautifully until the day the Philistines decided to make war on Israel. David's bluff was about to be called, for this time he would have to fight, if fight he did, under the watchful eye of Achish and the Philistine lords! So when Achish told David, '**You must understand that you and your men will accompany me in the army**,' (28:1) it must have made his head spin, as he searched about for an answer to the dilemma it posed for him. If he fought against Israel, he would be sinning against the Lord and the Lord's people and, indeed, it would be the radical denial of his calling to be the King of Israel. On the other hand, his practical situation was that if he refused to fight against Israel he would be guilty of treachery against Achish and his life would certainly be forfeit. He was 'damned if he did and damned if he didn't'.

David was already living a lie among the Philistines. If they had found out what he had done already, he would have been in serious trouble. Still, as long as he brought

back plenty of plunder from his raids, his Philistine masters
would be happy and as long as he took no prisoners they
would be kept in the dark about his duplicity. Thus the
Canaanites died for David's country and his Philistine hosts
thought they had an ally! (27:8–12).

What could David say? How could he resolve his
dilemma? He had no intention of fighting against Israel but
he had no obligation to put his head on a Philistine
executioner's block. So David did the prudent thing: without batting an eye-lid, he gave a politician's answer and
played for time! '**David said, "Then you will see for
yourself what your servant can do**"' (28:2). David was
trapped in his own web of deceit. He had so compromised
his commitment to the Lord that he was unable to testify to
Achish that it was impossible for him to take the field
against the armies of the Lord of hosts. The 'chickens had
come home to roost' for David. The day of decision was at
hand.

The lesson in David's predicament is surely that pragmatic compromise with the world and its ways, however
small it may seem at the time, is *always* the 'toe in the door'
for greater defections from biblical principle in the future.
Compromise is the prelude to apostasy. 'You have to be
practical,' is sin's Trojan horse for the modern Christian.
David was being 'practical' when he went to Gath and lied
to Achish. We can understand his reasons. His actions were
certainly intelligible in the circumstances. The pressures he
faced were very real. We would, perhaps, have been crushed
by them, whereas David only bent a little! Yes, but in
bending as he did, he made his faith a private, internal
matter at the expense of a consistent public witness to the
claims of God over every aspect of life – his life and the lives
of the Philistines. The 'private' believer has, in effect,
surrendered the field of his public life to the enemy. His
public behaviour is, to one degree or another, hostage to the
world's standards. He has no witness to the world's sin, for
if he says anything to the man who is up to his neck in it,
that man turns round and says, 'But you are up to your
ankles and you haven't been complaining!' Arthur Pink put
it so well when he wrote, 'Satan rests not satisfied for the
Christian to yield one "little" point, and knows full well our

doing so greatly lessens our resistance to his next temptations.' He highlights some examples, especially with respect to young Christians: 'To go anywhere we ought not, will bring us into temptations it will be almost impossible to resist. To seek the society of non-Christians is to play with fire, and to accept favours from them will almost certainly result in our getting burned. . . For a young lady to accept the attentions of an undesirable young man, makes it far harder to reject his later advances. . . Then go slow, we beg you, in accepting favours from any, especially from those who are likely to take an unfair advantage of you.'[2]

Deliverance [29:1–11]

The Lord never deserts his people, especially in the need that their own foolishness has generated. This is the essence of his salvation. 1 Samuel 29 illustrates a basic biblical principle which received its definitive statement in 1 Corinthians 10:13: 'No temptation has seized you except what is common to man. And God is faithful; he will not let you be tempted beyond what you can bear. But when you are tempted, he will also provide a way out so that you can stand up under it.' The fact that we may see no way of escape is no limitation on the Lord's ingenuity. So, as the dusty columns of men and horses marched north from Aphek and David wondered how he could be extricated from this dilemma, the Lord was already working to effect his rescue.

1. Objections against David (29:2–5)
The 'wild card' which, in the providence of God, 'took the trick,' was the collective attitude of the other rulers of the Philistines. They were as suspicious of David as Achish was trusting and they were sensitive to the potentially devastating consequences should a unit of 600 experienced and well-led soldiers change sides in the middle of a battle. What better way for him to regain favour with Saul than to turn the tide at just the right moment? Was not this the man who had slain his 'tens of thousands'? The argument was irrefutable. In any case, Achish was outvoted. David had to go.

2. David's dismissal (29:6–11)

With evident regret, Achish dismissed David and ordered him and his men back to Ziklag. David, now a 'practised deceiver',[3] duly acted the part of the disappointed vassal, knowing full well that he had been let off the hook in a most remarkable way. In yet another as yet unsuspected twist of providence, his return to Ziklag was to give him further cause to be thankful to the Lord. For as David's men retraced their steps to Philistia, the Amalekites descended upon Ziklag and carried off their families and their possessions (30:1–2).

Several points emerge from this extraordinary turn of events.

First of all, it illustrates that God is faithful to his promise that he will save his people from their sins. This is no encouragement to anyone to go on sinning under the convenient but illusory supposition that grace will increase. The point is that the Lord knows those that are his. And those that are his are 'dead to sin' and know, in the deepest struggles of their Christian consciences, that they cannot go on living in a way that flies in the face of the Lord they love (Romans 6:1–2). David was a believer who was in trouble. He knew he was in an ethical and spiritual corner. And, although we are not told about his prayer life in this crisis, it is difficult to imagine that he did not cry to God for help on many an occasion. Every Christian has known that sense of crisis at some time or other and remembers how that preoccupation broke into every waking moment and brought forth repeated groanings for the relief that seemed beyond reasonable hope. The Lord who watches over Israel will neither slumber nor sleep (Psalm 121:3). He keeps the feet of his saints (1 Samuel 2:9). And he has not appointd them to suffer wrath 'but to receive salvation through our Lord Jesus Christ' (1 Thessalonians 5:9).

Secondly, God is Lord over all. The hearts of the Philistine kings were 'in the hand of the Lord' and he directed them 'like a watercourse' according to his pleasure (Proverbs 21:1). God used his enemies to deliver David! God's sovereignty is not restricted by human unbelief. I once came across a tract that stated that God used 'only believers' to build his kingdom (on earth). I was working for the summer in a church in the American mid-west corn-belt at the time and I showed it to the godly old elder in whose home I was staying. He was a man of very few words, but they always weighed a great deal. He read it, was silent for a couple of minutes, then looked at me and said, 'My shepherd, Cyrus.' Only three words from an octogenarian Iowa pig farmer! But they exposed the theological incompetence of that tract, because that reference to Isaiah 44:28 brought out the truth that the Persian king Cyrus was used by God to 'build God's kingdom on earth' by restoring the exiles from Babylon to Jerusalem in 536 B.C. The perspective of God's absolute sovereignty means that, far from hindering God's purpose, the unbelieving will actually be used to facilitate the advance of God's cause and kingdom. And because the risen Christ is 'head over everything for the church, which is his body' (Ephesians 1:22), Christians have a mandate to live for him in holy confidence and the assurance that they will be kept by his power.

Thirdly, whereas the friendship of unbelievers can be a great snare, their hostility can sometimes be a blessing. In David's case, it was the distrust of the Philistine rulers that, as Matthew Henry put it, 'befriended him, when no friend he had was capable of doing him such a kindness'. The antithesis between light and darkness makes for clearer issues and the opposition of the world can help us know where we stand and actually help us to stand.

Fourthly, our actual safety is not a function of our sensual perceptions about our security. While we worry, the Lord is surrounding us with his angels. David was delivered before he knew what was happening. The conclave of the Philistine rulers unwittingly did God's work while David still wondered what the future held. But faith runs to Christ, when, to all appearances, the odds are stacked against us: 'We know that God causes all things to work together for good to those who love God, to those who are called according to his purpose' (Romans 8:28 NASB).

Devotion [30:1–31]

When the cat's away, the mice will play! While David and his men were with the Philistine army, the Amalekites had descended upon his base at Ziklag, laid it waste and captured all the women and children, presumably for future ransom or sale into slavery (30:1–2). The only mitigating factors in this catastrophe were the absence of dead bodies and the likelihood that the Amalekites did not have too much of a head start. But when calamity strikes, we are too numbed to think coolly about what to do next. David and his men were devastated and '**wept aloud until they had no strength left to weep**' (30:4).

1. Recrimination and renewal (30:6–8)
When there is no strength left to grieve, there always seems to be some energy left for recrimination and revenge. There is a fickle mindlessness about this search for a scapegoat. And invariably the 'stab in the back' theory wins the day – the culprit is one of us, even our leader, whom we thought to be faithful all these years! The men turned on David and began to talk about stoning him! Was not the general responsible for what happened to his command? He must be to blame! After all, he brought us to this country and took us off to Aphek with the Philistine army!

Part of the burden of leadership, particularly in the aftermath of a set-back, is to face the criticism of people whose frustration has overwhelmed their rationality. People who can't balance their cheque books become experts on the nation's economy when they feel insecure and afraid. Public opinion polls chart perceptions and fears, not informed judgements. People flail around precisely because they cannot cope with the situation. They are 'prisoners of the passions of the moment'.[4]

David, therefore, had cause to be '**greatly distressed**'. And even though he was not to be blamed for the Amalekite raid, he certainly was responsible for responding to it in as effective a way as possible. It is no use if a leader – and in a church, that means a pastor – rolls over and gives up when his people complain. The reasonableness, or otherwise, of their complaint is irrelevant. This is, in the last analysis, why they are followers and he is the leader. They are only proving why they need a leader. His task is to prove he has the mettle to be their leader! That is why leadership demands real spiritual, moral and even physical fibre.

Christian leadership requires the gifts and the filling of the Holy Spirit.

The crisis was, however, God's means to concentrate David's mind on the real issue – his relationship to and dependence upon the Lord. In spite of, or perhaps because of the problems he faced, David '**found strength in the Lord his God**' (30:6). This pregnant expression reminds us of 23:16, where Jonathan helped David find 'strength in God'. David, like the prodigal son in Jesus' parable, had come 'to his senses' (Luke 15:17). His deliverance from the Philistine service had not done this, but the disaster of Ziklag did – it rekindled in his soul a renewed devotion to the Lord. He immediately sought to discover the Lord's will. To that end he called for Abiathar and the priestly ephod – the garment in which the priest officiated before the Lord. The Lord told him – how exactly, we are not informed – that he should pursue the Amalekites, and that he would overtake them and succeed in rescuing their captured families (30:7–8).

2. Rescue and retribution (30:9–20)

For men who had already marched the 120 miles to Aphek and back in the course of about a week, the pursuit of the Amalekites must have been a veritable Via Dolorosa. 200 men were too exhausted to continue and were detached to look after the baggage train at the Besor Ravine, some fifteen miles from Ziklag (30:9–10).

David pressed on with 400 men and then, in one of those not uncommon twists of providence that has transformed a seemingly dismal situation, they discovered an Egyptian in a field! The poor fellow had been abandoned by his Amalekite masters, who apparently did not anticipate his transformation into an intelligence coup for the Israelites! Since he had not eaten for three days, he was pretty near the end of his tether. Once fortified by some welcome food and drink, he was ready to take David to where the Amalekites were camped (30:11–15).

The Amalekites were enjoying the fruits of their reprehensible labours when David caught up with them. The fighting seems to have lasted long enough – '**from dusk until the evening of the next day**' (30:17) – which, in view of the exhausted state of the Israelites, bespeaks the wonders that victory and adrenalin can do for tired muscles! The slaughter was great, some 400 young men escaped on camels and all the captives were liberated and the plunder repossessed! So overwhelmed were the men with their triumph that, instead of thinking about stoning David, as they had been only forty-eight hours before, they now waived their share of the booty and declared with extravagant generosity, '**This is David's plunder**.' The Lord had retrieved the apparently irretrievable.

3. Return and reward (30:21–31)

It was not all over bar the shouting. The return posed further leadership challenges for David. And he rose to them in a truly regal manner.

The first question concerned the sharing of the spoils of war with the men who had dropped out of the pursuit at the Besor Ravine (30:21–25). The more rascally element among David's followers did not want to divide the plunder with them. Those that stayed with the baggage were non-combatants. They had not, to use a New Testament expression, 'borne the burden of the work and the heat of the day' (Matthew 20:12) in battle. David, with magisterial authority, immediately established the principle that all – combatants and non-combatants – would share alike (30:24).[5] The army was a team! Like the church, which is described by Paul in 1 Corinthians 12:14–26 as a body made up of many complementary and interdependent parts, the various components were to be seen as indispensable to the effective operation of the whole.

The second, closely related point, at which David showed he had 'come of age' as the king-in-waiting, was in his distribution of gifts to the elders of Judah who had been his friends and the towns where he and his men '**had roamed**' (30:31). These were in the nature of the 'thank-you' gifts we give to those who have opened their homes to us and shared their table and their fellowship. David made a gesture of gratitude to those who had helped him in his darkest days.

Step by step

Step by step, the Lord led David from a low period in his life to the higher ground of a faith exercised with all the joy that knowing the presence of the Lord and his hand of blessing must always generate. There is a picture here of what he has done again and again in the lives of Christians. David is a window on the way the Holy Spirit woos believers – sometimes, to be sure, this can be a rough wooing! But this is how the Holy Spirit often brings us to a closer relationship of faith, obedience and devotion to the Lord. We have all had our sojourns in some spiritual Philistia. Our spiritual life was flat, our prayer life stale and stuttering, our sense of the nearness of God's love almost a dream of long-lost days of forgotten joy. The Lord first let David go. He let him entangle himself in the lilliputian threads of micro-compromises until the poor man was so encased in the accumulated folly of his life of lies that the only way out was a mighty intervention of God's gracious providence. Rocked by the disaster at Ziklag, David was brought by the grace of God to renewal of the faith which had long been indelibly engraved upon his being by the Spirit of God. Then the windows of heaven opened and the blessing poured out was more than could be contained by the Lord's servant. The Lord's promises have not changed. His Word is near you, says Paul. "It is in your mouth and in your heart," that is, the word of faith we are proclaiming: That if you confess with your mouth, "Jesus is Lord," and believe in your heart that God raised him from the dead, you will be saved' (Romans 10:8–9).

References

[1] The order is not rigorously chronological. The events of 1 Samuel 29 actually took place between 28:2 and 28:4. That is, the Philistines assembled (28:1–2), entered Israel at Aphek (29:1) and then moved north to Shunem (28:4; see map). It was on that line of march that David was sent back to Ziklag. The action recorded in the next chapter (30) must have occurred at about the same time as the battle of Mount Gilboa (31). Clearly, chapter 29 was moved to heighten the drama of Saul's dénouement by placing the account of David's deliverance (29:1–30:31) between the episode with the witch of Endor (28:3–25) and the death of Saul on Mount Gilboa (31:1–13). Incidentally, 28:3 (the death of Samuel

and Saul's suppression of the spiritists) is also out of chronological order – it is only a reminder of earlier events (25:1), placed here to enable us to understand the meaning of Saul's visit to the witch. The literary structure is determined by the theme and while the correct chronology is made obvious for the reader, it was not the first concern of the inspired historian.

[2] A.W. Pink, p. 191.

[3] R. P. Gordon, p. 198.

[4] D. F. Payne, p. 152, reminds us of the way the Jerusalem crowd hailed Jesus in his triumphant entry on Palm Sunday and called for his crucifixion before the week's end.

[5] J. C. Laney, p. 81, notes that David's decree (30:25) was still being followed in the Maccabean era (c. 150 B.C.), according to the Second Book of Maccabees (Apocrypha).

25.
How are the mighty fallen!

Please read 1 Samuel 28:3–25; 31:1–13 and 1 Chronicles 10:1–14

'Saul died because he was unfaithful to the Lord; he did not keep the word of the Lord, and even consulted a medium for guidance, and did not enquire of the Lord. So the Lord put him to death and turned the kingdom over to David son of Jesse' (1 Chronicles 10:13–14).

While David was successfully disposing of the Amalekites on the southern border of Judah, the closing chapter of Saul's unhappy reign was unfolding in Israel's far north. After David and his men had been dismissed by the Philistine commanders, the Philistine army had continued to march north to the plain of Jezreel – both the bread-basket of Israel and much better country for their chariots than the Judean hills. Saul, denied thereby the traditional Israelite advantage of fighting in the hills, was forced to concentrate his forces at the eastern edge of the plain, near Mount Gilboa. There he awaited the approaching clash of arms.

From the very beginning of the biblical record of these events, there are intimations of impending doom. The air of these chapters is heavy with spiritual darkness. The end, when it comes, is so clearly the righteous judgement of God upon implacable apostasy. This does not seem, on the face of it, a particularly encouraging note on which to conclude! We tend to look for happy endings and upbeat exhortations! So, some explanation is perhaps in order, that we might have a clear understanding of the place of this grim passage in relation to the overall theme of 1 Samuel.

First of all, it must be remembered that the division of the one Book of Samuel into two books is one of many little ways in which God's inspired Word has been touched up by 'helpful' translators, purportedly to make it easier for us to use. Chapter and verse divisions were added for the same reason. The original Hebrew text of Samuel, however, is a continuous history of Israel from the period of the Judges to the closing days of David's reign. 1 Samuel 'ends' but the text has no break. 2 Samuel goes on without any ado to complete the story! In fact, the climax to 1 Samuel is to be found in 2 Samuel! The establishment by God of the monarchy under David is the central theme of the inspired historian. We are actually only halfway through the exposition of that theme.

Secondly, there is nevertheless an appropriateness to the way in which this segment of God's dealings with Israel ends. It marks both an end and a beginning. Saul's death brings to an end what may be termed 'the people's monarchy' and makes way for the man after God's own heart (13:14). God had taken his time, but he had let Israel begin to regret their thirst for a king and had, almost literally, given their king enough rope to hang himself. The predicted abuses of monarchy had exacted their burdensome toll and the unhappy division between Saul and the popular David opened fissures in Israelite society which were never to heal.[1]

Thirdly, even in the judgements of God upon wickedness, there is an overture of grace to all who witness them. Herman Bavinck reminds us that 'In Scripture God's remunerative justice is much more prominent than his retributive justice.'[2] In other words, the righteousness which punishes the wicked also rewards the godly and it is the latter that is the more prominent theme in the Bible! The righteousness of God, adds Bavinck, has a purpose to save sinners and surround their lives with blessings, through the Lord Jesus Christ's perfect atonement for sin.[3] God's dark clouds point to his silver linings. The law is a schoolmaster to lead us to Christ. God takes no pleasure in the death of the wicked, but rather that they turn from their ways and live. Saul's self-destructive commitment to his opposition to

God was confirmed by the descent of divine wrath upon him. But in the context of God's unfolding plan of redemption, this fearful sentence points away from itself towards the better way and says, 'This is the way of the Lord. Walk in it!' He who will by no means clear the guilty is, in Jesus Christ, keeping mercy for thousands!

If this last act of the drama of 1 Samuel seems grim, hopeless and forbidding – like the ending to a modern film – then understand what the Lord is saying in these events: 'There is a way that seems right to a man, but in the end it leads to death' (Proverbs 14:12). But there is another way: Jesus said, 'I am the way. . . ' (John 14:6).

The seeds of declension [1 Chronicles 10:13]

It is a supreme irony that what should be the greatest of blessings so often are turned into the worst of curses. This is one of the ever-present and ever-painful realities of the human condition. Men take the gifts that should be used to generate genuine good and healthy happiness – and turn them into dust! Political power enables the 'servant of the people' to become a ruthless tyrant; wealth and property do not provide the joy and the 'meaning' that they were supposed to, and even the gospel of Jesus Christ – never mind false religions – has been used by unscrupulous men to cover the most sordid of life-styles.[4] Man's natural way is to exchange the truth of God for a lie and without his grace and a changed heart, the best of gifts will be to no good effect.

God had promised Israel a king. But he was to be God's man. And he was to be given in God's good time.[5] The people had, however, insisted on the appointment of a king according to their own timetable. And so, after rebuking their attitude and warning of the consequences of their course of action, the Lord granted their wish and gave Samuel the go-ahead to give them a king (8:22).

1. Chosen and gifted
In spite of this less than auspicious beginning, the monarchy was actually inaugurated on a bright and positive

note. The first king, Saul, was a fine figure of a man and the early days of his reign amply fulfilled the expectations of the people and promised great things for the future. He was 'an impressive young man without equal among the Israelites' (9:1–2). He received the acclamation of the people (10:24). The Spirit of God came upon him with power and he led a successful campaign to save Jabesh Gilead from the Ammonites (11:6–11). In modern parlance, Saul had everything going for him.

2. Tested and found wanting

The obligations of political power afford the severest tests to any man's mettle. As a theocratic king, Saul was responsible not primarily to his subjects but to his God. And unlike the public opinion polls, the Lord is never impressed by our promises. He commands our obedience to his good and perfect will. In many respects, Saul appears to have been an able king. The reverses suffered by Israel during his reign were no worse than those experienced during the period of the judges. They were probably considerably outweighed by the advantages of a relatively strong centralized government. For most of his forty-year rule, Saul governed Israel effectively. It was, perhaps, in the last ten years that the cracks really began to appear in the foundation of his rule and his personal life. These years were peppered with calamities. But even then, there is little hint from Scripture that his rule was excessively oppressive or that there was civil unrest throughout the country. After his break with David, however, there was a steady deterioration in the situation which clearly laid the groundwork for the divisions that erupted into civil war after his death.

From God's perspective, however, there are higher criteria of effective kingship than, to use an anachronism, keeping the trains running on time. The ultimate test of all rulers, ancient and modern, is what they do with the fact that they are to serve, not themselves, not only the people, but, first and foremost, the living God himself! It was not only the kings of Israel who were charged to serve the Lord. Civil government is an institution of God for the blessing of human society (Romans 13:1–7). The psalmist gave voice to that truth in one of the most challenging words of prophecy

in the Old Testament when he sang in praise of the coming
Messiah:

> 'Therefore, you kings, be wise;
>   be warned, you rulers of the earth.
> Serve the Lord with fear
>   and rejoice with trembling.
> Kiss the Son, lest he be angry
>   and you be destroyed in your way,
> for his wrath can flare up in a moment.
>   Blessed are all who take refuge in him'
>
> (Psalm 2:10–12).

This inspired song is about the mediatorial kingship of the
Lord Jesus Christ over the institutions of government of the
nations of the earth. The 'powers that be' are responsible to
God for the way they govern. Whether they recognize it or
not, they will answer to him. His Word will be the measure,
not the Gallup poll or some abstraction like 'the verdict of
history'. And the risen Christ – the one who, by his own
death and resurrection has triumphed over sin and death
and is exalted to the right hand of God in glory – *is* the King
of kings, presidents and dictators alike. They must answer
to Christ and that answer involves their response to the
gospel of salvation through his blood shed for sin. Omin-
ously for world unbelief, it is elsewhere declared that 'He
waits for his enemies to be made his footstool' (Hebrews
10:13; Psalm 110:1). The Lordship of Christ over civil
authorities is a universal principle for all of human history
and cannot but be the fundamental principle of all Christian
political involvement.

The Israelite monarchy, however, was the particular
repository on earth of God's sovereign, gracious and redemptive rule over human society. As the theocratic king of
the covenant people of God, the Israelite monarch was in a
unique relationship to God. He was the Lord's anointed and
the very institution he served looked ahead to the one true
King, the Lord Jesus Christ. Israel, as the church of that era,
was in its political organization and administration as well
as its religious institutions, a prophetic foreshadowing of
the New Testament church. It pointed ahead to the domin-

ion of Christ – the head of the church and head over
everything for the church (Ephesians 1:22–23).

Unless we grasp this theological perspective, we will fail
to understand both the nature of Saul's failure and the
meaning of his rejection by God. Saul did not just make a
few slips or suffer some lapses in spiritual discernment or
doctrinal knowledge. He was not just a personal sinner in a
public position. Neither was it a case, like almost all
political scandals today, of his compromising public confidence by some indiscretion that didn't 'fit the mould' for a
public official. Rather, he radically denied his calling as the
Lord's anointed king, put the Lord to open shame and cast a
shadow upon the Lord's redemptive programme for his
people. When Saul offered the burnt offerings himself,
because he was too impatient to wait for Samuel, as he had
been commanded by the Lord (13:9), and when, also against
God's will, he spared the Amalekite king, Agag (15:9), he
exposed a layer of contempt for the Lord and his revealed
will, which had hitherto lain hidden in his heart. Hence, the
Lord said to him that 'To obey is better than sacrifice, and
to heed is better than the fat of rams.' Significantly, he went
on to say, 'For rebellion is like the sin of divination, and
arrogance like the evil of idolatry' (15:22). Here was the
Lord's definition of Saul's sin and the reason for his
rejection of Saul as king. The literal 'sin of divination' was
to be the immediate precursor of his death (28:3–25).

The sin of divination [28:3–25]

Though rejected by God, Saul reigned on unchallenged for
many years and, indeed, to an advanced age – he may have
been about seventy years old at his death. He did not,
however, improve with age. The Lord had departed from
him and he had become increasingly set in his ways.
Evidence of a reprobate mind began mount as time went
on. There were the repeated attempts to murder David and
there was the mass-murder of the priests at Nob. And then,
on the day before his death, he had recourse to a medium at
Endor. From rebellion that was 'like the sin of divination'
(15:22), Saul had descended to the 'sin of divination' itself

and, although he would not have said this was his intention, he was, in effect, seeking the aid of Satan for the preservation of his life and kingdom!

1. Why did Saul seek out a medium? (28:3–7)
Because the result of Saul's visit to the witch of Endor was a posthumous encounter with Samuel, the background is set out with succinct completeness. We are told that '**Samuel was dead, and all Israel had mourned for him and buried him in his own town of Ramah.**' We are also told that Saul had, at some point in his reign, '**expelled the mediums and spiritists from the land**' (28:3). Since this was in accord with the law of God,[6] Saul's subsequent action is seen as the most bare-faced hypocrisy and apostasy.

When Saul saw the Philistine army he '**was afraid; terror filled his heart**'. He sought the Lord's will, but received no answer '**by dreams or Urim or prophets**'. The Chronicler says he 'did not enquire of the Lord' (1 Chronicles 10:14). This, argues R.P. Gordon, is 'probably intended as a generalizing comment on the direction of Saul's life' and need not be seen as a contradiction of Saul's action on this occasion.[7] The Spirit of God had ceased to strive with Saul (cf. Genesis 6:3). He was left to himself. And in his wicked desperation, he turned to the dark world of spiritism (28:4–7).

2. The meeting with Samuel (28:8–19)
Saul went incognito to the medium and, after overcoming her suspicions that it was a trap to secure her condemnation under the king's decree, he asked her to call up Samuel from the dead. The medium did as he asked and, to her terrified amazement, Samuel appeared before her eyes!

There has been great debate over this incident. Was it a vision of the prophet? Was it Satan masquerading as Samuel? Was it an appearance of the glorified spirit of Samuel – as with Moses and Elijah at the transfiguration of Jesus? Or was it a clever trick that fooled the over-wrought king?[8] The best answer would seem to be that it was a real appearance of the glorified spirit of Samuel. There is no evidence of either satanic trickery or a mere vision in Saul's mind. And the medium herself, apart from being powerless to bring anyone from the dead, was clearly not pulling a stunt, for she was shocked by Samuel's appearance (28:12). No! It was an intervention of God, which, paradoxically, demonstrated the powerlessness of evil to stand against the Lord. It was a very solemn matter, as Matthew Henry noted, that 'God permitted, on this one occasion, the soul of a departed prophet to come as a witness from heaven, thus sending him to confirm the word he had spoken on earth.' The Lord gave Saul what he wanted but, as we shall see, not what he wanted to hear.

Samuel's words serve to confirm that this was a mighty intervention of the Lord. He rebuked Saul for seeking him, when he knew that the Lord had rejected him. If the Lord would not hear him, why would his prophets, living or dead, be able to answer? Samuel also reiterated the prediction that the kingdom would be given to another and identified him as David. He further predicted that Saul would be defeated by the Philistines and that he and his sons would die on the battlefield (28:16–19). It was a divine epitaph upon a sorry life.

3. A fearful expectation of judgement (28:20–25)

Saul had asked Samuel what he was to do (28:15). The answer was that he could do nothing. It was all over. Sentence had been passed. He was finished. Saul was prostrated with terror, as well he might be. He could not eat and it was only the kindness of the medium and the coaxing of his men that made him eat a meal before returning to the Israelite camp.

The starkness with which the realities were laid before Saul should not be allowed to obscure a solemn truth that applies to everyone who opposes the Lord with his dying breath. It is that 'If we deliberately keep on sinning after we have received the knowledge of the truth, no sacrifice for sins is left, but a fearful expectation of judgement and of raging fire that will consume the enemies of God' (Hebrews 10:27). Today, if you hear the Lord's voice, do not harden your hearts (Hebrews 4:7). Jesus came that men and women might have life and have it abundantly. Believe on the Lord Jesus Christ and you will be saved. Do nothing and a lost eternity will be yours.

The day of reckoning [31:1–13]

With the Battle of Gilboa, the curtain fell on Saul and his
kingdom. The Philistines won a total victory, all but eliminated the house of Saul and occupied the northern towns of
Israel. Samuel's posthumous prophecy was fulfilled (28:19)
and the throne was vacated in readiness for the accession of
David.

Saul and his sons evidently fought hard that day. The king
stood his ground when his sons were dead[9] and much of his
army had fled. Critically wounded and facing certain death,
Saul decided he must not fall into the hands of the enemy. He
ordered his armour-bearer to kill him. When the man could
not bring himself to kill his king, Saul fell on his own sword
and died a suicide's death.

In such circumstances, Saul's suicide seems very understandable, perhaps even strangely laudable. Probably
because of the Japanese practice of hara-kiri, especially in the
context of their defeat in World War II, the idea that suicide
can be honourable has gained some credence. Even the
suicide of Adolf Hitler – which was almost certainly for the
very same reasons as that of Saul – has gained a tinge of
propriety as a kind of Wagnerian hara-kiri.

From God's point of view, however, suicide is self-murder.
It is a gross sin and a clear breach of the Sixth Commandment.
Of the four instances of suicide in the Scriptures – Saul,
Ahithophel (2 Samuel 17:23), Zimri (1 Kings 16:18) and Judas
Iscariot (Matthew 27:5) – not one is, as Pink puts it,
'extenuated by ascribing the deed to insanity'.[10] Those who,
sadly, take their own lives while in the grip of mental illness
are not true suicides in any ethical sense. Let no one think that
any and all suicide is unpardonable sin that ushers the soul
directly into a lost eternity. In all of the biblical cases, as in all
true self-murder, wicked men perished in their sins by their
own hand. And that kind of suicide is, as Herman Hoeksema
wrote, 'principally rooted in enmity against God and hatred of
the position in which God had placed man. . . The suicide is
not a brave man, but a wicked coward, who has not the moral
courage to stand and function in the position in which God has
placed him. . . and who simply removes himself from that
position to open his eyes in hell.'[11]

There is a day of reckoning for every human being. The death of Saul reminds us all that we must all appear before the judgement seat of Christ so that each may receive what is due to him for the things done while in the body, whether good or bad (2 Corinthians 5:10). The death of Saul calls to mind the last moments of the film version of Christopher Marlowe's play, *Dr Faustus*. Faustus, who had sold his soul to Mephistopheles (Satan) for youth, vigour and the enjoyment of the pleasures of the flesh, is finally faced with the bill for all his indulgences. His life is over. He belongs to hell. In the final scene Faustus (played by the late Richard Burton) is dragged screaming into the fires of hell and the camera pans over to a copy of the Latin Bible and lights on the words: '*Stipendium peccate, mors est.*' These are the words of Romans 6:23: 'The wages of sin is death'!

But even in this sombre truth lies the seed of the way to life. For the Lord says to the human race, 'Just as man is destined to die once, and after that to face judgement, so Christ was sacrificed once to take away the sins of many people; and he will appear a second time, not to bear sin, but to bring salvation to those who are waiting for him' (Hebrews 9:27–28).

References

[1] The civil war which followed Saul's death anticipated the division of Solomon's kingdom, after his death, into the northern kingdom of Israel and the southern kingdom of Judah.

[2] H. Bavinck, *The Doctrine of God*, (Edinburgh: Banner of Truth, 1977), p. 215.

[3] *Ibid.*, p. 218.

[4] The 1987 scandal involving the PTL TV ministry in the USA, and its founders Jim and Tammy Bakker, is a case in point.

[5] See chapter 8 above.

[6] Deuteronomy 18:9–14; Leviticus 19:31; 20:27; 2 Kings 21:6; 23:24; Isaiah 8:19–22.

[7] R. P. Gordon, p. 194.

[8] E. H. Merrill, *An Historical survey of the Old Testament*, (Nutley, N.J.: Craig Press, 1969), pp. 211–212, documents various opinions.

[9] Three sons were killed at Gilboa – Jonathan, Abinadab and Malki-Shua (31:2). A fourth, Ish-bosheth, survived to be the puppet-king of a short-lived kingdom organized by Abner, Saul's general (2 Samuel 2–4).

[10] A.W. Pink, pp. 229–230. Samson died as a result of his own action, but it was an act of war against the Lord's enemies and not self-murder and was, indeed, an act of faithfulness to the Lord.

[11] H. Hoeksema, *The Triple Knowledge*, (Grand Rapids: Reformed Free Publishing Association, 1972), Vol. 3, pp. 311–312.